# Guerrillas, Unionists, and Violence on the Confederate Home Front

# Guerrillas, Unionists, and Violence on the Confederate Home Front

Edited by
Daniel E. Sutherland

THE UNIVERSITY OF ARKANSAS PRESS
Fayetteville 1999

03   02   01   00   99      5   4   3   2   1

*Designed by Liz Lester*

♾   The paper used in this publication meets the minimum requirements of the American National Standard for Permanence of Paper for
Printed Library Materials Z39.48–1984.


LIBRARY OF CONGRESS CATALOGING-IN-PUBLICATION DATA

Guerrillas, Unionists, and violence on the Confederate home front /
    edited by Daniel E. Sutherland.
        p.      cm.
    Includes bibliographical references and index.
    ISBN 1-55728-549-7 (cloth : alk. paper).   —ISBN 1-55728-
550-0 (pbk. : alk. paper)
        1. Confederate State of America—Social conditions.
    2. Confederate States of America—Politics and government.
    3. United States—History—Civil War, 1861–1865—Public
    opinion.  4. United States—History—Civil War, 1861–1865—
    Underground movements.  5. United States—History—Civil War,
    1861–1865—Social aspects.  6. Dissenters—Confederate States of
    America.  7. Public opinion—Confederate States of America.
    8. Guerrillas—Confederate States of America.  9. Violence—
    Confederate States of America.  I. Sutherland, Daniel E.
    E487.G84    1999
    973.7'1—dc21                           99-23240
                                              CIP

# Contents

# Contributors

VICTORIA E. BYNUM is a professor of history at Southwest Texas State University. She is the author of *Unruly Women: The Politics of Social and Sexual Control in the Old South* (1992) and *Mississippi's Longest Civil War: Memory, Community, and the "Free State of Jones"* (forthcoming).

BENJAMIN FRANKLIN COOLING is a research director in the U.S. Department of Energy and a professor of history at the Industrial College of the Armed Forces (National Defense University). He is the author or editor of fifteen books on military and naval history, most recently *Monocacy: The Battle That Saved Washington* (1997), and *Fort Donelson's Legacy: War and Society in Kentucky and Tennessee, 1862–63* (1997).

MICHAEL FELLMAN is a professor of history at Simon Fraser University. He is the author of several books on nineteenth-century America, including *Inside War: The Guerrilla Conflict in Missouri during the American Civil War* (1989) and *Citizen Sherman: A Life of William Tecumseh Sherman* (1995).

NOEL C. FISHER is a freelance writer and independent scholar who resides in Columbus, Ohio. He is the author of *War at Every Door: Partisan Politics and Guerrilla Violence in East Tennessee, 1860–1869* (1997).

DONALD S. FRAZIER is an associate professor of history at McMurry University. He is the author of *Blood and Treasure: Confederate Empire in the Southwest* (1995) and general editor of *The United States and Mexico at War: Nineteenth-Century Expansionism and Conflict* (1998).

LESLEY J. GORDON is an assistant professor of history at the University of Akron. She is the author of *General George E. Pickett in Life and Legend* (1998) and *The Sixteenth Regiment Connecticut Volunteers in War and Memory* (forthcoming).

ROBERT R. MACKEY, a captain in the U.S. Army, is an instructor of history at the United States Military Academy. He received his M.A. in American history at Texas A&M University and is currently completing work on his Ph.D.

JONATHAN D. SARRIS is an assistant professor of history at Appalachian State University. He has published several essays on the Civil War in Georgia, most recently in *The Civil War in Appalachia: Collected Essays*, edited by Kenneth W. Noe and Shannon H. Wilson (1997).

DAVID PAUL SMITH is chair of the Social Studies Department at Highland Park High School in Dallas, Texas. He is the author of *Frontier Defense in the Civil War: Texas Rangers and Rebels* (1992) and *Perspectives in American History*, 2 volumes (1997).

DANIEL E. SUTHERLAND is a professor of history at the University of Arkansas. He is the author or editor of eight other books, including *Seasons of War: The Ordeal of a Confederate Community, 1861–1865* (1995) and *Fredericksburg and Chancellorsville: The Dare Mark Campaign* (1998).

JON L. WAKELYN is a professor of history at Kent State University. He is the author or editor of several books on nineteenth-century U.S. history, including *The Web of Southern Social Relations: Women, Family, and Education* (1985), and *Southern Pamphlets on Secession, November 1860–April 1861* (1996).

# Guerrillas, Unionists, and Violence
# on the Confederate Home Front

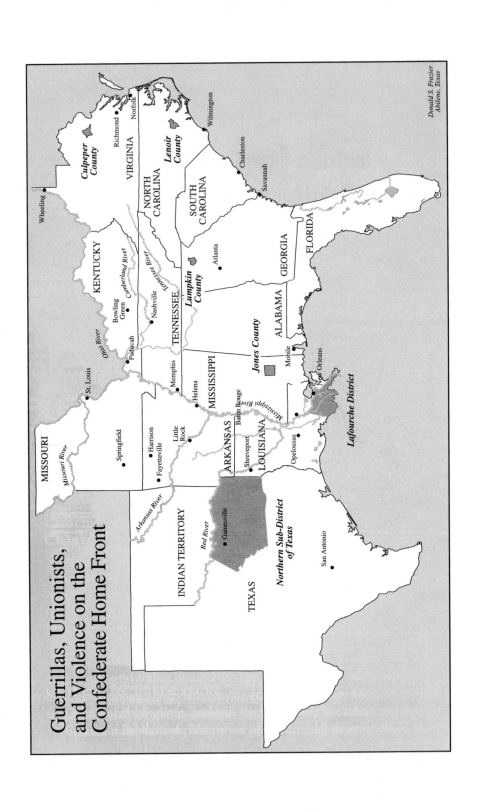

## Guerrillas, Unionists, and Violence on the Confederate Home Front

**MISSOURI**
- Wheeling
- St. Louis
- Springfield
- Harrison
- Fayetteville
- Little Rock

*Missouri River*
*Ohio River*
*Arkansas River*
*Red River*

**KENTUCKY**
- Bowling Green
- Paducah
- Nashville

*Cumberland River*
*Tennessee River*

**TENNESSEE**
- Memphis
- Helena

**VIRGINIA**
- Richmond
- Norfolk

*Culpeper County*

**NORTH CAROLINA**

*Lenoir County*
- Wilmington

**SOUTH CAROLINA**
- Charleston
- Savannah

**GEORGIA**
- Atlanta

*Lumpkin County*

**ALABAMA**

**FLORIDA**

**MISSISSIPPI**

*Jones County*
- Mobile

**ARKANSAS**
- Baton Rouge
- Shreveport
- Opelousas

*Mississippi River*

**LOUISIANA**
- New Orleans

*Lafourche District*

**INDIAN TERRITORY**
- Gainesville

**TEXAS**

*Northern Sub-District of Texas*
- San Antonio

*Donald S. Frazier*
*Abilene, Texas*

# Introduction:
# The Desperate Side of War

## Daniel E. Sutherland

T HE CLASH of Northern and Southern armies during the Civil War is traditionally lamented as a tragic episode that sometimes found brothers fighting brothers. Yet even more tragic, and far more pervasive, was the relentless, frequently bloody internal struggle to control the Confederate home front, a struggle that pitted families and neighbors against one another. The essays, all but one published for the first time in this volume, explore important dimensions of this most brutal and desperate side of the Civil War.

Scholarly interest in the Southern home front goes back at least to the first third of this century. Studies by Albert Burton Moore, Ella Lonn, and Georgia Lee Tatum spoke to issues of conscription, desertion, and disloyalty, issues that had received scant attention in broader military and political histories. A turning point and forcible boost to recent interest in what had happened behind the lines came in 1984 with publication of *Why the South Lost the Civil War*. This collaborative effort by four military/political scholars asserted that Confederate defeat came not only as a result of battlefield losses but also from a collapse of will at all levels of Rebel society. An earlier scholar, E. Merton Coulter, building on the work of Moore, Lonn, and Tatum, had said much the same thing in 1950, but *Why the South Lost* revitalized in more sophisticated fashion the premise that vital social, cultural, and intellectual dynamics within the South were as important as military and political ones in determining the outcome of the war.[1]

Within this web of tangled interpretations, several more finely focused interpretive trends have also emerged, three of which—Southern Unionism, the meaning of community, and the upheaval caused by guerrilla warfare—hold immediate relevance for the essays in this volume. Oldest of all is the effort to explain the role of Southern Unionists in the war. Unionists got their due in Tatum's 1934 book, although she tended to explore organized resistance to Confederate rule rather than individual clashes between Unionists and secessionists or the meaning of Unionism. Still, except for a tantalizing look at the subject by Frank W. Klingberg in the 1950s, Tatum's work stood alone for forty years, until Carl Degler directed our attention to the whys and wherefores of Unionism in *The Other South: Southern Dissenters in the Nineteenth Century*. A number of historians followed Degler's lead by testing the meaning of Southern Unionism at the state and local level. North Carolina—birthplace of the militant peace organization Heroes of America and home to outspoken Unionist leaders like William W. Holden—received the most attention; but scholars examined other Unionist strongholds, too, including portions of Alabama, Arkansas, Georgia, Tennessee, and Virginia.[2]

Despite all this energetic probing, we still lack a comprehensive history of Southern Unionism, a fact that may be explained in no small part by our inability to agree on a satisfactory definition of the subject. The problem stems partly from the different phases and objectives of Southern Unionism. Unionists and cooperationists inspired widespread opposition to the Confederacy during the early, pre–Fort Sumter, secession crisis. Yet these early expressions of anti-Confederate sentiment differed in important ways from the variety that developed during the war. Generally speaking, they were political expressions that embodied rational, well-articulated, well-defined, and closely argued ideological positions. Even so, they remain hard to define, largely, as Daniel W. Crofts suggests in his excellent study of Unionism in the Upper South, because they "vanished abruptly."[3]

Wartime Unionism, the phase of unionism considered by several essays in this collection, sometimes had a political dimension; but here, too, the dissenters divided. The most staunch wartime Unionists—the so-called "tories"—endorsed Union political ideology, encouraged hostility to the Confederacy, and sought to end the war at all costs. This sort of political opposition found its most effective expression in places like East Tennessee and West Virginia, where many Unionist leaders in the secession crisis continued to hold sway. But another strain, and seemingly the dominant one, emerged when many loyal Confederates, appalled by the mounting human and material costs of war, called for a peaceful settlement of the conflict. The Unionism of these peace advocates was more pragmatic than ideological, and it was fostered more by war weariness than by political considerations. They did not object to seeing the Union rejoined, but, unlike the tories, they feared any peace settlement that failed to protect Southern interests. Further complicating matters, some peace advocates were also pacifists or religious dissenters. The Quakers of the North Carolina piedmont and some German communities in Texas offer good examples of people whose loyalties were defined by a mixture of political, social, and cultural factors.

Then there were what may be called the "antigovernment" Confederates. Many of these people were indistinguishable from the peace advocates. They believed the Confederate government had bungled the war at an enormous cost to the citizenry. What was more, they opposed the centralizing policies of the Confederacy, most especially conscription and confiscation. They became bitter, even to the point of sometimes aligning themselves with the tories, yet they parted company with any group of dissenters who considered reunion an acceptable solution to the war. Antigovernment Confederates welcomed an armistice but not a surrender. They wanted Confederate policies altered but did not want the Confederacy toppled. It is a fine line, to be sure, but then that is what makes this business of Unionism and Confederate opposition such a slippery proposition.

Another indication of the complexity of this issue may be seen in the fact that these Unionists sometimes expressed conflicting sentiments. Some contradictions were inevitable, inspired as they were by changing military and political fortunes over four years of war. One day, people might be fervent and firm in their desire to see the nation rejoined. A few months later, the shifting fortunes of war and altered personal circumstances could make the same people more cautious, less certain that the Union should be repaired without political or constitutional guarantees being extended to the South. Not a few Southerners battled with dual, simultaneous loyalties. A Missouri farmer balked when asked to prove his devotion to the United States by signing an oath of allegiance: "I have never acknowledged allegiance to any other government than that of the U.S. & would prefer taking the oath to being imprisoned to the injury of my health & the distress of my family," he insisted, "yet I protest against the right of the state to impose any involuntary oath upon us. The constitution prescribes no oath to private citizens or persons not in the official employment of the Government."[4]

So the question remains: Who were the Unionists? Stephen V. Ash, in a series of articles and two books on the occupied South, has contributed most to our understanding of Unionism across the Confederacy. In *When the Yankees Came: Conflict and Chaos in the Occupied South, 1861–1865*, Ash skillfully integrates discussions of Federal military policy toward civilians, the physical and emotional disruption of communities, and the clash of competing factions within the Confederacy. Although he sidesteps the sticky issues of East Tennessee and West Virginia—the Confederacy's two most active Unionist regions—as well as large portions of other Unionist bastions that were not occupied by the Federals, he successfully summarizes current historical thinking by identifying three principal "wellsprings" of Unionism. Southern Unionists, he says, were most likely either Northern emigrants to the South, former Whigs, or small—and generally poor—farmers. The fact that any one of these three groups could be diametrically opposed to another but further illustrates how complicated the issue can be.[5]

More detailed studies of Rebel communities blur even these distinctions. W. Todd Groce has suggested that the principal differences between Unionist and secessionist leaders in East Tennessee were age and occupation. Unionists tended to be older than secessionists, Groce contends, and they were agriculturalists rather than merchants or professional people. Martin Crawford believes that the socioeconomic profiles of volunteers for the Union and Confederate armies in one North Carolina county support the more traditional view, as presented by Ash; but he also admits that there were virtually no social or economic differences between people living in Unionist and Confederate regions of the county. As for politics, Crawford warns against easy generalizations: "For most southern mountaineers, the war did not resolve itself into a neat argument between diver-

gent political ideals or social allegiances." The same caution should be
used in handling the complex issue of social class. The war divided social
classes, says Richard N. Current in his admirable study of the eighty-six
thousand white Southerners who joined the Union army, as surely as it
splintered families and communities. Loyalists differed "*with* the rebels
much more than they differed *from* them," he concludes perceptively.[6]

This emphasis on state and local studies of Unionist and antigovernment Confederate activity coincides with a decided trend toward the study
of communities as a means of understanding the war, and it represents a
second important theme in this volume. Neither the United States nor the
Confederate States was a genuinely united nation. Each had its naysayers,
peace advocates, draft dodgers, and traitors. The most easily spotted weak-
ness in earlier studies of Unionism, such as those by Tatum and Degler, was
a tendency to speak in generalities. Their sweeping conclusions about
Unionism and Unionists require verification at the community level. The
Civil War was a struggle not just between two blocks of states but among
states, and it can be comprehended only through the collected experiences
of individual states. Even more to the point, it needs to be explored through
the lives of individual communities. The most revealing recent explorations
of the South's wartime experience—including Unionism—have been built
on studies of individual towns and counties. *The Civil War in Appalachia,* a
collection of essays edited by Kenneth W. Noe and Shannon H. Wilson,
which has several elements in common with the present volume, utilizes
this approach quite successfully. Even Ash's *When the Yankees Came,* while
treating the broad sweep of the Confederacy, is sensitive to differences in
local circumstances.

The advantage of local studies in coming to grips with the clash
between Unionists and secessionists is the wealth of detail they can provide. By dealing with limited numbers of people, historians can carefully
investigate the social, economic, and political status of individuals and
the competing segments of their communities. By getting to know these
people intimately, scholars can better understand what motivated them
and interpret their behavior with more confidence. They can flesh out
local stories to provide insights denied them when taking the longer view
of events. The best way to understand the impact of the war on the South
is to examine it at this level, where one may watch, weigh, measure, and

evaluate the consequences of war as they affected a single, concentrated area and the people, both soldiers and civilians, who witnessed the war there. Moreover, local studies can infuse our understanding of the war with the gritty experience of real people, people with names, and families who wondered what each day would bring, how long the war would last, and how much more chaos, destruction, and suspense they would be asked to endure. This is one area of research where it is important not to miss the trees for the forest.[7]

A common desire to control communities produced acts of suppression and violence that erupted into guerrilla warfare—the third ingredient of these essays—on many parts of the Southern home front. The Rebels employed a variety of means to keep Unionists in check, including intimidation by Confederate soldiers, militia, conscription and impressment agents, and watchful secessionist neighbors; but nothing was as effective in controlling dissidents as the threat of retaliation by Rebel guerrillas. Not coincidentally, the most momentous confrontations between Unionists and secessionists came in the hills and mountains of Appalachia and the Ozarks. Richard Current estimates that 75 percent of all Unionists lived in those hills and mountains. Unfortunately, that rugged terrain was also home to the largest bands of Rebel guerrillas. A collision was unavoidable. From their mountain bases, Confederate guerrillas could harass and embarrass Federal armies; but they also preyed on civilians, particularly the despised Unionists.[8]

This is not say that Unionists were always hapless victims, for they often retaliated against Rebel neighbors. Even though outnumbered in most places, they struck back whenever possible at symbols of Confederate authority and fought to maintain control of their communities, sometimes as guerrillas. Unionist guerrillas appear to have congregated in smaller bands than the Rebels, and perhaps more of them operated as lone bushwhackers in picking off enemy soldiers and civilians, but they added a marked degree of precariousness and uncertainty to everyday life. In areas occupied by or within range of the Union army, the Federals recruited Unionists to form counterguerrilla units. They realized, quite rightly, that Unionists, with their knowledge of the terrain, the Rebel rendezvous points, and the identify of Rebel sympathizers, were perfectly suited to root out a common foe.

Interest in the guerrilla conflict has grown steadily over the past few decades, but only recently have we begun to understand the rank-and-file guerrilla, whether Union or Confederate, and the nature of the South's guerrilla war. During the 1950s and 1960s, historians were interested primarily in the exploits of famous partisan leaders, such as William C. Quantrill and John S. Mosby. Albert Castel went beyond this popular fixation in the 1970s to explore both the extent of the guerrilla war and the motives of Confederate irregulars, but two historiographical trends not directly related to guerrillas have had the most dramatic effect. In 1976, John Keegan rallied an entire generation of military historians to what soon became known as the "new" military history. The experiences of the common soldier and the broader meaning of combat, rather than grand strategy and the deeds of generals, became the new focus. Then in 1989, Maris Vinovskis, suggesting that the study of the Civil War was too important to leave to military historians, called on scholars to employ the insights and techniques (often quantitative) of social history to learn more about the impact of the war on soldiers and their families, on civilians and their communities.[9]

On all three counts—as military history, as social history, as community history—the guerrilla war perfectly suited these new directions. A model for examining this side of the war soon appeared in the form of Phillip Shaw Paludan's *Victims: A True Story of the Civil War*, a powerful tale about the execution of thirteen North Carolina Unionist guerrillas by the Rebels. Equally dramatic was Michael Fellman's *Inside War: The Guerrilla Conflict in Missouri during the Civil War*, published the same year as the Vinovskis article. Since then, numerous historians have boldly entered the guerrilla arena. The best of their work explores the wartime tensions between Rebel guerrillas and Unionists, especially the duel to control and preserve Southern communities. Several essays in *The Civil War in Appalachia* incorporate those themes, as do recent books by B. Franklin Cooling and Noel C. Fisher. As further evidence of the tension between military and social history in the guerrilla story, the contributors to the present volume are evenly divided between military and social historians.[10]

But some lesser themes should also be considered in looking at violence and conflict on the Confederate home front. For instance, the role played by geography has already been offered as one explanation for the

bitterness of the Unionist versus secessionist clash, with the violence of
that collision being most evident in the rugged terrain of Appalachia and
the Ozarks. But some historians have suggested yet another geographical
factor to distinguish *between* those two regions, or, indeed, between
Appalachia and the entire Trans-Mississippi. The Confederacy west of
the Mississippi River represented more of a frontier region than the mountains of Virginia, Tennessee, and North Carolina or the hills of Alabama
and Georgia, say these scholars. A tradition of vigilante justice and frontier hooliganism still prevailed in the West. The region was still largely
untamed and populated by rough characters who carried guns as a matter of course. Hostile Indians threatened the security of the Texas border, and Bleeding Kansas seemed to represent a western solution to
political problems.[11]

Chronology also seems to have played a hand in the violence. Simply
put, both the intensity and scope of the violence appear to have grown
as the war progressed. There were early clashes, to be sure. The prewar
mayhem of the Kansas-Missouri border war spread alarmingly fast through
the border states. Rebels retaliated with ferocity against the "bridge burners" in East Tennessee. Urban violence broke out in Baltimore, St. Louis,
and even Jacksonville, Florida, during the first months of the war. In
Texas, the "great hanging" of more than forty Unionists at Gainesville
occurred in October 1862. But not until 1863, and most especially in 1864
and 1865, did the violence become systematic and systemic. Quantrill
first organized his band of cuthroats in 1862, but the infamous raid on
Lawrence, Kansas, did not come until August 1863. The Jeff Williams
band of Arkansas Unionist guerrillas did not form until September 1863;
most of North Georgia's several Unionist bands did not organize until
1864; Ezekiel Counts's Confederate partisans did not begin operations in
southwestern Virginia until 1864; and William H. Thomas's band of
North Carolina Cherokees, though organized in September 1862, did not
begin serious operations against Unionist troublemakers until 1863.[12]

Several factors help to explain the shift. First, Confederate guerrilla
operations against the Union army had become widespread by 1863. It
was an easy matter, while disrupting Federal communications and harass-
ing Federal troops, for these Rebels to strike as well at perceived threats
on the home front. Second, Union war policy had become less concili-

atory by 1863, aimed as much at Rebel civilians as at Confederate soldiers. This escalation, which, in fact, came much earlier in some parts of
the South, was bound intrinsically to the effectiveness of the guerrilla war
against Union forces, especially in the Trans-Mississippi and Western
theaters, and it is not easy to determine the extent to which Rebel guerrillas had already targeted Unionist neighbors.[13]

Third, the Conscription Act and Partisan Ranger Act, both passed by
the Confederate Congress in April 1862, altered Southern perceptions
about how best to defend the home front. Historians have yet to appreciate the large numbers of loyal Confederates who left the army after their
original short-term enlistments had expired in order to join guerrilla bands.
In the eyes of the government, these men had deserted, for the Conscription
Act required men already in the army to fight for the duration of the war.
But to their own way of thinking, these men remained steadfast Rebels, and
they used the Partisan Ranger Act to legitimize their new mode of fighting. Unionists also took to the bush when it appeared they would be forced
to fight for the Confederacy, and both secessionists and Unionists embraced
irregular warfare as the surest way to defend their homes, maintain law and
order, and wrest control of their neighborhoods from the enemy.[14]

Finally, and perhaps most importantly, the war weariness and anti-
Confederate sentiment that inspired so much dissent and overt Unionist
reaction against the Confederacy did not find widespread expression until
1863. Not by chance, eight of the eleven essays in the present volume
focus on community violence and the guerrilla threat during the last half
of the war.

The first three essays in this volume demonstrate how the struggle for
community autonomy had evoked ugly reactions by 1864 in Mississippi,
Georgia, and North Carolina. Victoria E. Bynum begins by offering a different slant on a well-known story, the "Free State of Jones." Bynum uses
the results of a Confederate cavalry raid against Jones County Unionists to
illustrate the roles of myth and memory in history. After the war, she says,
former Confederates insisted that every Southern man, woman, and child
had been loyal to the Confederacy. The self-proclaimed Unionists of Jones
County, according to ex-Confederate recollections of events, had been
thugs and bandits who used Unionism as an excuse to rob and pillage. But
were they such bullies? Bynum explores the twists and turns surrounding

the death of one Unionist guerrilla, a man named Ben Knight, to reveal the powerful force of myth in shaping the past.

Jonathan D. Sarris shows how and why Unionists in northern Georgia suffered for their beliefs by examining the important issue of community control. The great political and social catch phrases of Union, states rights, slavery, and abolition were secondary for many Southerners, whether Unionists or Confederates, says Sarris. What most concerned them was the breakdown of law and order in their communities. Unionists believed that Confederate conscription, confiscation, impressment, and similarly oppressive measures were extralegal actions taken by an illegitimate government. They responded by enlisting in Union service and forming guerrilla bands to oppose the usurpers. As a result, whirl became king, anarchy threatened, and both sides engaged in a brutal internal war to bring the other side to heel.

North Carolina, with perhaps the most ornery population of any Confederate state, saw its share of violence, too. Lesley J. Gordon relates a frightfully brutal tale of Unionist suppression that deals, as does the Sarris essay to some extent, with issues concerning the rules of war. In early 1864—roughly the same time period examined by Bynum and Sarris— General George E. Pickett executed a band of Confederate deserters. More than deserters, maintained Pickett, the men were traitors who had subsequently enlisted in Union service. The accused men insisted that they had been tricked or bullied into serving the Confederacy (most of them as state militia or partisans) and that they deserved to be treated as prisoners of war, not deserters.

Jon L. Wakelyn shifts the focus away from physical violence to a war of words between Unionists and Rebels in Virginia. Unionist leaders in the Old Dominion, concentrated in the upper and western portions of the state, worked desperately to maintain political control of their region. They succeeded in spectacular fashion by creating the loyal government of West Virginia. In order to achieve that mighty feat, tory leaders wrote and distributed pamphlets to encourage their followers to resist intimidation by Rebel neighbors and guerrilla bands. In so doing, they used the rhetoric of violence to forge a powerful political identity. Thus Wakelyn shows how the language and image of violence were used to wage war and how they can help us to understand yet another dimension of the South's internal civil war.

Daniel E. Sutherland looks at the divisions between Rebels and Unionists in Confederate Virginia. He is principally concerned with the role played by social class in defining the Unionist-Confederate split and the ways some historians have used class divisions to explain the collapse of the Confederacy. He finds that class had little to do with either issue in Culpeper County, Virginia. He also notes the absence of violence between neighbors in the community. Culpeper had Unionists, to be sure, but they were few in number and relatively prosperous. The factors that steered them toward a Unionist or antigovernment position were most often the size of their families, a sentimental attachment to the Union, self-interest, and a growing realization that the South could not win the war.

Noel C. Fisher discusses both political and military resistence to Confederate authority by Unionists in East Tennessee, one of the few regions of the South where tories outnumbered their Rebel neighbors. Militarily, Unionist partisans sabotaged railroads and telegraph lines, bush-whacked Confederate troops, terrorized Rebel civilians, and did battle with their Rebel counterparts, although Fisher also emphasizes that most loy-alist men preferred to join the Union army rather than haunt the hills as guerrillas. In any case, Unionist success allowed political leaders such as Andrew Johnson and William G. Brownlow to reassert Federal authority in East Tennessee by 1864.

B. Franklin Cooling maintains that the guerrilla war is the key to understanding the broader "civil" war of 1861–65 in the rest of Tennessee and in Kentucky. The guerrillas "linked war and society, . . . politics, eco-nomics, culture and violence in a holistic manner," he says. Irregular war-fare became the face of conflict seen most often by noncombatants in the region. Southerners who seldom caught a glimpse of conventional armies became all too familiar with the violence and oppression of guerrilla and counterguerrilla operations. Yet, like several other contributors, Cooling suggests that, despite appearances, most irregulars engaged not in random violence but, rather, in purposeful action that was intended to maintain law and order in their communities. He also asserts that the effectiveness of Confederate guerrilla operations, perhaps more than any single factor, pushed the Union army toward a harsher policy of repression against Southern civilians.

Moving to the Trans-Mississippi, David Paul Smith finds an equally complex, though very different, situation in Texas. The problem most

often confronted by Lone Star Confederates in dealing with dissent was
to distinguish between those people who presented genuine threats to the
security of the state and those who wished only to escape the destructive
force of war. Smith, like several contributors, poses the question of how
governments can ensure security while protecting democratic freedoms in
a nation at war. Northern Texas communities, in particular, says Smith,
bordered on chaos. By the final year of the war, thousands of deserters,
draft dodgers, and Unionists had joined with an even older foe of frontier
Texans, hostile bands of Comanches and Kiowas, to threaten any semblance of order and security. Confederate Texans were so worn down emotionally and psychologically by the constant threats of violence that they
lost interest in both the war and anti-Confederate dissenters.

Louisiana's rambunctious history, says Donald S. Frazier, made that
state "a land of blurred loyalties and simmering animosities" by 1861. War
only legitimized violence, anarchy, and guerrilla reprisals. As in most of
the rest of the Trans-Mississippi, both Union and Confederate military
leaders in Louisiana resorted to irregular warfare. The Confederates
needed guerrillas to supplement their outnumbered volunteer forces, and
the Federals relied on antiguerrilla units to counter them. In addition,
the Confederates formed partisan bands to operate as anti-jayhawker
units. Unhappily for Louisiana's civilians, neither side gave much thought
to the safety or welfare of noncombatants, regardless of their politics.
Geography again helped to define the boundaries of conflict, as home
front violence flourished most readily amid the rivers, streams, and bayous
of southern Louisiana.

While Frazier and Cooling only touch on the Union army's counterguerrilla operations, Robert Mackey examines this part of the war in detail
for Arkansas. Mackey believes that the only hope Confederate Arkansas
had for victory rested in a viable guerrilla war. Yet guerrilla resistance failed
in the state, in part because of Unionist-secessionist divisions within the
population, in part because of an elaborate counterguerrilla campaign
waged by the Union army. At first, the Federals pursued a policy of retribution against both Rebel guerrillas and their civilians supporters. When
that failed to work, they experimented with legal retaliation, enhanced
military security, the organization of Arkansas Unionists into antiguerrilla
military units, and the creation of fortified colonies.

The final essay, by Michael Fellman, maintains that the war between Unionists and secessionists produced nothing less than a "cultural catastrophe" in Missouri and that the brutality of their struggle had no equal in the war. Yet Fellman is not concerned so much with compiling another detailed narrative of violence in the land of Quantrill and Bloody Bill Anderson as he is with trying to understand the violence. The historian of the Confederacy's inner war, he declares in a singularly powerful and personal essay, confronts the same dilemma faced by the Civil War generation itself: How does one comprehend and cope with the barbarity of such acts? Fellman explores the ways in which both the victims and the perpetrators of violence in Missouri came to terms with their wartime environment and suggests how scholars can do the same.

None of these contributors contends that the meaning of the war can be reduced to a question of who controlled the Confederate home front. Famous generals, mighty armies, and wily politicians will always claim a prominent place in the story of the Civil War. Yet the impact of battles and elections cannot be entirely understood without appreciating the less visible struggle for survival on the home front. The actions of generals and politicians tell us something about why the war ended as it did; stories about Southerners and their wartime communities, whether Unionist or Rebel, explain the nature of the war and what it all meant to people far removed from traditional battlefields. The essays in this collection offer no definitive answers to the numerous questions that remain about conflict, violence, Southern loyalties, guerrillas, or the role of community; but they do nudge us closer to some reasonable conclusions. Equally important, they sometimes raise new questions.

# Telling and Retelling the Legend of the "Free State of Jones"

## Victoria E. Bynum

IN THE DAYS surrounding April 15, 1864, several deadly confrontations erupted on the borders of Jones and Covington Counties, near the Leaf River in southeastern Mississippi. A band of deserters headed by Newton Knight clashed with a company of Confederate cavalry led by Colonel Robert Lowry. By the time the skirmishes ended, one cavalryman had been killed and ten deserters "summarily executed" by the cavalry. Although all of the deaths have been described in various accounts of the clash, the gruesome killing of Newton's cousin, Benjamin Franklin Knight, has become legendary.

In an article published by the Jackson *Daily News* in 1974, Ruby Jordan recalled the story of Ben Knight's death as told by her uncle, Benjamin D. Graves. Jordan remained true to her uncle's version of Ben's death, told almost fifty years earlier at a community meeting in Hebron, Mississippi. At that gathering, seventy-five-year-old Ben Graves recalled his Civil War experiences. His memories were not those of a soldier, however, but of a twelve-year-old boy living in a war-torn community located near the Leaf River.[1]

Graves remembered awakening one morning to his brother's insistence that he had heard the firing of guns in the night. As the day progressed, he learned that twenty-seven-year-old Ben Knight, a neighbor,

upon hearing a noise, had risen from bed to find a group of Confederate
cavalry gathered near his home. Panic stricken, Ben ran "out through
them with his night clothes on." A cavalryman shot at him as he ran
down the road to Newton Knight's house. Breathlessly, he crossed the
bridge that separated his home from Newt's, only to find his cousin gone.
Instead, Ben found another cousin, seventeen-year-old Sil Coleman,
asleep at Newt's house. He woke Sil up and, together, they ran to nearby
Mason's Creek where they hid in the swamp.[2]

Graves then described the cavalry's capture of Ben. Run down by
bloodhounds, Ben was "torn up pretty bad" and craved water "like wounded
men always do." When he begged his captors for water, they refused and
prepared to hang him. Ben called on a merciful God to fill his grave with
cool water. Graves swore that "when they dug the grave right up on top of
the hill from where they hung him and Sil Coleman, water run into the
grave. I have heard people who saw it say so." The horrified community of
mostly Baptists and Methodists converted Ben's burial into a sacred baptism that gave meaning to the otherwise senseless loss of a young life.[3]

The story of Ben Knight's death is one of many folktales, ghost stories,
and scandals that grew out of the legendary Free State of Jones, where by
early 1864 deserters had become well organized and well known to the
Confederacy. Their self-styled military unit, the Knight Company, attracted
men from Jones and the surrounding counties of Covington, Jasper, Perry,
and Smith. The company's main hideout, Deserters' Den on the Leaf River,
is only one of many sites within the South where deadly civil wars were
fought between Confederate and anti-Confederate forces.[4]

Although Ruby Jordan repeated Ben Graves's version of Ben Knight's
death in her 1974 newspaper article, a new version in 1951 had already
eclipsed it. That year Ethel Knight, an amateur historian with deep roots
in the area, published *The Echo of the Black Horn*, her account of Newton
Knight and the Free State of Jones. Ethel, who was Newt's grandniece,
claimed that Ben was not a deserter at all, but rather a Confederate soldier who carried furlough papers in his pocket at the moment of his death.
Furthermore, she emphasized, the innocent Ben was murdered because the
cavalry believed that they had captured the guiltiest of deserters, Newton
Knight himself, to whom Ben bore an "unfortunate resemblance."[5]

Fiercely loyal to the Confederate cause, Ethel dedicated her book to the memory of the "Noble Confederates who lived and died for Jones County." She distanced pro-Confederate members of the Knight family from those who deserted by portraying Newt as a clever, shrewd, but half-crazed, murderous outlaw. In spite of a growing number of historical works during the 1940s and 1950s that subjected the Myth of the Lost Cause to withering criticisms, first-time author Ethel Knight zealously asserted all its chief tenets. Publishing her *Echo of the Black Horn* the same year as C. Vann Woodward's pathbreaking *Origins of the New South*, Ethel successfully packaged the Free State of Jones in a straightjacket of Lost Cause sentimentality, diatribe, and indignation.[6]

Among Mississippians today, Ethel's regularly reprinted history of the Free State of Jones reigns as the most widely known version. Her goal—to forever banish the notion that Newton Knight and his band of deserters might represent a principled opposition to secession and the Confederacy—encouraged her to reshape Ben Knight into a loyal Confederate soldier. By placing furlough papers in his pocket, she enabled "loyal" white Mississippians, especially loyal Knights like herself, to mourn his death yet deplore and disown the outlaw Newton Knight.

Despite Ethel's claims, there is solid evidence that Ben deserted the Confederate army and joined the Knight Company. Military records, for example, indicate that he was AWOL from December 1863 to February 1864 when his record ends. His name also appears on Newton Knight's handwritten company roster. Certainly, the Confederate cavalry had no doubts that he was in cahoots with the band of deserters they sought to vanquish. In a letter published in the Mobile *Evening News* on May 3, 1864, less than a month after Ben's execution, one of Colonel Lowry's men described the event. Ben Knight and Sil Coleman, he claimed, had attempted to ambush "another party of our boys" near the home of Newton Knight, just days after a sniper attacked three of Lowry's men in neighboring Covington County.[7]

In Covington County, the cavalry "promptly executed" Daniel Reddock, whom they identified as the sniper; they also shot to death Reddock's companion, Tucker Gregg, when he attempted to run from them. Convinced that they had nabbed the men who tried to ambush them, members of Lowry's band unleashed their hounds on Ben Knight and Sil Coleman, and then hanged them from the same tree. Explaining that the "condition of the community required it," the officer proudly proclaimed that "terror was struck" on the borders of Covington and Jones Counties.[8]

Contrasting versions of Ben Knight's death represent competing views about the Free State of Jones itself. Throughout the years, the legend of the Free State of Jones has been the subject of numerous essays, several books, a novel, and even a movie, its meaning periodically reshaped according to conflicts of the times. In fact, the earliest debates about the Free State began before the war ended when the Natchez *Courier* erroneously reported that Jones County had seceded from the Confederacy and declared itself the "Republic of Jones." From there the tale of a confederacy within a confederacy grew even taller.[9]

In 1886, G. Norton Galloway, a Northerner who billed himself as the "historian of the 6th Army Corps," published his version of the uprising in an essay. Galloway described a "Jones County Confederacy" that had produced its own constitution and elected "Nathan" (Newton) Knight as its president. He entertained Northerners and ridiculed Southerners with images of feuding backswoodsmen engaged in fratricidal war—"bloodcurdling in the extreme." Southern whites were portrayed as ignorant and illiterate brutes, no matter on which side of the war they fought. Plainly intending to endorse the civilizing effects of industrialization, Galloway ended by praising Northern capitalists' introduction of lumber mills into Jones County.[10]

In an era in which Northern and Southern elites clasped hands across the ruins of war to build an economically "progressive" New South, Confederate General Dabney H. Maury offered a Southern version of the Free State of Jones. In his 1894 memoir, *Recollections of a Virginian*, he, too, portrayed the deserters as hyper-secessionists, referring to the uprising as an "imperium in imperio." Like Galloway, Maury described the deserters as degraded poor whites, but from a class-based rather than a Northern perspective. Jones County, he explained, was part of the "vast piney woods that sweep along our seaboard from Carolina to the Sabine." For him, the area contained the "worst class of our population."[11]

In the wake of Galloway's article and Maury's memoir, twentieth-century journalists, folklorists, and historians time and again wrangled over whether Jones County truly attempted secession from the Confederacy. New South writers increasingly romanticized the Confederate cause and exaggerated the image of a "Solid [white] South" in an era of growing racial segregation. They found the notion that Jones's deserters attempted secession-within-secession more entertaining and believable than the notion that they supported the Union. Jones County deserters devolved into degraded, poor whites who responded savagely to any and all authority. Stung by the story's connotations of poor white ignorance and violence, local residents frequently denied that any such secession took place. Deserters and their descendants continued to assert that they had supported the Union during the Civil War.[12]

Certainly, most members of the Knight Company were not the knife-wielding "brutes in the forms of men," described by Galloway. Neither did they possess the most "vicious and cruel natures" found in North America, as Maury claimed. They did, however, live in a region periph-eral to national markets, and they participated only marginally in Southern political decision making. Piney Woods people were essentially farmers and herders who built strongly kin-based, church-centered com-munities. During annual or biannual trips to Mobile, they marketed their livestock, wool, and relatively small crops of cotton and rice. Economic independence was fragile; many in fact grew too little corn to be truly self-sufficient in order to devote more acres to grazing cattle and raising cash crops. Most Jones County farmers were descended from plain folk who fled or bypassed plantation regions of Virginia, North Carolina, South Carolina, and Georgia in favor of limited, selective access to mar-kets. By choosing to live in backcountry regions, they hoped to avoid direct competition with planters in Black Belt regions.[13]

The Knight Company consisted primarily of nonslaveholding yeoman farmers. Like many pockets of Southern Unionism, the Jones County region boasted few members of the planter class. In 1860, slaves comprised only 12.2 percent of Jones County's population. Of the total 116 slaveholders who claimed 407 slaves, 97 owned 5 or fewer. What most distinguished the deserter band's core members from their pro-Confederate neighbors was fewer slaves, and less wealth. Most of the approximately 95 men who joined Knight's Company owned land but no slaves; only 11 were slaveholders or lived with slaveholding fathers. Clearly, economic suffering contributed to men's decision to desert the Confederacy, particularly after the Union army's siege of Vicksburg from mid-May to July 4, 1863.[14]

Although most members of the Knight band were nonslaveholders, many were kin to slaveholders. In 1860 Newton Knight's grandfather, Jackie Knight, owned 22 slaves although neither Newton, who claimed land worth $800 and personal property worth $300, nor his father, Albert, owned slaves. Likewise, neither Jasper Collins nor William Wesley Sumrall owned slaves although some of their relatives did. Collins, age thirty-three in 1860, claimed $2,000 in real and $1,120 in personal property. Twenty-year-old William Wesley Sumrall lived with his forty-two-year-old brother, Harmon Levi Sumrall, a nonslaveholder who claimed $1,000 in real and $924 in personal property.[15]

By the mid-twentieth century, the debate over whether Jones County actually seceded from the Confederacy had waned. Many historians nevertheless doubted that a band of backwoods white farmers had challenged the legitimacy, as well as the authority, of the Confederacy. Ethel Knight vehemently denied that any but a few members of the Knight Company were Unionists. "In fact," she claimed, "the Knight Company hated the Union as much as did any Rebel." She correctly pointed out that several of its members came from slaveholding families, but simultaneously characterized the others as "riffraff." In her view, all of them were misguided, fearful dupes of a demented Newton Knight. Other historians continued to portray Newt and his followers as simple, pastoral people frozen in time, or, alternately, as desperadoes who preferred to murder, pillage, and lay out in swamps rather than fight for their "country."[16]

Unlike twentieth-century writers, however, Confederate leaders described Jones County deserters as both outlaws *and* Unionists. Lieutenant General Leonidas Polk reported to President Jefferson Davis that Jones's deserters called themselves "Southern Yankees;" he seemed to accept the label at face value. Captain W. Wirt Thomson of Company A, Twenty-fourth Mississippi Regiment, reported to Secretary of War James Seddon that a "Federal flag had been raised by [deserters] over the courthouse in Jones County."[17]

Colonel William Brown, a member of the Lowry expedition who spent a good deal of time observing and talking with the civilian population of Jones County, attributed Unionism to the agrarian influence of elder citizens. In a letter to Governor Charles Clark dated May 5, 1864, he described deserters as "misled by some old and influential citizens—perhaps their fathers or relatives—who have encouraged and harbored them. We find great ignorance among them generally and many union ideas that seem to be principles [held] by demogogues of the agrarian class."[18]

What Confederate leaders did not accept was the *legitimacy* of Unionist claims. Even before the explosive events of mid-April 1864, cavalry and deserters had clashed in Jones County. On February 7, 1864, Confederate lieutenant general Polk directed General Dabney H. Maury to order Colonel Henry Maury and five hundred men into Jones County to subdue deserters. In a letter to Confederate secretary of war James Seddon dated March 3, 1864, Dabney Maury emphasized that Jones's deserters were well armed and five hundred strong. "They have been seizing Government stores," he wrote, ". . . killing our people, and have actually made prisoners of and paroled officers of the Confederate army." Indeed, on the same day that Maury wrote to Seddon, Polk reported to Confederate headquarters that Jones County deserters had murdered a conscript officer, pillaged loyal citizens' houses, and launched a successful raid on government stores at Paulding, in neighboring Jasper County.[19]

Colonel Henry Maury reported from Jones county on March 12 that deserters were under control; "although," he wrote, "some few scattered outlaws are still lurking about in the swamps and will have to be hunted out with dogs." Appearances were deceiving, however; and the self-proclaimed "Southern Yankees" remained defiant. Polk was forced to send a second expedition, headed by Colonel Robert Lowry, into the region.[20]

Colonel Lowry regarded the Knight Company's punishment of Confederate soldiers by "death or banishment from home" as a shocking example of murder and treason. Colonel Brown expressed similar sentiments when he described to the governor the executions of "two brothers named Ates and two others named Whitehead." The men "were found guilty of desertion and armed resistance and were sentenced to death by hanging before a military court." In the Jones County region, wrote Brown, their deaths "made ten who have forfeited their lives for treason."[21]

Just as surely as Confederate leaders considered deserters guilty of treason, deserters did not accept the legitimacy of the Confederate government. In a 1921 interview with Meigs Frost of the *New Orleans Item*, Newton Knight bitterly denounced Colonel Lowry's executions of his men, complaining that he was "rough beyond reason. He hanged some of my company he had no right to hang." In 1870, Newt billed Congress for compensation on behalf of himself and selected men of the Knight Company, including the ten who were executed by Lowry's men.[22]

Newt supported his claims of Unionism with sworn testimony from several individuals, including Republican state senate nominee Richard Simmons. Simmons praised him as "a true Union man and a true friend to the Federal Government." B. A. Mathews, a former probate judge of Jones County, swore that "Knight and his men tuck shelter in the swamps & fought men & dogs day-by-day about twenty days" during Lowry's raid. "The men that Lowery murdered was as good citizens as the county afforded," he insisted; "all they had against them was because they weare fighting for the United States & did not deny it."[23]

In 1921, an aged Newt explained to Meigs Frost why he and his men considered themselves justified in deserting the Confederate army. Jones County voters had overwhelmingly opposed secession, he said, and had elected an anti-secession candidate, John H. Powell, to represent them at the 1861 state convention. Powell, however, switched to the pro-secession side after the first ballot. "Then next thing we knew," said Newt, "they were conscripting us. The rebels passed a law conscripting everybody between 18 and 35. They just came around with a squad of soldiers [and] took you." But, he maintained, "if they had a right to conscript me when I didn't want to fight the Union, I had a right to quit when I got ready."[24]

Newt claimed that he avoided the battlefield by enlisting as a hospital orderly, but his assertion is not supported by his military records. More likely, he developed Unionist views gradually, perhaps through contact with the militantly pro-Union Collins family. When the Twenty Negro Law was passed on October 11, 1862, exempting many large slaveholders from Confederate service, Jasper Collins immediately deserted his unit. According to Newt, Jasper told him shortly thereafter that the Twenty Negro Law had exposed the Confederate cause once and for all as a "rich man's war and poor man's fight." Newt concluded that Jasper was right.[25]

When Confederate leaders learned that the Knight Company controlled the county government by a combination of consent and terror, they sent special forces to the area. After Confederate forces rained down on them, Newt said, his company attempted to "break through the rebels" and join the Union army. His forces failed, however, and the Union army likewise failed to reach them. "Johnny Rebs busted up the party they sent to swear us in," explained Newt.[26]

Frost, Newt's interviewer, mistakenly concluded that Newt was referring to the Federal raid on Brookhaven, Mississippi, a raid that was routed by Lieutenant W. M. Wilson of the Forty-third Tennessee Infantry at Rocky Creek, near Ellisville, in Jones County. The Brookhaven raid occurred, however, on June 25, 1863, almost four months before the Knight Company was even formed. Conversely, historian Rudy Leverett cited the same Rocky Creek battle as evidence to disprove the popularity of Union sympathies in Jones County, because Lieutenant Wilson reported that Jones County citizens eagerly appropriated the "horses, arms, and equipments" of his Union prisoners. In a region beset by mounting food shortages and death tolls, however, the citizens' behavior need not have reflected a pro-Confederate stance. By 1863 Southern farm families were suffering mightily, and one would expect them to seize whatever goods became available.[27]

There is evidence, moreover, to support Newt's claim that the Knight Company intended to join Union forces. Although he had driven most deserters from the county, Colonel Henry Maury told General Dabney Maury, "[T]hey brag that they will get Yankee aid and return." On March 29, Captain W. Wirt Thomson reported rumors that "Yankees [were] frequently among" the Jones County deserters. Nine days later, and only one week before the Lowry raids, Daniel P. Logan warned Provost Marshal Major J. C. Denis that "large numbers" of Jones County deserters had "gone down Pearl River to and near Honey Island where they exist[ed] in some force . . . openly boasting of their being in communication with the Yankees." As late as August 14, 1864, Brigadier General W. L. Brandon reported to General Dabney Maury, "[A] Yankee lieutenant is now in Jones, entertained and protected by deserters."[28]

There were also twentieth-century voices—in addition to Newton Knight's—that insisted upon the Unionism of Jones County deserters. In 1912, Madison (Maddie) Prescott Bush, whose brother Scott had joined the Knight Company, explained his views on the Confederacy to a meeting of the Daughters of the American Revolution (DAR). He confessed frankly to his patriotic audience, "I was no secessioner, I will tell the truth about it." Even though he had participated in the great siege of Vicksburg, he explained, "I hope I didn't kill anybody. I had to go, but I didn't want to go." He conceded that some men and boys were eager to go to war because "they thought it was big to get the big guns on," but he insisted that anti-secession men like himself volunteered for service in the Confederate army "rather than be conscripted and be put in companies where [they] didn't want to go."[29]

Ruby Huff, kin to deserter and Reconstruction sheriff Thomas Jefferson Huff, wrote a history of the Lowry raid during the 1930s for the Works Progress Administration (WPA). Several decades of Lost Cause education apparently had little effect on Huff's reverence for the Knight band. Toward the end of her unpublished essay, Huff editorialized, "[T]his spirit of the South gets so unsouthy as to want to clap my hands and say three cheers for the most daring troop that ever tramped the Southern soil—the Deserters."[30]

B. R. Sumrall, kin to deserter William Wesley Sumrall, told a WPA interviewer in 1936 that members of the Knight Company "said that they were not deserters because in the first place their country [county] did not vote to ceceed [sic]." Sumrall offered both economic and ideological reasons for the county's anti-secessionist stance. First, he explained, most Jones County residents did not own slaves. Second, he claimed, paraphrasing Lincoln, those opposed to secession believed that "a house divided against itself cannot stand." Anti-secessionists feared that if the South seceded, "England would take the advantage of their discension [sic] and [they] would be again under the British yoke." Knight's Company, he said, required members to repeat the phrase "I am of the Red, White, and Blue" before entering camp. The company, he boasted, was made up of "the best men in Jones County."[31]

One might dismiss such claims as nothing more than attempts by descendants to defend the motives of the deserters, but even some pro-Confederates attributed the desertions to political principles. For example, Ben Graves, whose father owned ten slaves and supported the Confederacy, grudgingly conceded that political motives underlay Newton Knight's opposition to the Confederacy. "I believe in giving the devil his due," he said. "Newt was a mighty sorry man. . . . But he was a poor man and didn't own any Negroes. . . . He felt that the [Twenty Negro] law wasn't fair; that it enabled the rich man to evade service and that it wasn't right to ask him

THE LEGEND OF THE "FREE STATE OF JONES"

to risk his life for people who rated themselves so far above him." After the war, Graves pointed out, Newt "called himself a Union man and was a full-fledged Republican."[32]

Although Ethel Knight denied Newt's Unionism, she admitted that the family of Jasper Collins was overwhelmingly Unionist in its sympathies. It could hardly be denied. Sumrall, for example, described how Jasper's older brother Riley once "called a meeting at old Union church in Jones County where he made a great speech" in which he condemned the "injustice" of secession. Riley urged the men of Jones to "not fight against the union; but if they had to fight [to] stay at home and fight for a cause in which they believed." He fled to New Orleans during the Lowry raid, joined the Union army, and died of disease five months later.[33]

Riley's brothers, Jasper and Vinson, revealed Unionist sympathies well before and after 1861. Jasper Collins named a son born in 1855 "Henry Clay" and another, born in 1867, "Ulysses Sherman." Vinson, who named a son born in 1852 "Clay Crittenden," served in the Mississippi State Convention of 1868 as Jones's delegate. Yet another Collins brother, Simeon (Sim), harbored his three sons as deserters. Father and sons were all members of the Knight Company. Finally, in the Big Thicket region of eastern Texas, three additional Collins brothers headed their own band of pro-Union deserters.[34]

The ongoing debates over whether Unionism or mere banditry gave rise to the Free State of Jones did not initially include debates over the manner in which Ben Knight died. Other than those provided by Confederate cavalrymen, I have found no descriptions of his death before that given by Ben Graves in 1926. Deserters and their kinfolk rarely discussed it in interviews conducted before Ethel's book appeared, probably because Ben was only one of ten men killed by Colonel Lowry's band in the space of a few days. It seems that Ethel Knight was the first to link Ben's death to arguments over whether the Knight Company was a band of Unionists or outlaws.

It is easy to see why she would do just that. A decade after Graves told the story, it had became ever more vivid and detailed, and Ben ever more Christlike. In 1936, WPA writer Addie West reported that when the cavalry denied Ben water before they executed him, he prayed to the Lord, "Forgive them, for they know not what they do." Martha Wheeler, a former slave of the Knight family, told West that when her husband helped the family bury him, he witnessed firsthand the water that "gushed up. . . . Two men could not keep it dipped as fast as it ran in." "All old people knew this for a fact," wrote West, and there "is awe in each voice that repeats the story."[35]

Ethel Knight built on these accounts when she created her own version of Ben's murder. She elaborated on Graves's description of Ben's torture, describing how bloodhounds "bit and tore his legs as the soldiers dragged him mercilessly by the neck to the place of hanging." She altered, however, Graves's description of the sequence of events leading to Ben's hanging. In her version, Ben was taking an afternoon walk to visit relatives in another neighborhood; he was not furtively darting through cavalry in the middle of the night to reach Newt's home. Nor did Ethel place Ben in the company of his cousin Sil Coleman at the time of his capture; she claimed instead that Ben was ignorant of skirmishes between deserters and Confederate cavalry. Most importantly, she claimed that he was "home on furlough, and carried his credentials in his pocket" on the afternoon of April 15, 1864. Her Ben Knight was a loyal Confederate soldier, killed only because the cavalry mistook him for his lawless cousin, Newton Knight.[36]

Having established Ben's innocence, Ethel described his hanging. Once again she reshaped the story, this time by painting the Confederacy in the best light possible. In her version, Colonel Lowry silenced soldiers who jeered the captured Ben, granted Ben a last chance to pray (but denied his request for water), and removed the rope from his neck just before he died. Lowry and his men became "ashy-faced and silent" when they discovered furlough papers in the dead man's coat pocket.[37]

Ethel also reworked the story of Ben's burial by disputing ex-slave Martha Wheeler's claim that her husband had helped to bury Ben. An avid segregationist, Ethel applied Jim Crow principles to the Civil War scene: white folks alone prepared the grave of the "innocent soldier," soon to be baptized by a regenerative spring of clear water. "The Negroes were too superstitious to be of much assistance," she wrote, "and it took persuasion to get any help out of them."[38]

Ethel Knight thus managed a difficult political and genealogical task in The Echo of the Black Horn. She vilified her hated kinsman, Newton

Knight, while claiming the sanctified Ben Knight for the loyal side of the family. Newton's controversial postwar behavior, however, considerably lightened her task. Not only did he support the carpetbag administration of Governor Adelbert Ames, but two of his children married the children of Rachel Knight, a former slave who had assisted Newt and the deserters during the war. The intermarriages of their children created a mixed-race community in which Newton lived until his death in 1922. Many whites believed, as Ben Graves did, that "what he did after the war was worse than deserting."[39]

Ethel Knight eagerly made these scandals a centerpiece of her book, in the process disarming those kinfolk who took a certain pride in their colorful ancestors. But not quite. In 1994, I talked with eighty-nine-year-old Earle Knight, the grandson of Ben Knight's brother, William Martin Knight, nicknamed "Dicky." Earle seemed far more interested in telling me how his great-uncle Ben slashed the throats of two or three bloodhounds with his knife before the cavalry brought him down than in speculating about whether Ben carried furlough papers in his pocket. Earle enjoyed telling how grandpa Dicky, who fled to the Union army in New Orleans after Lowry's raid, often laughed that he would be "the only Yankee buried in Big Creek cemetery."[40]

Under Ethel's guiding pen, Ben Knight achieved sainthood while Newton emerged as his evil twin. Her demonization of Newton thus turned an important episode of Southern history into a lurid tale of lust and murder. The ongoing contest over the meaning of the Free State of Jones also has contributed to historians' failure to analyze the origins of this yeoman uprising. It is time to let Ben Knight rest in peace as a man who was killed because he refused to fight for the Confederacy. Most importantly, it is time to release Newton Knight, who flouted both the rules of war and the conventions of race, from the Lost Cause mentality that holds him, and the important story of the Free State of Jones, its prisoner.

# "Shot for Being Bushwhackers": Guerrilla War and Extralegal Violence in a North Georgia Community, 1862–1865

## Jonathan D. Sarris

URING THE FIRST spring of the Civil War, Miss Fannie Boyd received a disturbing letter at her home in Dahlonega, in the north Georgia county of Lumpkin, nestled at the foot of the Blue Ridge Mountains. In the nearby community of Lincolnton, Fannie read, a mob had threatened to lynch a drunken man who was suspected of voicing pro-Union sympathies. "If it had not bin that he was drinking and his friends interceded for him . . . he would have bin hung," the letter concluded. In May of 1861, before the war had extracted more than a few drops of blood, Miss Boyd was deeply shocked at the mere threat of intra-community violence directed against fellow Georgians. But three years later, far more grisly events would occur in Dahlonega, events which Boyd did not even find notable enough to write about. In October of 1864, Lumpkin County militia captured three young north Georgians— Solomon Stansbury, William Witt, and Iley Stuart—who had betrayed the Confederacy by enlisting in the Union army. Local authorities jailed the three men briefly and charged them with "bushwhacking." The captives were offered no trial. On the evening of October 22, 1864, a squad of Georgia militia tied the three and led them in a column through the small north Georgia community to the banks of the Chestatee River.

There the prisoners halted and a firing squad readied. It was over in a moment. Solomon Stansbury, Iley Stuart, and William Witt were shot to death and their bodies hastily buried.[1]

The differences between these two incidents—both in the way they occurred and the way locals reacted to them—reveals much about the effect of guerrilla warfare upon one nineteenth-century community's mores and values. Over time, the people of the southern Appalachians experienced and interpreted the Civil War in different ways. In 1861, a time before war had ravaged the community, the Lincolnton man who was thoughtless enough to utter anti-Confederate comments suffered threats from the mob, but he faced no actual violence. The would-be lynchers in that instance were likely restrained by a sense of legality and due process which still affected their actions early in the conflict. Attitudes had changed dramatically three years later, when Stansbury, Stuart, and Witt lost their lives to a firing squad. These three men were never officially charged with any crime, but few residents of Dahlonega quarreled with their summary execution in the autumn of 1864. Three years of guerrilla war and community dissention changed the atmosphere entirely, and the community quickly sacrificed these men in order to restore stability to their society.

Although no Yankee or Rebel armies marched over north Georgia's blue mountains, and no major battles scarred its farmlands and homesteads, the Civil War left its mark upon the region. In mountain Georgia, the Civil War took the form of vicious local struggles between Confederate deserters, Unionist guerrilla bands, outlaws, and scattered militia companies. This bitter internecine conflict often divided counties, neighborhoods, and families, and atrocities like the Dahlonega executions were commonplace. Combatants in this inner civil war found motivation in a variety of sources—ideology, economic self-interest, and community politics. But transcending all of these factors was an omnipresent concern with law, order, and stability. From the beginning of the conflict, both Unionists and Confederates identified their enemies with the forces of lawlessness and disorder, and, as we will see, criminal imagery dominated local rhetoric throughout the period. Ironically, in the process of fighting for law and order, north Georgians soon found their concepts of justice under assault, their notions of propriety and morality challenged. As the war dragged on, mountaineers increasingly justified their own brutality with the rhetoric of legalism. And ultimately, in the crucible of conflict, these highlanders constructed a peculiar definition of justice which allowed them to commit the most heinous acts in the name of law and order.

As was the case in much of southern Appalachia, north Georgians experienced divided loyalties during the secession crisis of 1860. This was especially true of Lumpkin County, where residents voted by a margin of almost four to one against leaving the Union in Georgia's secession convention of January 1861.[2] Sitting astride the southern spur of the Blue Ridge, Lumpkin residents were caught between two worlds—one commercial, developed, and outward looking and the other traditional, isolated, and community oriented. These divisions manifested themselves in divided loyalties during the controversy over disunion. Much of local resistance to disunion stemmed from the conservative nature of Dahlonega's business community, the relatively low slave population, and the historic Unionism of local political leaders. For a brief period after Fort Sumter, most Lumpkin residents fell into line behind the Confederacy, as dissent temporarily succumbed to the same martial frenzy that subsumed the entire South. But rumblings of disaffection continued, and the deep divisions which rent the mountain region could not be contained. Those who opposed secession refused to enlist and attempted to dissuade those who did. Dissenters flew United States flags from homes and court houses and wrote Georgia governor Joseph E. Brown vitriolic letters denouncing disunion. Pro-secessionists branded these malcontents as "tories," comparing them with pro-British collaborators of the American Revolution. Sometimes, as the unfortunate man from Lincolnton who was mentioned in Fannie Boyd's letter learned, secessionists responded with violence or threats of violence.[3]

But in the early stages of the war, upcountry Georgians were too preoccupied with concepts of legality to engage in spontaneous extralegal violence against their enemies. They defended their own causes with appeals to the law and excoriated their opponents as criminals. And, in general, they tried to adhere to the formal channels of protest and action which the letter of the law demanded. In the spring of 1861, one north Georgia tory wrote Governor Brown a critical letter castigating secession as illegal as well as immoral. The correspondent decried the procedures of the state's secession convention, in which elected delegates had voted in secret to leave the Union instead of submitting the question directly to the people. "[W]e do not intend to submit to the secession movement," the Unionist wrote, "which has been taken out of the hands of the people and has fallen into the hands of Dimegougs." Secessionists were not simply wrong, according to the angry mountaineer, but common criminals, "pick-pockets and vagrants." The writer asserted that mountain Georgia would secede from the rest of the state if necessary: "We have the right to leave the South as much as the State has to leave the Union." This man thus framed a crude but coherent dissent in legal and even constitutional terms. He spoke of rights and electoral procedures and expressed indignation over the illegal behavior of his opponents. And although he did threaten violence— promising to resist secession "with flint and steel"—this dissenter was clearly interested in exhausting traditional channels of protest first.[4]

Those who supported secession were equally convinced of the law-lessness of the tories. But despite their suspicions, mountain Confederates at first tried to maintain a commitment to the legal process and made a conscious effort to avoid mob violence or lynching of dissenters. Letters to Governor Brown during 1861 evince a sincere concern with due process, concern which would seem outdated even a year later. Highland Confederates bombarded the governor's office with requests for delineation of the "proper" treatment of tories, insisting that communities would observe strict legal proprieties, even when dealing with alleged traitors. "What is the process to make a suspicious person take the oath?" wrote one upcountry secessionist, "as we still have a few of that sort hear that should be attended to." Another stated, "[W]e wish to know what way for us to pursue the case of people talking or acting contrary to the Southern Confederacy. There has been some cases . . . which we have acted upon *as we thought according to law*. We would like you to state . . . what way to arrange our community and upon conviction what to do with them." And when the citizens of one mountain county formed a home guard to watch over domestic enemies, they made an explicit promise to defend due process, pledging to "try and pass sentence according to the evidence on all suspicious characters." Even those who wished they could deal harshly with the tories felt limited by the structure of the law. One mountain Rebel castigated some of his disloyal neighbors and mused,

"[W]e have some that ought to be punished in our section." But he admitted that the dissenters would have to be "spared the salutary influence of hemp" because they had committed no "overt act of treason" and the law would not allow for punishment without a specific statutory violation. While these letters evince a profound uncertainty about how to deal with tories, they also show that early in the war north Georgia Confederates were trying to accommodate to prewar legalism and procedure.[5]

This began to change as north Georgia devolved into internal civil war. The catalyst for violence was the passage of the Confederate Conscription Act of 1862, a policy which sent draft dodgers and deserters flooding into the mountains of north Georgia. Some of these erstwhile Confederate solders were outsiders who simply used the mountains as a convenient refuge. Others were locals who were "laying out" in the Blue Ridge country in order to be near home. These deserters, forming armed bands for self-protection, subsisting off the countryside, and defying the efforts of state militia and regular troops to compel their return, proved to be an incendiary factor. By 1863, open combat was beginning in the region. Lumpkin County was particularly hard hit, torn by a bloody internal struggle as draft dodgers, deserters, and Unionists waged a running battle with Confederate troops, local militia, and secessionist civilians. Sporadic fighting would last until well after Appomattox.

For the deserters and others who dissented from the Confederate establishment, the intrusive Southern military machine represented a destabilizing force which disrupted communities, abused legitimate state authority, and violated common understandings of justice. An examination of their rhetoric and actions shows that Lumpkin's anti-Confederates chiefly opposed the state's unwarranted taking of private property and the compulsory enlistment of all military age men. Tories defined these offenses as crimes.

Military conscription was the most onerous burden for Lumpkin dissenters to bear. More than the draft itself, the strict draft-enforcement procedures adopted in the county inspired particular resistance. When Lumpkin men evaded the draft or deserted in droves, authorities responded harshly. Confederate troops from Atlanta invaded the county twice in 1863. The soldiers quartered themselves in private homes and used Dahlonega as base from which to launch attacks on tory bands. Troops arrested hundreds of military-age men, forcing the them into the army or transporting them to Atlanta for criminal trial. For many residents, this represented an unendurable intrusion, an illegitimate and illegal use of state power. It only increased dissenters' resolve to avoid military service. One Lumpkin County deserter, on trial for resistance in 1863, echoed the sentiments of many residents when he said that "he would not fight if he could help it."[6] Others took a less passive stance in their opposition to the Confederacy. They hid in the mountains and formed guerrilla cells, ambushing conscription agents and state militia units.

Conscription was not the only example of Confederate "lawlessness" which dissenters had to endure. Early in the war Confederate authorities had instituted an impressment system which empowered officials to seize needed supplies from citizens with only minimal compensation. Later, Richmond enacted a tax-in-kind program under which farmers were obliged to give one-tenth of their produce and livestock to the government, in addition to other taxes.[7] Impressment officials, militia, and Confederate troops often took these policies as licenses to plunder at will, especially from families rumored to be in some way "disloyal." In depositions before the federal government's Southern Claims Commission soon after the Civil War, anti-Confederate civilians spoke of their oppression by troops. Civilians accused state troops of taking livestock and crops, breaking into homes, and stealing personal belongings. When one north Georgia victim complained about this looting, he was told that he "was a tory and they had a right to take stock or anything else from that sort." Another civilian stated that after troops had finished "taking and destroying everything in the place," they proceeded to steal the shoes off of his children's feet. When challenged, troops often responded with violence. "They threatened to burn my house," charged one north Georgia resident, and when he protested, troops "knocked down and badly hurt" his daughters and "badly abused" his wife and other children.[8]

Thus, many Lumpkin County residents saw the Confederacy's policies as essentially illegal and unconstitutional. In the name of secession, authorities invaded civilian homes and violated the security of property and family. The traditional arbiters of law and order—constables and local militia—had transformed into brutal organs of state-sponsored terrorism. Some mountaineers were hopelessly confused by the new order. One wrote a plaintive letter to Governor Brown wherein he demanded to know where civilians stood in their battle with rapacious impressment officers: "Would it be safe to resist the [militia]?" If so, he asked, "[H]ow far would resistance be justified? I also wish to know what is a legal order? What Officer must issue it?" In this pathetic search for answers, this civilian was hearkening back to an earlier notion of legality, one which he found superseded by the remorseless, violent logic of war.[9]

Sion Darnell exemplifies this rhetoric of the state-as-criminal perfectly. Darnell was a north Georgian who opposed the Confederacy and ultimately joined the Union army in 1864. In a postwar speech to the Grand Army of Republic, Darnell told the story of mountaineers like himself who had fought against the Confederacy. Darnell compiled a long list of Confederate transgressions, including such property crimes as "robbery, plunder, and destruction," to justify his Unionism. He claimed that secessionist authorities knew no law but "the law of force" and that "those who exercised authority in the region appeared to have lost all sense of reason and humanity." Darnell, and, one suspects, many north Georgia dissenters, found motivation for resistance in the conviction that his enemies had violated citizens' fundamental rights to legal protection from their government. When the Confederacy abandoned these protections, it lost its legitimacy in the eyes of many highlanders.[10]

By 1864, anti-Confederates in Lumpkin County were in open rebellion against the secessionists. In October of that year, a lone Union army officer from East Tennessee infiltrated the mountains north of Lumpkin and organized an armed revolt of local dissenters. These anti-Confederates traveled across north Georgia, rallying locals to their cause with public speeches decrying the criminality of the state authorities. The tory raiders reminded north Georgians that "the rebels . . . were robbing the citizens" and urged mountaineers "to protect their homes." Many locals concurred with this logic and joined the raiders in a destructive spree through the region, targeting any civilians deemed sympathetic to the Rebels. In the words of a later U.S. government report, the raiders "took the opportunity of repaying past injuries, if not on those who inflicted them, on their abettors." By the autumn of 1864, anti-Confederates had come a long way from the passive resistance and moral suasion which characterized their earlier tactics. Now tories sought their own form of justice through indiscriminate violence.[11]

Even some mountain Rebels had begun to doubt the legality of their government's actions by 1863. Although these individuals remained loyal to the Confederacy, they did question policies such as the draft and impressment. One Lumpkin County militia colonel reacted angrily when Confederate troops from Tennessee came thorough his neighborhood, "stealing everything they [could] get their hands on," and asked the governor to send him some "pamphlets of the law" to distribute to visiting troops and remind them of proper behavior. Huldah Fain, a pro-Confederate north Georgia woman, felt that the impressment policy of her government encouraged general lawlessness and taught the poor that thievery was justifiable. When hungry women rioted in the streets of the state capital of Milledgeville, looting stores and shops, Fain was not surprised. If the state legitimized seizing of private goods for the war effort, how could they be surprised when needy women rioted for food? "I don't believe in 'pressing' [taking goods] unless suffering," Fain wrote, "and then I say take if it is to be had." The implications of the impressment policy were coming home to roost.[12]

Simpson Fouche was one of the most articulate Confederates to criticize his government's policies. In 1863, the northwest Georgia man authored a formal petition to Confederate general Braxton Bragg on behalf of secessionists in his region who had suffered at the hands of Bragg's impressment companies. "We have seen bodies of armed men traversing over our neighborhood," Fouche complained, "taking . . . from the families of absent soldiers the last animal fit for beef, and insulting all those who dared to claim their rights to food . . . or question the legality of the proceedings." Denouncing this behavior, Fouche lectured Bragg on the law: "These seizures are not impressments. Impressment is a legal power of the government. The government has proscribed the legal mode of exercising it. . . . Any other violent seizure without legal warrant is robbery." Fouche warned that this "cruel oppression" created a "*profound sense of injustice* and injury" among the populace. He concluded by asking for "the restoration to us of the protection of the laws, and the infliction of just punishment upon those" responsible for the illegal impressments. Fouche was no tory. He supported the Rebels wholeheartedly throughout the conflict. But he shared with the anti-Confederates a profound disdain for the outlaw behavior manifested by some of the more zealous of the Confederate States of America.[13]

But although some up-country Confederates feared the lawless elements within their own government, most argued that the tories presented the chief threat to law and order in north Georgia. Lumpkin County secessionists labeled dissenters as anarchists and common criminals who wilfully defied legitimate authority and used the war as an pretext to prey upon the helpless. And, as the experience of war eroded traditional ethical barriers, secessionists would seize upon extralegal violence in order to restore some sense of order.

Loyal Confederates had complained about the disorder in their midst since the beginning of the secession crisis. By 1862, Confederate north Georgians flooded Governor Joseph E. Brown's office with letters reporting violence and terrorism perpetrated by the so-called tories. In Lumpkin County, Josiah Woody reported to the governor, "[T]hese blue mountains . . . are filled with tories and deserters and thieves and runaway Negroes." Woody was particularly worried about the raiders' assaults upon women, children, and the family structure. The "tories ran wild," Woody wrote, "robbing soldiers' families . . . shamefully abusing" women and "even ministers of the gospel."[14] By 1863, the county seemed on the verge of anarchy. Another Lumpkin Confederate worried, with regard to the tories, "[T]here is no law to keep them from living better than they ever did." When Confederate troops from Atlanta entered Lumpkin that year to restore order, their commander echoed this rhetoric. Colonel George W. Lee saw his mission as a large law-enforcement operation. He called dissenters "lawless persons" and promised that "those who violate the laws of the State or Confederacy [would suffer] retribution due the crimes of which they [were] guilty."[15]

In 1863, Lumpkin's crisis was exacerbated by the failure of the established judicial system to maintain order. That year, two high-profile court cases rocked the county. Grand juries brought treason charges against John Woody and James Payne in separate trials. Woody was heard to have said that "he wish[ed] the Confederacy to be subjugated and that we should be whipped." Payne had stubbornly evaded the draft and had told neighbors that "he had no hand in bringing on the war and would not have anything to do with it." After a lengthy trial, both defendants were acquitted of all charges. Dahlonega elites must have been shocked at the legal system's failure to convict these dissenters, whom they saw as common criminals.

Rebels' confidence in their legal system was further shaken in 1864 when Lumpkin County judge Stephen Rice suspended all court proceedings due to what he called the "unsettled conditions in this peculiar crisis." Now the county was virtually without a judiciary and without formal means to deal with the lawless elements in its midst.[16]

For Lumpkin County's secessionist population, dissenters were nothing more than gangsters who threatened the stability of the community, the family, and state authority. Pro-Confederates in Lumpkin County felt besieged. Lawless elements ran rampant, the legal establishment seemed powerless to punish treason, and finally the courts disintegrated altogether. This environment was ripe for an outbreak of vigilantism.

Richard Maxwell Brown, one of the preeminent scholars of American violence, has argued that vigilantes historically acted as "a conservative mob," out to defend traditional values and property relationships. Although Brown argues that newly settled frontier areas were most susceptible to outbreaks of vigilantism, social disruption in a more established regions could also cause communities to commit extralegal violence. In these instances, the profound desire of elites to restore the status quo and eliminate crime led to mass killings of those alleged to be outside the law. Bertram Wyatt-Brown placed this analysis in a regional context with his work on Southern honor. Wyatt-Brown asserts that Southern communities were prone to employ mob violence if the normal judicial organs were perceived to have failed in their duty to punish criminals. In the final chapter of *Southern Honor*, entitled "Anatomy of a Wife-Killing," Wyatt-Brown gives a perfect example of this phenomenon, illustrating the dynamics which led an antebellum Southern mob to lynch a man charged with a heinous crime but acquitted by the regular courts. In this instance, the community's need for justice contradicted the findings of the legal system—mob violence resulted.

Vigilantism has long been part of the stereotype of the Appalachian South, of which north Georgia is a part. Much of this image sprang from the turn-of-the-century media depictions of the Hatfield-McCoy feud, which portrayed quick-tempered mountaineers too impatient to wait for court-dispensed justice and eager to take the law into their own hands. Recent scholars such as Altina Waller have disputed this interpretation. But Waller did find in her study of the Hatfield-McCoy feud that highlanders did resort to extralegal violence if they felt they had no recourse in the courts, or if outside forces threatened to remove the reins of justice from community control.[17]

All these analyses speak to the conditions in Civil War–era Lumpkin County. The area suffered social dislocation and, by 1864, a breakdown in the formal justice system. Lumpkin County was both mountain and Southern, and thus heir to a certain legacy of extralegal violence endemic to those regions. In response to the perceived lawlessness of the tories and the breakdown of legal authorities, Lumpkin's pro-Confederate residents decided to take justice into their own hands.

Local secessionists had been on the verge of vigilantism for some time, and opinions regarding the proper treatment of "traitors" began to harden among Lumpkin's Confederates by the war's third year. The vicious progress of the conflict thoroughly embittered Mrs. Nancy Wimpy, wife of a prominent attorney in the county seat of Dahlonega. When state troops executed a deserter in the county in August 1863, she stated matter-of-factly, "I think all deserters from state service ought to be shot, for they know nothing about suffering and hardship yet." Angered by the tory assaults on the social order, Wimpy advocated savage retribution. She even wished that Cherokee Indians from nearby western North Carolina could be turned loose on the anti-Confederate dissenters: "It would be a good thing if they could get those Indians in N.C. after the tories. They would treat them just about right."[18]

By the time William T. Sherman had begun his march across Georgia, many had concluded with Mrs. Wimpy that any means were justified to stamp out dissent and restore stability to their fragmented community. The last straw proved to be the Unionist raid of autumn 1864, discussed above; the raid marked a culmination of a vengeful tory campaign intended to strike back at the draft and impressment. When word came from north of Lumpkin County that raiders, led by an U.S. Army officer, were "stealing horses and robbing houses," local secessionists reacted quickly and violently. Militia took the field on October 20, 1864, and arrested three of the raiders, Solomon Stansbury, Iley Stuart, and William Witt.[19]

For pro-Confederates, the course of action seemed clear. Lumpkin County was a community living in terror, cut off from the rest of the state by Sherman's forces, surrounded by actual or imaginary bands of tories.

The civil authorities were unable to keep order. Accordingly, the colonel of the Lumpkin militia, who had become the de facto leader of the community after the collapse of the courts, ordered his militia to summarily execute the three Unionists on October 22, 1864. The only evidence of a formal charge was the colonel's curt order that the three were to be "shot for being bushwhackers."[20] In the next two weeks, the militia caught and hanged twelve more dissenters in the area. For the time being, Lumpkin County was secure.

These executions may have been outside the bounds of legality, even in wartime. However, this does not mean that the killings were perpetrated without regard to justice. Whatever else may be said of their actions, it is clear that Lumpkin's pro-Confederates acted out of a profound concern for law and order. And even though the three tories were given no trial before their executions, there were certain pseudo-legal proprieties observed. For example, when the militia captured the raiders, they did not simply gun them down on the spot but instead went through the inconvenience of transporting them to the county seat for judgment by the local military commander. They were jailed for two days while their fate was deliberated. When the officer on the scene issued his verdict, the three were taken out and executed by firing squad in a quasi-formal military ceremony.

As Joel Williamson has observed, ritual was very important in Southern extralegal violence. Williamson focused on lynching, and the racial dynamic which dominated that subject is clearly absent in the case of the Lumpkin County executions. But there are similarities. The Dahlonega firing squad shared with lynch mobs of a later generation a common concern for justice and a common determination to follow certain formalistic behavioral patterns to lend the weight of custom to their activities. In both cases, it was vital for the killers to feel community sanction for their activities, to feel that they were serving the greater ends of justice. In Civil War north Georgia, the executioners indulged in some of the trappings of legalism for this very reason. What happened in Lumpkin County in October of 1864 was somewhere between a lynching and a legal, state-sponsored execution. If the Unionist victims did not enjoy a formal trial, they did experience an informal process of community judgment.[21]

In an ironic coda to the story, legitimate judicial authority eventually intervened to pass judgment on the wartime vigilantism of Lumpkin County's Confederates. During the first postwar session of the Lumpkin County Superior Court in 1866, the government of Georgia decided to try the men who had carried out the wartime execution of Stansbury, Stuart, and Witt. But a grand jury refused to indict the group. Although no record of their deliberations exists, the jury's rationale for the acquittal can be found in another war-crimes decision they issued that summer, in which the same jury asked the prosector to desist from pursuing "all old war prosecutions." The message was clear. Peacetime concepts of justice could not be applied to the disruptive experience of war. The grand jury legitimized the wartime atrocity on the grounds that the greater ends of justice had been served.[22]

Even though the Civil War is one of the most studied conflicts in history, the question of what motivated Americans to fight in that war is still actively debated. Indeed, one of the most prominent scholars of the war has recently authored a book entitled *What They Fought For,* in which he tries to answer this basic question. Various historians have posited the primacy of economics, ideology, religion, family and gender relations, and other factors. Phillip Paludan has argued that the American Civil War can be considered a "crisis in law and order."[23] He asserts that, for Northerners, the image of the constitutional Union defiled by an illegal act of secession was too much to bear, and so the war came.

In a different sense, the Civil War as it played out in the mountains of north Georgia can be considered a crisis in law and order. For north Georgians, the war was not an abstract struggle over legal concepts but rather a conflict among local factions, each convinced that it was defending the most basic functions of law and order in the community. Anti-Confederates saw the imposition of near-martial law as a fundamental violation of the most elemental motions of justice. Pro-Confederates saw dissenters as traitorous bandits. Both were convinced that their enemy posed a fundamental threat to community stability.

The war also challenged and reformulated notions of legal and illegal behavior. Internal guerrilla conflicts tend to be extremely brutal, with combatants "othering" their enemies in order to validate the most horrific acts of retribution, all the while clinging to some legal or moral pretense.

In the heat of battle, both sides in north Georgia's civil war claimed to defend home, family, and community. They dehumanized their opponents as criminals or bushwhackers or tories. Both sides seized upon bloody, even illegal methods to defend their concepts of justice. This does not make them hypocrites. It only illuminates the power of war to make malleable virtually all social values and codes of conduct.

# "In Time of War": Unionists Hanged in Kinston, North Carolina, February 1864

## Lesley J. Gordon

DURING THE DARK early morning hours of February 1, 1864, Federal soldiers at the Beech Grove outpost four miles outside New Bern, North Carolina, awoke with a start. Confederates were crossing the Neuse River at Bachelder Creek. Fog was thick and there was a light drizzle. Signal communication was useless. Two Union couriers died trying to reach Beech Grove with orders to fall back. As Confederates attacked coastal New Bern, the post commander remained in position. A small detachment arrived with scant reinforcements, but Confederates soon cut off the post from the rest of the Union line. After two days of sporadic fighting, Confederates retreated from New Bern. On their march west, they stopped at the grove and demanded surrender. Federal officers yielded, and Confederate troops quickly rounded up men and ransacked the Union camp.[1]

Prisoners were marched thirty miles west to Kinston, North Carolina, in Lenoir County. The journey took two days and weather remained cold and damp. Rustic log cabins lined the road, and as the motley procession passed by, curiosity seekers came outside their homes to watch. Several women instantly recognized prisoners as former residents. Confederates discovered that they had captured nearly two dozen North Carolinians who had served in the Confederate army but deserted to the Union. Most of these Union soldiers and their families lived in Lenoir or surrounding counties. Some were former members of the same units that were now their captors. In fact, it is possible that Confederates specifically targeted Beech Grove, fully aware of North Carolinian Union troops stationed there. "God damn you," Major General George E. Pickett reportedly exploded at prisoners after learning their status. "I reckon you will hardly go back there again, you damned rascals; I'll have you shot, and all other damned rascals who desert."[2]

Within two weeks, Confederates tried and hanged twenty-two of the prisoners captured at Beech Grove. The executions took place near the center of Kinston on apparently three separate occasions, although the exact dates are unclear. The last of the three hangings consisted of thirteen to fifteen victims, including two sets of brothers. Family members and friends watched the executions in shock and horror. Confederate officials including Pickett affirmed the justice of the deaths; Union commanders expressed horror and dismay. After the war the federal government tried to indict George Pickett for war crimes, but failed partially due to the interference of Ulysses S. Grant. Grant admitted that the Kinston hangings were "harsh" but argued that "it was in time of war and when the enemy no doubt felt it necessary to retain, by some power, the service of every man within their reach."[3]

Wars do inflict great cruelties beyond the pale of the battlefield itself, and historians are now just beginning to illuminate these dark and forgotten margins of Civil War history. Atrocities such as guerrilla warfare and mass executions reveal not only deep and disturbing aspects of the war but divisions within Southern society. Traditional romanticized narratives of the Civil War, however, typically make no room for incidents like those at Kinston. In the public's collective memory of courageous leaders, selfless soldiers, and honorable causes the harsh reality of Kinston is forgotten.

Some parts of this story are easier to recover than others—particularly in setting the scene. The fact that the incident occurred in North Carolina helps; there has been a good deal of work done on the state's internal divisiveness. Scholars have documented the prevalence of desertion and disaffection among North Carolinians and noted that by 1864 tensions were particularly high. Bands of destitute deserters roamed the Tar Heel State, plundering homes and wreaking havoc, often upon their own neighbors. Confederate conscription, Jefferson Davis's suspension of habeas corpus,

tax-in-kind and impressment laws, military defeats and economic hardships
—all of these things stirred discontent among North Carolina's nonslaveholding white population. Division intensified under the governorship of
Zebulon Vance, an outspoken Davis critic. Vance had his own political
enemies, and one of the most vocal was Raleigh newspaper editor William
W. Holden. Holden and his conservative "Peace Movement" demanded
that North Carolina pull out of the war and out of the Confederacy.[4]

Southern Unionism has also been increasingly well documented,
although its causes are not easy to explain. Unionism was not the same
as formally fighting for the Federal government, and disloyalty to the
Confederacy did not always mean Unionism, nor did disaffection. One
of the earliest scholars to recognize Unionism, Georgia Lee Tatum,
delimited "disloyal" white Southerners as "persons living in the Confederacy, who not only refused to support the Confederate government,
but who also appeared to be actively working against it." She called "disaffection" a passive opposition to the Confederacy. In 1955 Frank Klingberg
pointed to "southern internal sectionalism" that predated secession and
was not a result of war weariness or suffering. "Southern Unionism," he
wrote, "drew strength from the ties of blood, of education, of religion, of
politics, and of a common history that could not be wiped out at a single
blow." Philip Paludan's 1981 book, *Victims,* traced Unionism in western
North Carolina to a variety of sources including class resentment, absence
of slavery, isolation, and family and neighborhood traditions. William T.
Auman found an "outlier-militant Unionist faction" in Randolph County,
North Carolina, a faction that included those "disaffected and dissatis-
fied with the Confederacy, and pro-Union elements for political reasons
as well as for purposes of self-defense." Richard N. Current has offered the
only comprehensive study of Southern Unionism to date, but even he
notes that motivations varied among white Southerners who formally
fought for the Union. Current shies away from abstract ideological expla-
nations and concludes that some white Southern soldiers were blatant
mercenaries or opportunists and others had a "strong sense of old fash-
ioned patriotism," but he fails to define exactly what this term means.
Stephen Ash has aptly observed, "Unionism in the Confederate South
was a complex phenomenon, not easily defined or explained."[5]

Unionism, whatever its cause, splintered counties in western and piedmont North Carolina, but its appearance was also apparent in coastal regions close to Federally occupied New Bern. Residents suspected of Union sympathies suffered violent harassment by pro-Confederate residents and Confederate officials. President Davis periodically ordered military sweeps to round up deserters and quash Union sentiment. Arrests, punishments, and executions of Unionists sometimes included women and children.[6]

Lenoir County, where the majority of the victims resided and where the hangings took place, reflected the state's bitter inner strife. Lenoir was one of North Carolina's few counties that counted more blacks than whites; Lenoir's residents included a minority of wealthy planters and many poor, propertyless whites. In 1860 Kinston numbered about 1,000 residents, and the county just over 10,000, with 4,902 whites and over 5,000 slaves. Lenoir County planters grew cotton, corn, and tobacco and raised pigs. In 1861 the majority of the county's voters were secessionists, but as the conflict dragged into its third year, discontent grew. War brought economic growth, industry, and activity, as well as fighting; but it also seemed to aggravate tensions among whites. The proximity of Union troops in nearby New Bern apparently stirred anti-Confederate sentiment. A Virginia soldier described Kinston in October 1863, "We're among a set of people who are considerably under the influence of Holden and consequently quite disloyal."[7]

Census records from 1860 indicate that the men hanged at Kinston were mainly nonslaveholding small farmers, laborers, and carpenters. Jessie Summerlin was an overseer and Stephen Jones was a painter. Most were married men with young families. Several were illiterate.[8] Records also show that early in the war these men joined the Eighth Battalion of North Carolina Partisan Rangers. The battalion was not part of the regular Confederate army but instead acted as a local home guard unit that scouted, provided outpost service, guarded bridges, and offered intimate knowledge of the region to the Southern military. Members remained close to their families and away from large-scale battles. J. H. Nethercutt, the battalion commander, later recalled Confederate officials assuring the men that they would "never go out of the state or locality." They stayed at home through most of their service. "[A] good deal, for soldiers," Nethercutt attested.[9]

Confederate need for manpower and conscription, however, required consolidating such home guard units into the regular Southern army. In August 1863, Nethercutt's battalion merged with another unit of rangers to become the Sixty-sixth Regiment of North Carolina Troops. Its new colonel, A. Duncan Moore, was a West Pointer and a stern disciplinarian, described as having "remarkable appearance and soldierly bearing."[10] Moore was initially unpopular among his officers, and perhaps among his men — especially among men not used to military regulations and restrictions. The Sixty-sixth Regiment left Kinston during the fall of 1863 and headed for Wilmington. There the troops drilled and awaited further orders, but dissatisfaction grew among Nethercutt's former unit. In October Governor Vance tried to return the men to their previous position, but Major General W. H. C. Whiting, commander of the Cape Fear district, demurred. He dismissed the charges of discontent as "greatly exaggerated" and spread by a single individual for "private needs." "The discipline of the command has been very bad," Whiting stated, "and in my view of the case, it is better for the men themselves, the service and the country that they should be removed from their farms locality and placed in this present organization."[11] But inquietude continued to fester among Nethercutt's former unit, and several members decided to desert. Instead of returning home and risking capture and punishment by Confederate officials, they fled to nearby New Bern and enlisted in Company F of the Second North Carolina Union Volunteers.

What exactly compelled these men to join the Union army? The twenty-two prisoners captured and hanged at Kinston left little behind to explain their actions, other than the actions themselves. One can only speculate that their sudden Unionism was due to a combination of desires and fears: perhaps class resentment and draft evasion. They may have based their decision purely on self-interest; once they perceived that the Confederacy failed to serve and protect their personal needs, they switched to the Union. Confederate conscription threatened to take them far from their homes, expose them to large-scale combat, and force them to fight for a cause they little understood or supported. The timing of their desertions does seem significant; most of them deserted the same month that Abraham Lincoln issued his Amnesty Proclamation. These North Carolinians may have believed that enlisting in the Federal army would keep them closer to their homes and away from the front. They did receive a sizable bounty, perhaps as much as three hundred dollars. And they did return to duty similar to what they had done in Nethercutt's battalion—scouting and providing valuable information of the region to military officials. But despite promises made by Union recruiters, the men must have realized that this was particularly hazardous work for Confederate deserters. Their service in the Union army clearly placed them and their families in great personal jeopardy. Although Federals sent expeditions to try to rescue families from behind Confederate lines, most of their wives and children remained in hostile territory. Whatever their reasons, this had to have been an agonizing and perhaps hasty decision for them to make. Perhaps the consequences of their actions only began to dawn on them as they marched past familiar faces and familiar scenes into Kinston.[12]

Anger, outrage, and dismay tinge all firsthand descriptions of what happened next. What may have been a harried decision on the part of a handful of discontented individuals now took on greater meaning. The public nature of the executions was a determined attempt by the Southern army to stifle Unionism and deter desertion. The Confederacy sought to make an example of them. Soon after arriving in the town, Confederates locked the men in the local jail. News spread quickly and family members and friends gathered outside the cells. Confederates apparently allowed prisoners limited personal visits and little food or coverings. Wives brought bedding and begged for mercy. A Union chaplain incarcerated in the same jail two months later described the cells as filthy, dark, and rat and roach infested.[13]

Departmental commander George Pickett ordered court-martial proceedings to try the captured men for desertion and treason. The court-martial may have been entirely made up of Virginians, although the actual names of the officers remains a mystery. Confederate staff officer Walter Harrison asserted that the men were fairly "tried by that court in strict conformity with the principles and practice of Courts Martial General and under the articles of war, the same as those of the U.S. Government."[14] But in actuality the court denied the men legal council, clemency, or witnesses, and in what one scholar calls "uncommon haste," they found twenty-two prisoners guilty of treason and sentenced them to death by hanging. Acquittals were only granted to individuals who had not served in the Confederate army.[15] Union officials tried pleas and threats to pre-

vent Confederates from treating the men any differently than other prisoners of war. Pickett responded by making his own threats of retaliation.[16]

Chaplain John Paris of the Fifty-fourth North Carolina provided
some of the most complete firsthand descriptions of the prisoners and
their state of mind. He kept a diary, wrote an open letter to a North
Carolina newspaper, and preached a special sermon, all narrating the
Kinston hangings. But his words seethed with disapproval, distrust, and
disgust. In the dark and dirty Kinston jail, he interrogated most of the
men, demanded their confession, and offered baptism. Several were illiterate, and Paris wrote letters for their family and friends. He denounced
them as ignorant, corrupt, and hopelessly deluded. Still, Paris strongly
believed that some "bad and mischievous" outside influence had turned
formerly honest and hardworking North Carolinians into traitors. He
alleged that a few named the "authors of their ruin." "I told them," Paris
wrote, "they had sinned against their country, and their country would
not forgive them but they had also sinned against God, yet God would
forgive them if they approached him with penitent hearts filled with a
Godly sorrow for sin and repose their trust in the atoning blood of Christ."
When one avowed that he already was a Christian, Paris scoffed at his
hypocrisy. He did, however, feel some compassion toward the victims'
families. On February 15, 1864, he wrote, "The distress of women and
children was truly great." But his righteous indignation remained. In a
sermon given to Brigadier General Robert Hoke's North Carolina brigade,
Paris again furiously blasted these "twenty-two unfortunate yet wicked
and deluded men" and declared that their greatest crime was betraying
their native land.[17]

Even the Confederacy's treatment of the corpses had clear symbolic
implications. Pickett allowed his troops to bury unclaimed bodies in a
mass grave at the foot of gallows. Some were allegedly used for "experi-
menting surgery."[18] A Union chaplain who came to Kinston soon after
the hangings described the grave: "A rude pit of gravel without the form
of a grave, without headboard, or memorial marks the place."[19]

In the weeks that followed, the executions at Kinston gained wide
attention in the North and the South, and both sides sought larger political meanings from the event. Confederate newspapers echoed Paris's
sentiments, and, like his sermon, used the hangings to bolster support and

silence dissent. Pro-Confederate North Carolinian papers praised the court-martial's sentence, although some accused Holden's *Standard* and his followers "for the blood of these poor misguided men." On February 16, the Raleigh *Daily Confederate* paper attacked the "poor & ignorant men" who "had near relatives & all of them had friends" and left service on "some fancied wrong." But they again blamed Holden for the "deplorable crime." Even Holden supported the sentence and firmly denied playing any part in encouraging desertion. The Raleigh *Daily Progress* on February 11, 1864, proclaimed: "Let the fate of these men be a warning to others; and let every man who enters the army realize that everything—family, business, home and all must give way to the stern requirements of military law, and that his duty to his country rises high above all other considerations." It would have been better for the men and their families, the paper maintained, had they died in battle. "The fact that their homes were in the hands of the enemy was no excuse for desertion. On the contrary, they should have fought all the harder to rescue them and drive the insolent invaders from the soil."[20]

During the summer of 1864, a member of the Third North Carolina Cavalry spread his jaundiced tale of Unionism and desertion in coastal North Carolina through his novelette, *The Deserter's Daughter or Dark Deeds of Dover*. Loosely basing his story on the Kinston hangings, William D. Herrington narrated the fate of an innocent and beautiful daughter betrayed by her disloyal father. After witnessing her father's gory death, she fell in love with his killer, a Confederate officer. Marriage to her husband's murderer, the author claimed, redeemed the heroine and freed her of her father's unforgivable crime. A large group of North Carolinian deserters captured in Union uniforms made a short but dramatic appearance in the romance. Herrington scornfully cast them as "vile" "scoundrels" who "met a very merited end, that is the end of a rope."[21]

Northern reaction was the polar opposite. Union officials, newspapers, and soldiers responded to the hangings with shock and fear, casting the Confederates, rather than the dead deserters, as the brutal villains. News of the executions severely demoralized North Carolina Union soldiers in New Bern. Generals John J. Peck and Benjamin Butler protested directly to Confederate officials, to no avail. Butler maintained that once these men formally joined the Union army they were no longer deserters, and thus the

Confederacy had defied the "law of nations" and "belligerent rights" by hanging them.[22] Peck argued that the men were loyal but were forced by "a merciless conscription" to join the Confederate army. They "with tens of thousands [of others]," Peck maintained, "seized the first opportunity to rush within my lines and resume their former allegiance."[23]

Northern newspapers were full of furious denunciations and wild exaggerations. The New Bern North Carolina Times published a letter from Lieutenant Colonel Charles Foster of the Second North Carolina Union Volunteers, denouncing the "late barbarous and inexcusable massacre" and promising revenge. Although he recognized desertion to the enemy as the "supremist infamy," requiring a death sentence, Foster denied the legal right of the enemy to declare these men deserters and mete out punishment. The Rebels had no legitimate government, he explained, with no sovereignty, no international recognition, and no "legal being." Thus he asked, How could these men desert from something that did not exist? This was not a war between nations, Foster stated, but a war for the restoration of Union. He concluded, "The hanging of these loyal North Carolinians at Kinston was utterly unwarranted by the law of civilized war. It was pure . . . unadulterated assassination."[24]

On March 11, 1864, the New York Times informed readers of the "cruel massacre." The article described a sympathetic crowd moved to tears by the hanged men's "unflinching fortitude and determination" and "sublime exhibition of loyalty." The author added a new victim, a fifteen-year-old drummer boy, Ira Neal, who never even served in the Confederate army. The paper attested that the executions caused more Confederate desertions and vows of revenge on the part of Union soldiers. One week later, a "line officer" of the Second North Carolina wrote another article with more details of the hangings. Just before all twenty-four men were hanged at once, the paper stated, one prisoner stepped forward and announced that they would die as they had lived: as "Union men." The writer urged Northern readers to show similar sacrifice and keep the faith.[25]

After the war two federal military boards of inquiry met, first in New Bern, then in Raleigh, to investigate what had happened in February 1864 and again tell the story of Kinston. From October 1865 until March 1866, they collected sworn statements from ex-Confederate military and political leaders, townspeople, and widows. Investigators concentrated on determining whether these twenty-two men were ever in the regular Confederate army, whether Confederate officials treated them according to the "rules of war," and if not, who was to blame. The boards determined that service in a local home guard did not constitute membership in the regular Rebel army and that their enlistment into the Confederate military was entirely involuntary. Blaming George Pickett for mistreatment of the prisoners, Judge Advocate Joseph Holt recommended the ex-Confederate general's arrest and indictment for war crimes. Pickett never was brought to trial; the intervention of Ulysses S. Grant, and his desire to heal war wounds rather than aggravate them, stopped the proceedings. Kinston faded from public consciousness.[26]

For victims' families and friends, the memory of February 1864 lingered. During the postwar years they told their versions of what happened during the federal investigation and retold them again when family dependents filed for pensions. Several widows lived into the twentieth century, and when Congress raised pensions, they again made sworn statements describing their losses. Their words conveyed lasting pain, bitterness, and desolation. And they put human faces on the otherwise forgotten victims of Kinston.[27]

These statements by family members were intended for federal officials seeking to indict ex-Confederate officials for war crimes or to justify government pensions. In either case victims' widows, children, and parents risked continued persecution by hostile neighbors in publicly avowing their Unionism. To obtain pensions they had to endure lengthy investigations and acquire support from lawyers, neighbors, and local residents. This was not necessarily an easy process, nor were they guaranteed of winning their cases. But these recorded memories by mainly illiterate, poor widows are charged with powerful emotion recounted in deeply personal terms. The same men whom Chaplain Paris condemned as unfeeling, corrupt, and vile, appear in these statements as devoted family men, broken and embittered by war, torn by the demands of the Confederacy and their strong desire to stay home. Widows testified that whiskey and threats of physical harm coaxed their husbands into the Southern army. Some recalled Confederate soldiers visiting their homes and forcibly taking their husbands away. Victims' families described feeling powerless and caught in a complex web of personal, familial, local, and national loyalties. Desertion was not a simple matter of right and wrong, as others had attested, but very much a desperate act by desperate men worn down by war, poverty, and fear.[28]

Pension records and sworn testimonies from the military investigations also dramatically demonstrate that each hanging had broad and lingering effects on victims' families. Wives, children, parents, and siblings not only experienced the horrific spectacle of watching the hangings but also faced taunts and jeers of Confederate soldiers when they tried to recover bodies for proper burial. Most victims' families remained in the vicinity and endured continued harassment by pro-Confederate residents and Confederate officials. And many women described themselves as robbed of their sole economic provider.

These personal accounts deserve hearing if only to demonstrate the diverse and individual human histories lost beneath the larger, more generalized corporal one. David Jones's invalid mother, Comfort, explained in her pension file that her twenty-year-old son deserted the Confederacy to join the Union army so that he could continue to support her financially. Widowed and abandoned by her other three sons, Comfort Jones owned no property. Before the war David had leased his labor to neighboring farmers. Conscription, his mother insisted, had forced her son to enlist in the Confederate army. As soon as he was able, his mother claimed, he deserted to Union lines near New Bern, where he continued to visit home and send Comfort his bounty and monthly pay. Losing her youngest son made Comfort Jones entirely dependent on charity. Between October 1861 and February 1864, Joseph L. Haskett had mourned the death of his wife and three children. By the time he went to the gallows, his only surviving daughter, Triphenia, was two years old. A guardian raised the girl and in 1866, due to Joseph's service in the Union, obtained a modest government pension. Lewis C. Bryan was like David Jones—he was single and childless, but his death put his crippled mother at the mercy of sympathetic neighbors. Celia Brock and her eight-year-old son lived four miles from Kinston; they were poor and propertyless. She was present at her husband, John's, execution but later attested, "I could not look at him being hung." She buried John at her mother's home: "He had nothing on but old cast off clothing." Celia Cuthrell described her husband, Charles, as a "Union man in sentiment." Just before her husband's death, her only child died. With no family left, she sold her land and moved permanently beyond Union lines to New Bern. She found work as a seamstress and never remarried. Mary Freeman and her four children had already fled Kinston after her husband, John, enlisted in the Union army. One year after the execution, Mary and three children died in New Bern from severe illness; only twelve-year-old Mary B. survived. A Northern couple, Sarah and Lafayette Clapp, renamed Mary "Bessie" and raised her as their own. The Clapps recalled Bessie carrying a "small tin bucket, which contained a few personal affects which she said her mother had told her to keep." Among these keepsakes was a torn leaf from the family Bible; it listed her parents' wedding date and her siblings' births. For Andrew Britton's family, like that of John Freeman's, the cycle of death did not end at the gallows. Within one month of her husband's death, Elizabeth Britton lost a child. In June 1865, her two surviving children died within one week of each other. After the hangings, Nancy Jones had difficulty obtaining help and a conveyance to carry her husband's body to her home twelve miles distant. She recalled that "plenty would have been glad to have assisted me, but did not dare to for fear of being called a Unionist." When she finally retrieved William, he "had nothing on but his socks." Catherine Summerlin was five months pregnant in February 1864. She spent less than two hours with her husband, Jessie, before he died. While she awaited his execution, a Confederate colonel harassed her and her four children at their Lenoir County home. The colonel confiscated her horse and provisions; after Jessie's death only an armed guard kept other Confederates from disturbing her. The Confederacy had seized her property, drafted her husband, and hanged him. She told federal officials after the war, "They took all I had."[29]

These individuals and their fates are largely unknown to present day Kinstonians. Despite growing scholarship on Southern Unionism, local histories of the region are silent about the hangings. William S. Powell, in *The Annals of Progress: The Story of Lenoir County and Kinston, North Carolina*, describes Unionism in the region prior to Fort Sumter but states nothing of lingering Unionism or dissatisfaction; nor does he mention the hangings. "It is reasonable to believe," conclude Talmage C. Johnson and Charles R. Holloman in *The Story of Kinston and Lenoir County*, "that it was the same here as elsewhere throughout the South—certainty of a righteous cause, assurance of an early triumph, jubilation over victories won in battle and minimizing of defeats, long years of attrition bravely endured, and finally exhaustion and surrender." The authors describe "hundreds of Kinston and Lenoir men and boys" who fought and died heroically for the Confederacy, and they declare, "The women and all those who remained at home were as steadfastly loyal and courageous as those who went to the front." Clifford Tyndall's 1981 master's thesis, "Lenoir County during the Civil War," discusses the hangings, but the author admitted, "The 1864 hangings are still clouded in controversy and ambiguity." Jeffrey Crow has recently noted how an "anti-Confederate interpretation" of the war's legacy in North Carolina posed a "radical alternative to the adoration of men who had prosecuted the war and exposed the South to devastation and defeat." Ultimately North Carolina rejected this "radical past."[30]

On a recent visit to the area this author found no public record of the executions or the Unionism that divided the county. Historical markers and a state museum narrate Kinston's role in the Civil War and the battles that occurred there but state nothing about February 1864. The exact location of the hangings and mass grave remains unknown today. A few longtime residents were surprised to learn of the episode. One native Kinstonian maintained that the hangings were an "embarrassment" to descendants of victims' families still living in the region.[31]

In the March 11, 1864, *New York Times* account of Kinston, the paper sensed that Kinston might fade from people's minds and consciousness. Noting that in other "less tragic" times such an incident would weigh heavily on a nation's heart, the paper worried if civil war and its sufferings had numbed the nation and whether the glare of "great events" and large-scale battles had overshadowed this brief yet disturbing episode.[32] Historian Phillip Shaw Paludan asks similar questions about the Shelton Laurel massacre of thirteen Unionists in western North Carolina: "On the national scene the thirteen deaths were quickly overwhelmed by the mountains of dead. Fredericksburg, Chancellorsville, Gettysburg—What possible meaning was there in thirteen murders in the midst of what Whitman called 'this slaughterhouse'?"[33]

What meaning indeed? This single incident from the Civil War, one that occurred far from the battlefield and one that remains distorted by incrimination and selective historical amnesia, has significant meaning. It demonstrates the complexities of the Civil War in North Carolina; it was an inner struggle that pitted neighbor against neighbor and left deep communal and familial scars. But even the historical process of trying to reconstruct what actually occurred in Kinston in 1864 is insightful. Sorting through the contradictory and emotionally charged versions of the "truth" reveals people struggling to make simple moral and political sense out of something that was in fact quite complicated and perhaps even amoral and apolitical. We find individuals seeking to come to terms with the brutality, violence, and pain that happened "in time of war."

# The Politics of Violence: Unionist Pamphleteers in Virginia's Inner Civil War

## Jon L. Wakelyn

D URING THE CIVIL WAR, Virginia Unionist leaders from border
regions under Northern army occupation fought a war of words and
sometimes deeds against the Confederacy and its guerrilla insurgents.
From the eastern shore to Norfolk, greater Arlington along the Potomac
River, and the northwestern region (which became West Virginia), those
leaders, speaking and writing from Washington and their home districts,
sent pamphlets about the war to constituents and other leaders throughout their parts of the state. In those pamphlets, they employed a politics
of violence to protect themselves and other loyalists from the horror of
the destructive inner civil and guerrilla war in their regions. Those
Virginia Unionist politicians no doubt used the politics of violence to
sustain their own authority back home. More importantly, their efforts
reveal the interrelationship between leadership self-interest and the
actual plight of the victims of that violent inner civil war on the borders
of Virginia. Their pamphlets, thus, represent another major, but largely
untapped, source of how that guerrilla war in its complicated facets
affected those Virginians who clung to the Union.

Virginia Unionist political pamphleteers' focus on threats and acts of
physical violence against individuals, their homes, and their families is
consistent with what other witnesses discussed in their writings about the
Civil War at home. Those who lived through Virginia's inner civil war

wrote of little else. For example, in his diaries Lieutenant Colonel David Strother of the Third (West) Virginia Cavalry left perceptive and critical memories of the people he was assigned to save. He hated fighting the murderous "gangs of idle, dirty, and insolent boys" who made up the Confederate guerrilla forces. Equally, he detested the "viciousness" of Unionist treatment of local Rebels.[1] Virginia Unionist governor Francis Pierpont's daughter, Anna Pierpont Sivitar, also left a vivid account in her *Recollections of War and Peace*. Chillingly, she remembered when Rebels came to Fairmont to burn the Pierpont family home and her father talked them out of it by threatening that after the Union army took charge he would in turn burn them out. Sivitar also discussed in detail her father's charge that the U.S. Congress had given the Rebels the opportunity to ravage east coast Virginia Unionists. But what she remembered most about her father was how he employed a language of violence against foes and even so-called friends in order to protect Virginia border loyalists.[2]

Historians also have discussed Virginia's inner civil war and the behavior of its leaders. The leaders, said Edward Conrad Smith, sought to fill a gap left by the dearth of elected local officials back in the home districts. Smith remarked that Confederate threats of physical violence against Virginia's Unionist leaders often kept them separated from their allies. But the Unionist leaders fought back in behalf of the citizenry. One way they resisted the Confederates, claims Smith, was by writing pamphlets which they distributed in their parts of border Virginia.[3] Another historian, Richard O. Curry, insists that politicians employed images of a violent guerrilla war to argue for the creation of a separate state of West Virginia.[4] But for all the excellent commentary on why the leaders wrote to their constituents about the plight of those people back home, there has been little study of just what the leaders wrote, what their words reveal about the lives of the people back in the local communities or the motivation of the pamphleteers themselves.[5]

Yet, pamphlets have long been used in the nation's history by leaders to communicate with their allies.[6] To be sure, other forms of communication, such as ceremonies, conventions, county political meetings, militia speeches, and fast-day sermons, have also been effective. Often, the written descriptions of those gatherings and speeches were printed as pamphlets which then became useful means to reach a targeted audience. In the Union occupied regions during the Civil War, leaders sent pamphlets through the mails or had them hand delivered. Bound pamphlets, usually in five-by-seven-inch size, could fit easily into the pockets of political leaders, other opinion makers, and constituents, who would refer to them in their writings and oral discourse. In addition, newspaper editors often used ideas and arguments from pamphlets and reprinted them. Political leaders at a distance or close by thus could influence home-front opinion and policy makers.[7]

Virginia's Unionist leaders began their pamphlet war when they communicated to the home folks their opposition to the state's joining the Confederacy. Fears of the possibility of violent internal war concerned those who warned against secession. To be sure, those Unionists addressed other subjects such as the constitutional right to secede. But their major worry, as they informed friend and foe alike, was the fate of the people back home on the borderlands.[8] Their arguments about the fruits of secession, as seen in the issues they discussed and the images they created, no doubt reappeared in their wartime pamphlets on internal violence and thus require extensive commentary.

Even before the state convention had assembled, Judge George W. Thompson from the Wheeling Circuit warned of mob rule and anarchy if the state seceded. He called secession a violence against reason, as he feared the "uprooting of all forms of government and cohercion of society by revolutionary movements." The judge worried that Virginia as a border barrier state would be invaded in the event of civil war, and that would cause internal disruptions.[9] Likewise, Samuel McD. Moore from Rockbridge, who himself would be swallowed up in that brothers' war, charged at the secession convention that civil war would cause much harm to Virginia's border citizenry. Moore insisted that Virginia had nothing in common with the lower South, was attached to the Union, and that a war of opposing military forces would also create opposing interests at home.[10] At Washington, Sherrard Clemens, U.S. congressman from Wheeling, gave a nostalgic Unionist speech which he circulated as a pamphlet in western Virginia. In it he proudly stated that the western part of the state contained many loyal Unionists who opposed a Southern Confederacy. Like the others, Clemens predicted the Unionists would be forced into internal civil war.[11] Correct he was, and he himself would become a symbol to his friends of the plight of Virginia's border Unionists.

Two Unionist members of the state secession convention, men who themselves would spend the war in fear for their personal safety as well as that of their constituents, wrote pamphlets which stand out in the shocking images they created of the fate loyal Virginians would face trapped within a Southern Confederacy. One, John Snyder Carlile, was born in Winchester, Virginia, moved to Philippi and later to Clarksburg, and became a successful lawyer and civic leader in the Kanawa region. He served in the federal House of Representatives from 1855 to 1857, and again in the House as a representative of the Wheeling restored government of Virginia, and led in the early statehood movement for West Virginia. Carlile replaced Robert M. T. Hunter in the U.S. Senate and later turned against statehood, yet he became a U.S. senator from West Virginia in 1863. The other, Joseph Eggleston Segar, was born in King William County in the state's eastern coastal region, and became a well-known lawyer there. Segar entered the U.S. Congress as a member from the restored state of Virginia, but Republicans denied him a seat. Elected again to Congress in 1862 and finally seated in 1863, he opposed West Virginia statehood, was again refused a seat in Congress in 1864, and then served in 1865 in the U.S. Senate from the restored state of Virginia. Both of those Unionist's pamphlets written to ward off civil war were circulated widely in their home districts.[12]

Carlile began his pamphlet in the usual manner of a leader praising the courage of his loyal constituents. But he soon turned to his principal concern, his worries that western Virginians would be placed in an the unenviable position if Virginia joined the Confederacy. He knew that war would harm the innocent as well as the guilty, and have dire consequences for the rights of personal property, including domestic slavery. "What son of Virginia can contemplate this picture without horror?," he exclaimed. Mincing no words, using written images everyone could visualize, Carlile stated secession would result in endless John Brown incursions into border western Virginia.[13] The reality of an inner war, of Confederate invasion and Federal counterinvasion, soon would consume the resources of both Carlile and the people in his western homeland.

Likewise, Segar worried about how loyalists on the east coast of Virginia could be defended in the event of war. Knowing that the Federal government planned to send guns from the Bellona, Virginia, arsenal to Fort Monroe in his home district, and that the secessionist governor intrigued to seize those guns, threw Segar into a panic. For him, Confederate soldiers and Unionist sympathizers feuding in the east would result in "innocent children of Virginia in miseries and woes unnumbered." Enough loyal Unionists, including himself, lived in coastal Virginia, he said, "so that there must be a double war—a Federal war, and a war among ourselves." Segar predicted a Federal blockade, invasion, and threats to Unionist slaveholders. Thus for him secession meant a reign of terror that would create a region "deluged with blood and strewed with carnage."[14]

If the state's Unionist leaders in their pamphlets warned of chaotic civil strife in the event of secession and civil war, they soon gained personal knowledge of that violence. During the Virginia secession convention, those who had spoken out against secession endured hostility and even open threats to their persons. Those Unionist leaders did not hesitate to inform their constituents of the perils they faced personally as defenders of the Union and their people's interests. Perhaps they employed descriptions of their personal troubles to identify with the expected plight of their constituents.

In his June 14, 1861, speech at the Wheeling convention, Carlile characterized secessionists as criminals. He knew this well, he told the people, because he had been forced to sneak out of Richmond after the convention had ended. Confederate thugs had surrounded his hotel room and placed him under a deathwatch.[15] Likewise, Segar wrote in a pamphlet to his constituents on November 3, 1861, for the time being he had to remain in Washington because it was not safe for him to return to his home. Secessionists, he told them, had threatened his life if he went to Norfolk.[16] In a March 1862 pamphlet addressed to his frightened constituents, Carlile told them that marauding soldiers had attacked him at his home in western Virginia.[17] Even years later, Waitman Willey, U.S. senator from West Virginia, found it useful to remind his former wartime allies of a threat on his life after he had traveled to Alexandria in April 1861.[18] Perhaps the most spectacular account of personal fears, and evidence to explain his forced retirement, was the poem that appeared in the *Rebellion Record*, reprinted from a Boston newspaper of April 22, 1861, on Sherrard Clemens's sacrifice for the Union cause. With apologies to all devotees of literature, it bears reprinting. Urging Wheeling lads to defend Clemens against Richmond, it read,

> And must our Clemens die?
> The west shall set this matter right
> Though Richmond jail had Moultrie's guns,
> We'll set our Clemens free.
> Our Clemens, he's in keep and hold
> But here's twenty thousand freemen bold
> Will see the reason why![19]

Thus, the Unionist leader pamphleteers had turned their own experiences into a politics of personal violence which they described in their pamphlets. That fear of personal physical violence also became a part of their constituents' lives from the beginning of the war. Attacks on Unionist homes, burning of local businesses, even the shooting of Unionist organizers occurred along the Virginia border during the sham vote that the Confederate government staged to confirm secession. Despite Virginia Confederates' claims of support there, the border became a Unionist hotbed that the South would have to attempt to pacify politically and control militarily, lest it become an entryway for Federal invasion. Point of entry it became, and Unionists unleashed counterviolence.

Carlile and his allies began the Unionist responses to the Confederate advance when they invited Federal troops to the western border and planned to create a separate state of West Virginia. To their Unionist friends, the leaders claimed that those activities were part of their efforts to deter Confederate acts of violence. In his March 1862 pamphlet, Carlile explained his decision of May 1861 to support a Federal invasion and call for a separate state.[20] Though he lost that first battle for making West Virginia a state, and would oppose the second and decisive one, he reminded his friends and fellow sufferers that at the time statehood seemed to be the only way to achieve protection from violence. As the war progressed, he stated, "I have periled all, life itself, in defense of . . . the mountain region." He claimed to have remained at the statehood convention amidst the "yells and taunts, hisses and threats of the mob."[21] Thus dan-

gers to himself were mingled with dangers to his friends when he called
for Federal protection and statehood to assist them in their inner war.

In their early pamphlets, as is seen, those loyalist congressmen praised
the North for protecting the Unionist citizens of the border districts. But
they soon had reason to question how successful Federal policies had been
in securing their constituents' safety. The Lincoln government's late 1862
decision to abolish slavery, although seemingly not meant to apply to the
Unionist sections, threatened loyal border Virginians because they lived
in a state which had seceded. Many of their leaders discussed in their pamphlets in great detail the violence that could result from that Federal policy
to end slavery. Carlile even compared the antislavery movement to
Virginia's secessionist guerrilla's "unholy and wicked effort . . . to enslave
the people and make them subservient to their own wicked purpose."[22] No
doubt he linked aboltion with secessionist enslavers of Virginia's Unionists
to warn the Lincoln government of the harm that could result from further talk of ending slavery.

Virginia Unionist leaders also connected the slavery issue with Federal
protection for their constituents. One such leader was Waitman Thomas
Willey, Morgantown lawyer, wartime U.S. senator from the restored state
of Virginia, delegate to the West Virginia state constitutional convention,
and West Virginia Republican senator from 1863 to 1871. Willey claimed
to his friends that his vote to end slavery showed his and their strong support for the Union. But Willey also defended his vote as a way to obtain
additional Federal army protection for border Virginia Unionists.[23]
Conversely, to his constituents Carlile explained that his support for slavery actually was to combat the horrors of that inner civil war. Some western Virginia Unionists, he claimed, had been recruited or dragooned into
the Confederate army and forced to join local insurrectionists. Carlile
wanted those men to return to the Union side and fight for freedom.
"What," he said to Northerners and to loyal Virginians, "will be the effect
(of freeing slaves) upon the thousands that have been impressed into the
rebel army who are now anxiously looking for an opportunity to rush to
your standard?"[24] Both men, from opposite sides of the slavery issue, had
discussed the proposed Federal policy in terms of how to support their constituents against an internal insurrection.

Other Virginia pamphlet writers saw additional dangers in the struggle to end slavery in their state. One was Kellian Whaley, originally from New York but a longtime Ceredon, Virginia, lumber merchant, who served the Wheeling government as a U.S. representative and later served in the U.S. House from West Virginia. His own twist on Carlile's argument, as published in a July 1862 pamphlet, revealed Whaley's fear that loyal western Virginia's white laborers would have to compete with free black labor. Would this violent struggle over jobs send Unionists scurrying to the Confederate side? he asked Northerners and western Virginians.[25] Obviously, Virginia's Unionist leaders knew that ending slavery would sorely test Unionist loyalty on the western border.

Those leaders had even more to say about the issue of freedom after the Federal government ended slavery in Virginia. In his April 1863 pamphlet, Segar reflected on the government's proposal to use ex-slaves to fight Confederate marauders around Norfolk. He told his constituents that he desired a vigorous prosecution of the inner war to defeat the Confederacy at all cost. But he wanted them to know that he had voted against the bill to arm ex-slaves out of fear of a race war at home. To his colleagues in Washington and to his allies back home, he used violent imagery when he declared that, if he had voted for the bill, he would have expected them "to hang me from the nearest tree."[26]

In March 1864, Carlile, perhaps trying to curry favor with those who regarded themselves as victims of abolition, wrote to his constituents concerning what to do about fugitive slaves who had come into western Virginia. Some allies had suggested, he said, that slaves join with Unionists to strike at Confederate guerrillas. Those slaves who fought, he warned, would in reality strike a blow at the Unionists, and "its effect will be directly injurious to the public cause."[27] Virginia's Unionist leaders, such as Carlile and Segar, thus had real concerns that the end of slavery would lead to the use of armed ex-slaves in the guerrilla war.

The slave freedom issue had become the Achilles' heel of loyalist border leaders. That meant that in order to protect their own positions back home most of the border Virginia Unionist leaders had to oppose the abolition of slavery and the use of ex-slaves to fight the war. For them, the Federal government clearly had exacerbated the problem of race relations and thus increased the violence in Virginia's Unionist regions. That they invoked fear of even more internal violence in their pamphlets reflects just how much they worried about Federal government policy and their constituents' reactions to it. Indeed, on this issue images of internal violence resonated through their arguments.

Perhaps to ease their Unionist constituents' resentment of Federal antislavery policies, in other pamphlets Virginia Unionist leaders bragged about how the Washington government and the Union army assisted their allies in defending themselves. Early on in the war, Carlile had been pleased to inform his Unionist friends that he had persuaded the Massachusetts government to loan them two thousand weapons which were much needed in their war against Confederate guerrillas.[28] Governor Francis Pierpont, in an otherwise uncomplimentary pamphlet on the Union army, in April 1864 praised the Federal government for its support of border Unionists. He reminded President Lincoln, and also his constituents, that such assistance had allowed the arming of irregular Unionist troops in Wheeling, Alexandria, and Norfolk to fight alongside Federal soldiers in behalf of the loyal citizens. His people, he exclaimed, knew the blessings of Federal government assistance.[29] One wonders just who Pierpont was appeasing with these helpful words.

Segar, too, thanked the Federal government for its military assistance, and he found even more to praise when he linked Virginian's struggle for the Union with Federal government economic policies. In a February 1863 pamphlet, which he mailed to constituents, he explained his recent vote in Congress in favor of a bill to build ship canals on the Great Lakes. He maintained that his vote had been in the "nation's best defense." Now how, he asked, could Virginia's Unionists gain from this vote? Segar answered that he feared the disintegration of coastal Virginia's commerce if dredging bills were not passed to aid that region. Failure of eastern Virginia businesses, he maintained, would break up loyalist support there and make the people vulnerable to Confederate invaders. Segar also envisioned that major trade links with the northeastern states would lead to favorable legislation for coastal Virginians and bestir them to resist the Confederates.[30]

Indeed, Federal troops, military aid, and commercial support were a boon to Virginia's victims of Confederate aggression. But Virginia's Unionist leaders in their pamphlets also insisted that, in addition to the Federal government's antislavery policy, actions by Congress and the U.S.

Army had perpetrated other forms of violence on the state's loyalists. For one thing, almost all of the loyal Unionist congressmen maintained that they had been treated horribly by Northern and other border fellow congressmen. When Northern and border state congressmen questioned the Virginia leaders' credentials and accused their Unionist constituents of being pro-Confederates who did not deserve protection, Virginia Unionist leaders tried to refute those charges. For the Virginia Unionist congressmen and other leaders, the pamphlets they wrote to defend themselves to Congress and to home constituents alike revealed yet another kind of violence in that inner civil war.

An eloquent defender of his constituents' loyalty, Segar also artfully used congressional attacks on him personally to identify with the plight of his constitutents. In his January 1862 pamphlet, Segar seethed to his friends that Northern Republicans' refusal to accept his credentials as an elected congressman from the east coast of Virginia to the Thirty-seventh Congress had perpetrated violence against him. To calm enraged loyal voters as well as members of Congress, Segar insisted that refusal to seat him delayed the return of Virginia to the Union. He wished Northerners to realize that his Unionist constituents wanted him in Congress but that armed guerrillas had kept them from voting.[31] In May 1864, Congress again denied Segar a seat. Secessionist guerrilla threats against those who wanted to vote for him again had affected the turnout. But the situation was even more critical back home now, he claimed. Segar wanted Congress to understand that even in Union controlled areas, Rebels continued to intimidate the citizenry. In those very regions adjacent to the Potomac River where loyalists were not allowed to vote, he reminded Congress, supplies were carried from Maryland to the enemy. He pleaded with Congress to allow him to help stop that flow of goods of ruin and death. By its refusal to seat him, Segar claimed, the Federal Congress had behaved in a violent manner toward him personally and thus also toward his eastern Virginia Unionist allies.[32]

Other reasons existed to criticize Northern allies' insensitivity to the plight of loyalists in that violent inner war. Virginia's Unionist leaders well understood the tenuous grasp the Union had on the so-called occupied sections of Virginia and the problems the Union army caused for loyalists there. Restored state governor Pierpont, in his April 1864 letter to

President Lincoln, vigorously condemned the policies of Union military commander General Benjamin Butler.[33] Pierpont mailed copies of the pamphlet to members of Congress and to leading Unionists in western Virginia, the Alexandria area, and the Norfolk–Albermarle Sound borderland where Butler commanded the Union army. His object was to inform President Lincoln, the national Congress, and his Virginia allies of the political and social chaos Butler caused in his persecution of loyal citizens. It was a tale replete with violent language and images, as Pierpont described families torn apart and, most damaging to continued loyalism, the seizure of Unionists' private property.

Governor Pierpont began his pamphlet by reminding President Lincoln of Virginia Unionists' great sacrifices and of the loyalty of the Wheeling government now located in Alexandria. His litany of horrors clearly had the purpose of providing him the necessary loyalist credentials with which to attack the actions of General Butler. The governor insisted that "harmony has always existed between the civil and military authorities in unionist Virginia." The Union loyalists felt that they had a protector, until now. He warned that "butternut" Confederate sympathizers in Pennsylvania and Ohio were poised to invade Virginia if they received the signal that the Union army would no longer assist the loyalists. Butler, he claimed, made friends with Rebels, and together they abused the Unionists. Even worse, by playing favorites in local politics and business, General Butler divided local leaders. In Norfolk, insisted the governor, Butler took from the loyalists: "Is this right, is it just that these men, . . . with large families to support, and who have lost largely by the rebellion, should thus be blasted by the caprice of a commanding general?" Pierpont also claimed that he too had been violated when Butler personally humiliated him. How could the Union cause be so wounded "in the house of friends"? he asked the president. Pierpont concluded by declaring to one and all that he had confidence in presidential justice. But he also warned that if West Virginia had had such hostile Northern military rule as Norfolk and Alexandria many Unionist followers there would have become copperheads and secessionists.[34]

The comment of Pierpont's that West Virginia had benefited from Union military protection was correct, to a point. Unionist politicians from the west knew that, despite being in so-called safe territory, their constituents continued to suffer from that inner civil war. Accordingly, in their pamphlets they warned and admonished their Federal allies and continued to call for Federal action. After all, with the help of Federal troops, western loyal leaders had begun to defend their own people. In their struggle to form the state of West Virginia, the pamphleteers argued that bringing that border region into the Union would protect its citizens from guerrilla warfare. To defend their loyalists allies, but not without argument and disagreement among themselves, they employed the politics of violence to establish a separate state of West Virginia.

The most important political spokesman for a separate state was Waitman Thomas Willey, who had written a number of pamphlets on the inner civil war in his region of the state. Unfortunately, I have discovered no pamphlet of that period in which he commented directly on making a new state. It is known, however, that Willey had opposed the 1861 statehood movement because at that time he feared it would exacerbate internal warfare. But in 1862 Willey supported statehood and linked it to his opposition to slavery. He insisted that all of the slaves in the new state would remain in Union army hands, thus mitigating the threat of racial violence. The West Virginia statehood bill, known as the Willey bill, passed the U.S. Senate on July 15, 1862.[35]

If Willey did not write a pamphlet in behalf of statehood for western Virginia, Kellian Whaley, the Wheeling government's U.S. congressman from Huntington on the Ohio River, did. In his pro-statehood speech in the U.S. House of Representatives in July 1862, Whaley talked mainly about how statehood would mean peace. Whaley sent copies of his speech in pamphlet form to his loyal followers. To assist his case with the folks back home, he refreshed his audience's memory of the violence in the prewar relations between the Richmond government and the people of northwest Virginia. The congressman characterized the relationship with Richmond as one of continuous suffering in the west, which he insisted had been kept poor by a violent and hostile slave society. Easterners behaved like "our masters," he claimed. They opposed any chance for westerners to gain the free public schools so needed to rid them of the burdens of poverty. During the war, stated Whaley, Richmond had grown even more aggressive toward the west. In support of his claim for statehood he described with passion "the groans of our slain and imprisoned people, the

flames of our burning dwellings, the devastation of our farms and villages."
In short, Richmond had instituted a "reign of Terror" to stamp out "free
expression and the will of the people." "Safety, quiet, peace, and liberty,"
he believed, "can only be found by separation." Western Virginians had
acted to break that cycle of bloodshed, robbery, and imprisonment. Now,
he exclaimed, let Congress make it legal. His constituents, whom he also
sought to convince, had proved "our fraternity . . . by all that is difficult
and dangerous in the separation of our political ties, and by the resolute
endurance of all the cruelities of a civil war within our borders."[36]

But not all of Virginia's Unionist politicians supported separate western statehood at that time. In 1862, Carlile's opposition, according to
Richard O. Curry, was based on fears of antislavery and Republican power
in western Virginia.[37] Perhaps Carlile also worried that discussion of statehood would stir up more internal warfare over slavery. Another loyal
Virginia congressman, Joseph E. Segar, explained to officials in Washington
why he had opposed statehood at that time. In December 1862, he sent a
pamphlet of that speech to his eastern Virginia constituents. Segar began
his argument with a recapitulation of the horrors of inner war for his followers and how he wanted the secessionists to suffer for their horrible
actions. He then insisted that the east and west Virginia borders had no
separate interests which divided them. Next, Segar revealed his primary
reason for opposing statehood when he asked rhetorically just who would
protect a divided Virginia: "What is to become of the people of the eastern shore, . . . and of those of York and Elizabeth City and other counties?"
Could a weakened Wheeling government protect them? To be set adrift,
to give way to anarchy and lawlessness, that is the image Segar conjured
for his listeners and readers of the results of creating two Virginias. "Let us
remain one and united," he exclaimed, "so that when the Union shall be
reconstructed, we shall be once more a band of brothers."[38]

Segar had believed that western statehood would hurt the coastal
counties. By 1864, a U.S. senator from West Virginia, Peter G. Van
Winkle, a Parkersburg lawyer and railroad president, wanted to make certain that the Federal Congress would continue to protect from Confederate
guerrilla attacks the new state it had created. Irked by comments from a
Kentucky congressman who had tried to deny him his own seat and had
claimed that West Virginia should not be made a state, Van Winkle spoke

to his Senate colleagues on April 21, 1864. Of course, he promptly sent home many copies of that speech to his constituents to display for them his continued concerns for their welfare. Reciting the usual litany of horrors, he described the violent life in his own town of Parkersburg, which recently had been burned out by Confederate guerrillas. He then reminded his colleagues and constituents of April 1861, when for his faithfulness to the Union cause he had been insulted, threatened, and "spat upon." His support in 1862 of those who had wanted to create a separate state, he told his audience, had subjected him to "threats of personal violence." His purpose in relating personal peril to the statehood struggle, stated Van Winkle, was to show that Unionist legislators had been the legitimate leaders who called the statehood convention, despite threats to their lives. After he established his own loyal credentials through comments about attacks on his person, Van Winkle concluded with praise for his followers' present actions. By 1864, he claimed, thanks to statehood, the leaders and people were beginning to restore peace to the region.[39]

With that concluding refrain, Van Winkle emphasized what may have been the central political theme of those Unionist pamphleteers who described in such vivid terms the violence of that inner civil war. As the war neared its end, they continued to relate personal comments about their own peril to specific acts of violence against Unionist constituents and recounted vividly the Confederate guerrillas' willful destruction of their part of the Union. They claimed that from the beginning their goal in writing pamphlets was to save the Union. Those leaders, then, described tales of horror to hasten the restoration of the Union, to make Virginia again peaceful.

Van Winkle himself maintained that the only way to ensure the safety of the loyal citizens of West Virginia was to "suppress" rebellion.[40] In his May 1864 retelling of his own troubles with a Federal Congress bent on depriving him of his constitutionally elected office, Segar said emphatically, "in the name of the Union, do not ignore our young and maybe feeble government, by denying us representation" in public life. How else, he asked, could Union and peace be restored?[41] Reflecting on his joy over the war's end, in June 1865, Segar revealed why he had regaled Northerners and tidewater Virginians alike with his many stories about violence perpertrated on them. Murder, want, ruin, bloodshed at "every step" had marked those who had sacrificed to save the Union. Now he said, "[T]he stream of brother's blood which has been reddening our waters for more than four years has ceased to flow."[42]

Indeed, the various topics which all those Virginia Unionist leaders discussed in their pamphlets on violence included their hopes for reunion and peace. From the war's beginning, when they asked Federal troops to come in to put down the guerrilla struggles, each of them worked in behalf of reunion. Even in their praise for Northern support and their admonitions to Northerners against causing trouble for them, each of them often in personal terms had called for reunion. Willey claimed that Southern secession forced on him what he called this "other war of opinion," this use of violent words and images.[43] Segar in 1862 insisted that the rupture of the Union had destroyed "all ties of kindred and blood." Loyalty to the Union, for him, was not disloyalty to Virginia. To his friends at a rally in Portsmouth in 1862, he shouted out, "[Y]ou must put an end to the war." He urged, with his tales of violence, that the masses of Norfolk and the rest of the coast rise up and fight back to restore the Union.[44] Whaley insisted his task was to put down treason and rebellion. Our young men, he wrote in one pamphlet, despite what happened to them, "rallied to return Virginia to the Union, to overthrow guerrillas and bandits." Even the statehood struggle for Whaley was a means to restore border western Virginians to the Union. "The Union rent and shattered by fractricidal strife," he stated, "must be reconstructed."[45] United in that goal, the Virginia Unionist political pamphleteers used the politics of violence to put down Confederate guerrillas and to restore peace to their divided Virginia border regions.

Virginia's loyalist leaders of course walked a careful path in creating that central image of a restored Union. That in part explains why in their pamphlets to their constituents they invoked such a vivid politics of violence. If the restoration of the Union meant an end to guerrilla war, the Unionist leaders from those border regions knew that the instruments of peace, the Union army and the Federal government, also posed a problem for the home front. Of course those loyal leaders sometimes accused Northerners of perpetrating another kind of violence to force additional assistance from their so-called friends. In addition, the Unionist Virginia leaders knew the danger of giving too much credit to Northerners for their safety. As the pamphleteers stated over and again, if their constituents hated Confederate insurgents, they also worried about the violence toward them from their Northern allies. All these defensive comments show that Virginia's inner war may have included a more complicated set of opponents than most historians have imagined.

A review of the many issues discussed in those pamphlets reveals that Virginia Unionist leaders' principal concerns even in their call for reunion were to assist the victims back home. To be sure, personal political survival in that chaos of governance and leadership back home motivated them and perhaps explains their seeming preoccupation with threats to themselves. Still, in their personal pursuit of peace, those men gave special attention to the fears of Union supporters in their own regions of the state's borderland. In their criticism of their Northern allies they always talked of the need to help the folks at home. Even those who discussed West Virginia statehood couched their arguments in terms of the violence perpetrated against their constituents. The pamphlets which they sent to constituents and colleagues indeed became a conversation of commiseration. Thus, the events and issues discussed in these pamphlets on the politics of violence reveal something of how oppressed that border slave state's communities, citizens, and leaders were and how they struggled with one another, with the Confederates and their guerrilla troops, and with their Federal allies.

# The Absence of Violence: Confederates and Unionists in Culpeper County, Virginia

## Daniel E. Sutherland

CULPEPER COUNTY, nestled in the heart of Virginia's northern piedmont, witnessed more than its share of violent upheaval during the
Civil War, but most of it was inspired by the Union (and occasionally
the Confederate) army. The county had relatively few Unionists or
antigovernment Confederates, and while divided neighbors sometimes
cursed or threatened each other, no one was physically abused. No competing bands of Rebel or tory guerrillas prowled the countryside, and the
people never witnessed the angry class divisions or social conflict some
historians have linked to Southern Unionism. Those links were tenuous
at best in Culpeper; this suggests that the county's Unionists were motivated by a more complex set of factors than income and social status.[1]

Culpeper County had 12,063 residents in 1860, 6,675 slaves and
5,388 free people, with 429 of the latter being black. Culpeper's wealth-
iest planters were moderately well-to-do, yet for every planter, the county
contained three to four small farmers and herders, and the principal towns
of Culpeper Court House (the county seat), Stevensburg, and Jeffersonton
held ample numbers of day laborers and artisans. These plain folk sub-
sisted on a few acres of land, much of it undeveloped woodland, or on a
small cash salary. In the presidential election of 1860, John Bell, candidate for the conciliatory Constitutional Union party, defeated Southern
Democrat John C. Breckinridge by in Culpeper by one vote, 526 to 525.

Popular opinion fluctuated over the next several months regarding the wisdom of secession, but Fort Sumter settled the issue for most people. On April 23, 1861, Culpeper County unanimously approved Virginia's secession ordinance with 1,051 votes, a number that accounted for 85 percent of the county's eligible voters.[2]

Yet this apparent wall of unanimity had cracks. Some voters opted for secession with more resignation than enthusiasm, and some fervent Unionists refused to vote at all. The total number of votes cast for secession was nineteen shy of the number of voters in November's presidential election; this suggests that at least nineteen people still resisted a plunge into the abyss. But most opponents of secession and war were too timid to speak out. Edward Elly, decided not to vote on the ordinance because, as he put it, "I was cautioned not to express my sentiments, and kept quiet." Had he gone to the polls, insisted Elly, he would have been "liable to injury and great abuse." James B. Kirk, who had only settled in Culpeper two years earlier, also chose not to go to the polls. "The people all around me were secesh with the exception of one family," he explained, "and I knew if I voted against the ratification of the ordinance, they would be down on me." Archibald Shaw, who had been born and bred in Culpeper, encountered an even stronger deterrent. "I was prevented from voting against it [secession]," he insisted, "by threats of arrest & of being tarred & feathered."[3]

Even those few souls courageous enough to speak publicly during the debate over secession saw the wisdom of holding their tongues once the ordinance had been passed; so not until July 1862, when Culpeper first experienced invasion, confiscation, and the widespread destruction of property by Federal troops, did the county's Unionists reemerge. As General John Pope's newly formed Army of Virginia carried the fury of war into Culpeper, previously cautious Unionists, eager to be liberated, stepped forward to supply U.S. troops with food and news of Rebel movements. Archibald Shaw, whose partial deafness spared him from being conscripted, suffered no disability that could prevent him from feeding Union soldiers and providing them with information "as to roads, fords, & the position of the enemy." Matilda Hudson provided Pope's army with nearly one thousand dollars worth of food, fodder, and livestock, including eight cattle and fatted calves.[4]

Who were these collaboraters? Some of them were free blacks; this is hardly surprising, but black Unionists aside, it is extremely difficult to find outright expressions of white class consciousness in Culpeper. Simeon B. Shaw, a forty-two-year-old tenant farmer with three children, best fits the image of a Southern class warrior. "I regarded the war as altogether wrong and unnecessary," insisted Shaw. "I considered it was carried on in the interest of slavery. I had no negroes and I told the sesech I was not going to fight for them. If the South had gained their independence, a poor man like me would stand no chance at all here." Delila Day held a more personal grudge against the Culpeper gentry. About five years before the war, the then Miss Delila Doggett bore a daughter who had been fathered by one of the locally influential Nalle family, but Johnson Nalle refused to marry the low-born Miss Doggett. Instead, he fulfilled his paternal obligation by purchasing a sixty-acre farm for mother and daughter. Delila was working the farm with her parents and five brothers when the war came. One of her two oldest brothers joined the Confederate army; the other was conscripted. Shortly thereafter, Delila married Lemuel Day, no doubt seeking security and protection in the great upheaval. Unfortunately, Day turned out to be "a good for nothing fellow" who drank, gambled, and physically abused Delila. This experience perhaps further impressed upon Delila her perilous position in life, a life that would have been very different had Johnson Nalle not deserted her. What seems certain is that she saw the war as a contest fought for the benefit of people like the Nalles. "The Southern people were so overbearing," she insisted, "it would have been worse than it was before the war: poor people and darkeys would [have] had no chance at all."[5]

But such statements are notable primarily for their rarity, and a profile of 65 identifiable white Unionists and antigovernment Confederates in Culpeper simply does not reflect a community rent by class divisions. To begin with, 46 (70 percent) of these people owned land, and 50 people (77 percent) claimed some amount of personal property (compared to 56 percent of the county's heads of household who owned real property and 87 percent who owned personal property). Thirty-five people owned or rented slaves, sometimes in large numbers. Indeed, 7 people qualified as planters (defined as holders of 20 or more slaves), and the average number of slaves per slaveholder was over 11 (compared to 9.5 for Rebel slaveholders). The majority of the group worked as independent farmers, with the remainder filling such varied occupations as tenant farmer (8), carpenter (4), hired hand (2), shoemaker (2), overseer, sawyer, blacksmith, wheelwright, physician, minister, steam mill owner, and merchant (1 each). While some of these occupations may appear to support a class interpretation of Unionism, only 4 people are known to have linked their sentiments to class rebellion.[6]

Neither do conscription and desertion, two of the most frequently cited pieces of evidence of class antagonism in the Confederacy, suggest a strong class influence. A review of Culpeper men who served in the army shows that only 40 of 323 men (12 percent) entered the army after the onset of conscription. Only 1 of those men is known to have been conscripted, and circumstances suggest that only another 16 were possible conscripts. Of the 65 identifiable Unionists, only 10 were drafted or had relatives who were drafted. Of those people, 5 were property owners, 4 were slaveowners, and only 2 expressed class resentment. So if conscription did add to anti-Confederate feeling, it could but occasionally have been expressed along class lines.[7]

There is less concrete evidence to measure the role of desertion — another possible expression of social discontent — but it is instructive. Most deserters probably did come from the poorer classes, but that is because the great bulk of the Confederate army consisted of such people. Some men undoubtedly deserted because they had grown weary of a war in which they had increasingly little interest. But men deserted for many reasons, not least of which was the proximity of the enemy to their communities and their own determination of how well the government was protecting those communities. Similarly, if a man already served near his home as invading armies approached, he would have more incentive to *stay* in the army, as demonstrated by a study of desertion in the Forty-fourth Virginia Infantry.[8]

Even men who did leave the army for financial reasons — usually to return home and support their families — did not necessarily stop supporting the Confederacy. They simply regarded their families as a higher priority than military service. They may also have blamed the Confederate government for failing to provide adequate relief programs for hungry civilians; but, once again, their unhappiness with the government would not necessarily be fueled by class resentment. As the desertion of men hoping to save themselves "from useless sacrifice" increased, those who remained in the ranks could not help but have second thoughts about the certainty of Confederate victory. Then, when letters from home told of high prices and inadequate provisions for relief, even loyal men pondered their "conflicting duties." It was perfectly reasonable, thought a Texas soldier in Culpeper, that a man who had "done his duty faithfully and bravely, as long as he could," should be tempted to return "home to his needy family."[9]

Likewise, there is a tendency to assume that Southern women who begged their men to return home, or beseeched politicians to grant their men discharges from service, became bitter opponents of the Confederacy when those men were not allowed to leave the army or when they were punished for trying to do so. Yet, not considering those cases where supplicants opposed the Confederacy even *prior* to their requests, very little evidence supports this interpretation. Indeed, there is far more evidence that women remained loyal despite the suffering. A Culpeper resident insisted in early 1864 that women in her neighborhood thought ill of men who deserted. The husband of a friend had not even deserted in the formal sense, only run away to avoid serving in the army, yet the wife was mortified. "She seems dreadfully cast down about it & says he ought not to have gone," she reported of her friend. "What an awful thing for a good honorable woman to be so disgraced." The husband also came to regret his hasty flight and remained away from the neighborhood because he was "ashamed" to go back.[10]

What, then, were the deciding factors in Culpeper Unionism? One obvious explanation runs absolutely counter to the class warfare interpretation. People who owned property, be it slaves, land, or businesses, believed that a war between the North and South jeopardized that property. One of Culpeper's most vocal Unionists, William D. Wallach, pinned his hopes for a permanent Union occupation in the summer of 1862 not on class-conscious Rebels but on prosperous citizens. When John Pope's disastrous policies of confiscation and martial law alienated Unionists, Wallach complained bitterly to the Federal government. These people could have provided enormous material and personal support to the occupying army, grumbled Wallach, had Pope treated them with some courtesy and had they been issued receipts for the "thousands of dollars" worth of wheat, hay, and livestock they freely donated to his army.[11]

Another factor, one seldom mentioned in discussions of Confederate disloyalty, is age. The average age of Culpeper's dissenters at the start of the war was forty-five (contrasted to a general population where only 39 percent were over forty). In other words, these were settled, middle-aged people with little enthusiasm for rebellion. While young firebrands used the image of the American Revolution to justify Southern revolt, some older people interpreted the significance of the Revolution differently. The Founding Fathers, they said, had forged a great nation that had grown and prospered in four score years. The memories of the nation's history and heroes had instilled a deeper, more abiding patriotism in a large portion of the older generation.

While historians have done very little systematic investigation of the connection of age to Unionism, there are some tantalizing hints. A recent study of disloyalty in East Tennessee, a recognized bastion of Unionism, stresses this age factor. Confederate leaders in that part of the South came from a rising "commercial-professional middle class," not from the established families or older citizens. Nearly three-fourths of those Tennessee Unionists were over forty years old. Some contemporaries also observed a connection. A Maryland Unionist reported in June 1861, "Generally the elderly men are for the maintenance of the Government: while the younger men and the women are for secession. The passionate and impulsive side with the rebels, while the more sedate and thoughtful are for the Union."[12]

Sentimental attachment to the old Union was widespread in Culpeper. Forty-five year old Martha Bailey, whose husband died in 1862, described herself as a poor, uneducated woman with five children. She seems a perfect recruit for the class war, yet when explaining her opposition she said simply, "When I found out what the war was for, I sympathized with the Union." Notice, she did not oppose the South so much as support the Union. Perhaps she thought along the same lines as John Brown, who claimed, "I spoke against it [the war] in public and private. . . . I told the people it would be the means of bringing destruction upon the country." Lucy M. Colvin, another widow with four children declared, "I had some relatives in the Confederate service and sympathized with their sufferings but had no sympathy with the cause they were engaged in." Even more revealingly, she added, "I was so sad and grieved. I could only pray. It seemed like a family slaying each other." Robert S. Thomas, in the words of a neighbor, "would have [had] his right arm cut off" before rebelling against the United States.[13]

People with children, people such as Bailey and Colvin, had another reason to balk at war. Forty-eight of the group of sixty-five Unionists had children residing with them when the war began, the average number of children per Unionist family being three and a half. This was slightly below the four children found in the average Culpeper family, but more than one Unionist mentioned their children as a reason for opposing the war. One shoemaker and father of five explained his reason for preferring peace to war this way, "I did not go with the state when it was voted out. I told the folks when they were voting the State out they were voting their children's blood away."[14]

William Soutter simply considered the size of the Northern population and the extent of Northern resources and realized that Southern independence was impossible. "I always felt that the North would conquer the South," proclaimed Soutter, "& so expressed myself." Similarly, Isham B. Chewning, a forty-six year old overseer and owner of seven slaves, insisted, "The result of the war was what I supposed it would be." Matilda Hudson, yet another widow, was forty-nine years old with four daughters to support when the war started. She lived on a five-hundred-acre farm given to her by her father when Mr. Hudson died. A brother managed the farm and directed the eleven slaves needed to work it. When he was conscripted, Mrs. Hudson might well have seen the Confederate struggle as one waged only for the benefit of large slaveowners. Instead, she continued to oppose the war for broader reasons. "I took the Union side because I thought it was right," she explained matter-of-factly. "I thought we had a good government and it was wrong to secede, and I was opposed to it from beginning to end."[15]

In point of fact, many people who regarded themselves as Unionists or who were so regarded by onlookers and neighbors only wanted the war to be over, regardless of the winner. Consider one barefoot, dirty, ragged, and hungry family that resided in the backwoods of Culpeper, called "poor white trash" by a New Jersey cavalryman. The mother of this family seemed, in the opinion of the Federal, "reconciled to the kindred sordidness of her life." She and her husband, continued the soldier, "lived in the labors of the day, caring for little outside their farm and homestead, letting the war pass on with no interest beyond that of the safety of their little [live]stock." When Union raiders snatched even that, the couple "looked on with an apathy which almost resembled indifference." Susan Hall, who lived with her husband on a rented farm four miles from Culpeper Court House, responded to the national crisis in similar fashion. She was forty-three when the war began and would be widowed in 1863. She had eight children, age four through twenty. "We were poor people and took no interest in politics," maintained Mrs. Hall, but her relative poverty (she claimed eight hundred dollars in personal property in 1860) did not dictate her politics. "I had so much trouble of my own that I scarcely knew which side succeeded in the battle," maintained the widow, "and for a long time I didn't know what they were fighting about." She pitied the "suffering and slaughter on both sides," but said, "[W]e had all we could do to provide for our children."[16]

This issue also raises the question of how to define the Southern poor. What, after all, is a "poor" person? Clearly, a farmer who owns ten acres and a single hog might consider a neighbor who owns a thousand acres, fifty slaves, and a hundred hogs to be rich. But what about the owner of five hundred acres, fifteen slaves, and fifty hogs? Is he poor? Certainly not, says the man with ten acres. Yet, when a revised conscription law in October 1862 exempted owners or overseers of twenty or more slaves from the draft, the man with only fifteen slaves might easily resent the "rich" for placing the burden of the war on him.

Even if clearly defined, there is the problem of identifying the poor. For instance, much of the evidence for the debilitating effect of class tensions in the Confederacy comes from Northerners. At least some Federals consciously used the language of class warfare to promote a rift between rich and poor and to create the impression of an irreconcilable social chasm between them. Even if honest in their reporting, many Northerners who attempted to define or describe Southern social classes and the Southern "poor" or "common" people must be viewed skeptically. So limited was their understanding of social conditions in the South, so often did they seek to contrast Southern society to what they had known in New York or Ohio, that they judged Southern conditions by Northern standards.[17]

In Culpeper, this problem is illustrated by the experience of a Federal reconnaissance party in May 1862. Major D. Porter Stowell reported being aided on this expedition by several of Culpeper's poor whites, but the only two men he identified by name were far from being that, and it is doubtful that they were Union sympathizers. One of these fellows identified himself as Bakham. "He was a very good Union man, and seemed very much pleased with the idea of Union troops coming forward," reported Stowell. Yet circumstances almost certainly dictate that this person was Beverly Beckham, the fifteen-year-old son of James A. Beckham (who owned fifty-six slaves) and brother of two officers in the Confederate army. One Culpeper resident later chuckled of Beckham's ruse, "Was he not 'soft soldering' the commanding officer, and did he [Stowell] not take it in beautifully?" The New Jersey cavalryman quoted above who had been so impressed by the apathy of Culpeper's "poor white trash" may have been similarly deceived. Perhaps the soldier's undisguised contempt for the herders blinded him to the possibility that their apathy was a pose. It was just such unassuming, apparently dispondent folk who could, under cover of darkness or the terrain, become deadly bushwhackers or saboteurs.[18]

Neighbors could be deceived, too. William and Mary Payne operated the Virginia House, one of Culpeper's three hotels. The couple owned slaves and had a son serving with General James E. B. Stuart. Yet the Paynes never embraced the Confederate cause wholeheartedly. The Northern-born Mrs. Payne claimed that they had inherited the slaves, and she had a son-in-law in the Union army. Thus her sympathies, if not her loyalties, were understandably divided. She nursed both Union and Confederate soldiers, and she felt neither happy nor sad about either Confederate or Federal victories. Rather, she remained "generally scared to death" during the entire war. "I was in hopes that the war would cease and that we would have no more of it," she explained. Her sentiments hardly constituted a ringing endorsement of the Union cause, yet even Mrs. Payne's most "intimate" neighbors grew suspicious of her and began to treat her "badly." One woman admitted that people considered Mrs. Payne a "curious" woman and continued to regard her as a Yankee sympathizer for years after the war.[19]

The wartime loyalties of Thomas R. Rixey and John S. Pendleton are likewise revealing. Rixey, owner of 750 acres and twenty slaves, is probably suspect as a genuine Unionist, for his sympathies fluctuated during the war. Yet his attitude was typical of many antigovernment Confederates. "I never felt interested enough in the war to rejoice or exult over anything in regard to it," he explained. "Only I felt very much oppressed, worn down, and . . . it was a hard matter for me to survive during the war." Pendleton, one of the county's most honored citizens, a former state legislator, Whig congressman, and diplomat, was fifty-eight years old when he opposed secession. He initially supported his state when Virginia left the Union; but, like Rixey, his shifting loyalties demonstrated a contradictory element. Both Confederate and Federal officers found Pendleton a congenial host, and he did not hesitate to seek favors and protection for himself and his friends from Federal authorities.[20]

Before condemning Rixey and Pendleton for blatent self-interest, one should acknowledge that most of Culpeper's citizens, whether Confederate or Unionist, likely acted in what they perceived to be their best interests. People were only trying to cope with the upheaval of war. As Rixey wisely observed, "A man cannot always say what his feelings were during three or four years. He may undergo many changes of feeling. It depends on his personal condition." William Heflin, a forty-seven-year-old sawyer and father of five, is a good example of the complexities involved here. Heflin was neither rich nor poor, neither a staunch Rebel nor a loyal Unionist. Neighbors described him as "a rather quiet man," "industrious except when he took an occasional spree." He took no sides in the war publicly. Not that it mattered. For Heflin "was not a man who carried any weight socially or politically." In addition to his job as a sawyer, he rented a 130-acre farm and owned enough livestock to be judged by neighbors as "comfortable during the war." Yet Heflin ensured his slim degree of comfort by "trafficking and trading with the Northern army, buying and selling them Tobacco, and other trade, poultry, etc."[21]

Speaking more broadly, William Wallach observed that many Unionists in Culpeper hesitated to support the North publicly because they were unsure of how the war would end. "I know two gentleman neighbors of mine," he maintained, "[who] would give half their estates to have the old flag permanently floating over them, and will gladly swear allegiance to the Government when to do so will not surely cause . . . their own prospective imprisonment in a Richmond jail." As for political affiliation, that was often no barometer at all. Asked to describe the political affiliations of one supposed Unionist, his Culpeper neighbor replied, "Well, I can hardly say that I can. He was at one time considered a whig, and at another time considered a democrat, and sometimes a little of one and then of the other."[22]

Of course, the longer the war dragged on, the greater the potential for demoralization. The heaviest blow for Culpeper came when the Army of the Potomac occupied the county between November 1863 and May 1864. Pope's invasion had caused havoc in 1862, but this winter encampment crushed whatever residue of spirit may have survived. "The Palatinate, during the wars of Louis XIV, could scarely have looked so desolate as this country," lamented a member of General George Gordon Meade's staff. "The houses that have not been burnt usually look almost worse than those that have: so dreary are they with their windows without sashes, and their open doors, and their walls half stripped of boards." Hundreds of acres of forest had been leveled, he elaborated, with once productive farmlands overrun by weeds and blackberry vines.[23]

Such calamity struck indiscriminately, and Culpeper's laboring classes never suggested otherwise. They never accused more affluent neighbors of exploiting them or of escaping the war's destructive force. Few men tried to avoid military service, although people with political influence did try to make their service as palatable as possible. Even fewer folk, rich or poor, escaped the war unscathed. "We cannot tell what kind of buildings stood between the great number of blackened chimney's on every side," reported a Confederate artilleryman upon entering Culpeper in October, 1863. "In addition, to these," he continued, "there is the framework of many a handsome residence stripped of all that could be useful to these fiends [the Federal soldiers]." Culpeper's citizen knew the identity of their true foes, and they mostly wore blue uniforms.[24]

The situation frankly puzzled both Confederate and Federal soldiers. A Rebel surgeon at Culpeper was appalled by how the surrounding countryside had been "totally devastated." "It is now nothing but one vast track of desolation, without a fence or a planted field of any kind," he informed his wife. "I do not understand how the people exists yet they do actually continue to live there. They are intensely hostile to the Yankees, and there is certainly no submission in them." A Union officer encamped at Brandy Station during the long winter occupation wrote to his wife in November

1863, "You cannot imagine the distress of the inhabitants in this part of Virginia. *Starvation stares them in the face.* . . . People here are actually lean and poor for the want of something to eat. A man told one of our officers yesterday that two of his children died of starvation." The Yankee could but ponder: "Why don't the Rebel masses rise up and outlaw the Rebel Government, hang the leaders, and put an end to this terable strugle?" He had no answer for that. He could only hope that prolongation of the war must eventually force a collapse of morale from hunger. "The want of bread," he concluded, "will do more towards puting [sic] down the rebellion than the bayonet." Ultimately, it took the two combined to do the trick.[25]

The physical sufferings of Culpeper could not be used as a wedge between the classes because local political leaders and those citizens still possessed of means did what they could to lighten the burdens of the poor, the weak, the destitute, and the hungry. Even as Culpeper first mobilized for war, its leading citizens had raised a contingency fund to support needy families whose menfolk had volunteered to fight the Yankees. Such relief efforts continued into the final year of the war. When the Army of the Potomac departed in May 1864, the county court, which had not met during Federal occupation, reassembled to put local affairs back in order. One of its first actions was to provide the county poor commissioner with nearly a thousand dollars (albeit, in Confederate currency) "to aid in maintaining the poor." Shortly thereafter the court appointed an agent to distribute salt to the people of the county. The salt shortage, a universal problem in the Confederacy, shows how basic were Culpeper's needs.[26]

In September, the court appointed two agents and authorized a twenty thousand dollar loan against the county's credit to procure necessary supplies for the indigent. The list of priorities began with needy widows and then descended to all women "whose husbands are in the Confederate service & then to such others as in their judgements are most needy." Unfortunately, and symptomatic of the depth of the county's poverty, no family, regardless of size or need, could be permitted more than a single barrel of flour, the bulk of which had been obtained from the Shenandoah Valley. With the onset of winter, the court acted again. Five days before Christmas 1864, it sent a resolution to Richmond asking exemption from the Confederate government's tax in kind. To justify its request the court stated, "The quantity of the necessaries of life produced in this county during the present year are not sufficient for the subsistence of the people of the county."[27]

Ultimately, Culpeper's Unionists, from whatever social class, realized that they were a pitifully small band. After Virginia seceded, one opponent of secession admitted that he just caved in and went with the majority. Thereafter, he believed, Unionists were "very scarce" in his neighborhood. Another observer said it was easy to spot the Unionists; they were the people who "kept quiet" during the war. "Things were so hot," he elaborated, "union men wouldn't dare to say they were such even privately. They didn't know who to trust." Another man felt the isolation. Surrounded by Confederates in his neighborhood, he declared, "I never left my premises at all during the war, except to go to the Court House when the federals were there. When the rebels had possession I had to be as quiet as I could." Another Culpeper farmer who initially opposed secession but eventually supported the Confederacy declared, "I wouldn't like to swear to the loyalty to the U.S. of many people there," even though some few people were "said to be loyal."[28]

So the waning of Confederate morale in Culpeper County had little to do with divisions among social classes. To the extent that the people of Culpeper came to oppose the war—and most remained remarkably loyal to the Davis government—it was not so much conscription acts, taxes in kind, or inadequate relief efforts that wore them down, but the dangers and privations of war, especially as imposed upon them by invasion, battle, and occupation. The community's handful of Unionists were too few to spread the cancer of demoralization. In any case, they were seldom poor. Their opposition to the Confederacy was based not on class antagonism but on factors that cut across class lines.

# Definitions of Victory: East Tennessee Unionists in the Civil War and Reconstruction

## Noel C. Fisher

A
S EARLY as the summer of 1861 President Abraham Lincoln had identified the eastern section of Tennessee as a key strategic target and had begun urging Brigadier General William T. Sherman, then in command in Kentucky, to seize and hold this area. Lincoln focused on East Tennessee for three reasons. First, the main railroad line connecting Virginia with the Gulf states, the one of only two trunk lines linking the eastern and western regions of the Confederacy, passed through the East Tennessee Valley. These tracks had already carried thousands of troops to the eastern theater, and they appeared to lie within easy striking distance of Federal camps in eastern Kentucky. Second, and probably more important to Lincoln, was the fact that East Tennessee was the home of a large Unionist population whose defiant rejection of secession was already well known in the North. Lincoln felt a great sympathy for these loyalists and wanted to bring them back under Northern control as soon as possible. He also retained hopes of reviving Unionist sentiments throughout the South and undermining the rebellion, and East Tennessee appeared to offer a promising chance to test this scheme. Finally, Lincoln, as well as several Union officers, believed that the loyalist population could considerably ease the task of retaking this portion of the South and add to Federal strength.[1]

The Northern hope that East Tennessee Unionists could become valuable allies was largely fulfilled. Unionists waged an effective war against both the secessionist population and the occupying Confederate troops, sent thousands of recruits to the Federal army, and provided other types of valuable aid. At the same time, Unionists and Federal officials would find many reasons to be disappointed in each other. It took more than two years for Northern troops to seize and hold East Tennessee, and Unionists suffered greatly under Confederate rule. Conversely, Unionist assistance sometimes fell short of what Federal officers expected. Further, while East Tennessee loyalists retained political control of their own region, they failed to expand their influence into the rest of the state.

Though East Tennessee maintained important economic and cultural ties with the rest of the South in the antebellum period, it remained a region set somewhat apart. Two sets of events early in East Tennessee's history had a profound influence on its political development. The original settlements, located in what is now northeastern Tennessee, lay in an area disputed between Virginia and North Carolina, and for a time neither state wanted to provide effective government or military protection to this area. Thus, in 1772 and again in 1784 the settlements established their own government and attempted to form a separate state. A combination of factional infighting and opposition from North Carolina doomed both attempts, and in 1796 East Tennesseans readily joined with settlements near Nashville to form the state of Tennessee. But East Tennesseans did not forget these initiatives toward self-government. The second formative event was the battle of King's Mountain. In 1781 British and loyalist forces secured control over much of North and South Carolina; and a loyalist officer, Major Patrick Ferguson, threatened to bring his forces over the mountains if the settlements there did not acknowledge British rule. In response, hundreds of volunteers from East Tennessee, along with men from western Virginia and western North Carolina, marched into North Carolina, surprised a considerable loyalist force at King's Mountain, and nearly annihilated it. This battle was followed by numerous other American victories in the Carolinas that ended the British occupation. East Tennesseans no doubt exaggerated the importance of King's Mountain, as well as their brief experience of self-government, but in the decades following the Revolution, East Tennessee retained a strong sense of patriotism, a fierce devotion to the Union, a

powerful sense of identity, and an instinct toward independent government that tended to surface in political crises.[2]

Geographic and economic factors further contributed to this sense
of distinctiveness. Though East Tennessee was not so isolated economically, politically, or culturally as many outsiders, both before and after the
war, believed, it was surrounded by mountain ranges that acted both as
natural boundaries and as barriers to transportation. East Tennessee's
rivers were too shallow and obstructed to allow effective shipping, and its
first railroads were not completed until the mid-1850s. Thus trade and
travel were more limited in this area than in many other regions of the
country. Largely due to the constraints imposed by geography, climate,
and the lack of transportation, throughout the antebellum period East
Tennessee remained predominantly the home of small farmers, tenants,
and laborers. Only 63 percent of East Tennessee white families owned
land in 1860, the mean farm size in this region was smaller than in Middle
and West Tennessee, and East Tennessee farms tended to have a significantly lower percentage of improved acres. It is true that the nature of
East Tennessee agriculture varied considerably with local geography. In
the fertile East Tennessee Valley, farmers cleared most of their acres, carefully cultivated their land, and raised large quantities of wheat, corn, other
grains, hay, and livestock. In most ways these farms did not differ greatly
from those found in the agricultural heartland of Middle Tennessee. But
in the mountain counties many more acres were left in pasture and timber, fewer families owned land, and the inhabitants depended more on
hunting, gathering, and open grazing. On the whole, East Tennessee was
somewhat less productive and developed, and considerably poorer, than
many other regions in the South.[3]

The most noticeable difference between East Tennessee and much
of the rest of the South was the scarcity of cotton and tobacco production and the relative absence of slave labor. Only one county, Monroe,
produced sizable amounts of cotton, and over half the counties grew no
cotton at all. Similarly, East Tennessee farms averaged only 27 pounds of
tobacco per farm, well below the state mean of 454 pounds. This lack did
not completely bar East Tennessee farmers from market production.
Throughout the antebellum period East Tennesseans drove cattle and
hogs to markets in North Carolina, South Carolina, and Virginia and

traded brandy, whiskey, hides, furs, honey, and other products for manu-
factured goods. Further, the completion of the East Tennessee and
Virginia and East Tennessee and Georgia Railroads in the 1850s allowed
East Tennessee farmers to send greatly increased amounts of wheat and
other grains to neighboring states. But the lack of staple crop production,
and to a lesser extent the lower level of economic development, prevented
the great majority of East Tennesseans from acquiring slaves. Only 10
percent of East Tennessee families owned at least one slave, and only .33
percent qualified as planters. The majority of slaves were found on the
larger farms in the valley and in the major towns, and many mountain
counties counted fewer than one hundred slaves. This does not mean that
most East Tennesseans held antislavery views; rather, they appear to have
harbored a strong animus against blacks and to have believed strongly
that slavery was essential for maintaining social order. Some pockets of
abolitionism did persist in East Tennessee in the late 1850s, but the more
widespread attitude was indifference to the fate of slaves. At the same
time, most East Tennesseans did not share the passionate fervor to defend
slavery, a fervor that motivated Southerners in other regions; and many
deeply resented the political influence held by large slaveholders.[4]

The strength and depth of Unionist sentiments in East Tennessee did
not become immediately apparent in 1860, and in fact South Carolina's
secession in December created an initial period of confusion. Despite their
attachment to the Union, loyalist East Tennesseans still saw themselves
as Southerners, and they had no wish to clash with their neighbors. But
several events quickly ended their indecision. On January 7 Governor
Isham G. Harris called the state legislature into special session, delivered
a passionate speech in support of immediate separation, and urged the legislature to authorize elections for a convention to take this step. The legislature agreed but also gave voters the power to chose whether or not the
convention should meet at all. Unionists, therefore, quickly faced a clear
choice of loyalties. At the same time, the loud and active campaigning of
local secessionist leaders such as physician and historian J. G. M. Ramsey
and Knoxville postmaster C. W. Charleton aroused Unionists' instincts
to defend the Federal government. Finally, Senator Andrew Johnson,
Knoxville *Whig* editor William G. Brownlow, and local leaders quickly
articulated coherent arguments against secession and rallied Unionist vot-

ers. Thus, 80 percent of East Tennesseans on February 9 joined a small majority in Middle Tennessee in voting down the convention and in electing a clear majority of anti-secession delegates. Unfortunately, their initial period of hesitation helped create the impression that voters in East Tennessee were manipulated into opposing secession by Johnson, Brownlow, and other loyalist leaders. That impression, based on an inability to believe that any Southerner could rationally chose to fight against his or her own section, was false, but it had unfortunate effects on Southern policies toward East Tennessee.[5]

The loyalist victory in Tennessee was short-lived. Tensions resulting from the standoff between Federal and Confederate forces at Fort Sumter and Fort Pickens, and the decreasing likelihood of a negotiated settlement, eroded Unionist support in Middle Tennessee, and the onset of war in early April eliminated it almost entirely. On April 30 the legislature passed measures for independence from the United States and representation in the Confederate government and immediately began mobilizing troops and supplies. The legislature again submitted these measures to the electorate, and 86 percent of voters in Middle and Tennessee on June 8 approved them. In East Tennessee, however, Unionists held firm and rejected secession by a vote of about thirty-three thousand to fifteen thousand. They also denied the right of the legislature to take the state out of the Union and refused to accept the results of the June vote as valid, thereby ensuring conflict with Confederate officials.[6]

Four factors were primarily responsible for the dangerous position that East Tennessee Unionists staked out. The first, and probably most important, were fears concerning the nature of the Confederate political system. Very early in 1861, Unionists became convinced that the new government would model itself on the conservative system of South Carolina, reserve office-holding and voting to men of wealth, and force small farmers into a position of submission and inequality. Brownlow asserted, "Let Tennessee once go into this *Empire of Cotton States*, and all poor men will at once become the *free negroes of the Empire*," while a group of loyalists from Clinton accused Governor Harris of "drilling his men for the purpose of awing, intimidating, and finally coercing [the loyalists] into subjection to him and his associated tyrants." These perceptions fed on a variety of factors: East Tennessee's relative lack of wealth; the contempt that leaders from states such as Mississippi and Alabama sometimes expressed toward this supposedly uncivilized region; resentment of the supposed inordinate influence of large slaveholders; and, more immediately, the manner in which some states had carried out secession. East Tennessee Unionists had already received numerous reports of intimidation of dissenters, voting fraud, and constitutional irregularities in Mississippi, Georgia, and Alabama. Further, rather than authorizing elections for a constitutional convention to debate secession, the Tennessee legislature had itself passed the measures for separation from the United States, immediately established contacts with the Confederate government, and authorized Governor Harris to issue officers' commissions and war bonds, without waiting for the approval of Tennessee voters. All these factors gave Unionists the impression that the Confederate government would use any means necessary to establish its power and would not secure the liberties of ordinary citizens in the way that the existing Union did.[7]

A second, closely related concern was the belief that the Confederate government would enact economic policies detrimental to East Tennessee's interests. Long-standing Southern positions made it clear that the Confederacy would establish free-trade policies beneficial to staple crop producers and would likely abandon central government funding for transportation improvements. Many East Tennesseans looked to the exploitation of the region's resources in timber, coal, and ore and to the development of manufacturing as the primary means to improve their economy and catch up with other regions. These hopes partly rested, however, on continued Federal protective tariffs and on possible state and Federal money for transportation improvements. Third, East Tennessee's memories of independent government and its strong sense of regional identity may have weakened its state loyalty and made it easier for Unionists to defy the state government and the voters in Middle and West Tennessee. Many Unionists even saw the secession crisis as an opportunity to establish a separate state made up East Tennessee and perhaps neighboring counties, in North Carolina, Virginia, Middle Tennessee, and Georgia, that had similar economic and political interests. The primary basis of Unionists' opposition to secession was ideological, but East Tennessee loyalists also clearly sought a political and economic system that more closely fit their interests and over which they had more control.[8]

The final factor, one that seems almost too obvious to mention but one whose power was critical, was the almost religious sense of devotion that Unionists displayed to the national government. The fervent sense of patriotism that emerged in East Tennessee during the Revolution seems to have continued undiminished through the entire antebellum period. When secessionists threatened the nation in 1860, Unionists not only instinctively came to its defense, they also employed the symbols and the language of the Revolution to justify their firm stance against secession. Unionists firmly believed that the government that the Revolution had created was the best the world had yet seen and that it constituted a secure bulwark against the erosion of their freedom. Loyalists almost certainly underestimated the length and severity of the war that they would fight and the suffering that they would undergo for that Union, but nonetheless their commitment to the preservation of the nation was deeply rooted and, in the majority of cases, unshakable.[9]

Unionist organization in East Tennessee was largely amorphous. Prominent leaders such as Johnson, Brownlow, Representatives T. A. R. Nelson and Horace Maynard, and Oliver P. Temple took the lead in developing and disseminating arguments against secession, organizing a network of regional and local leaders, and mobilizing Unionists into an effective political force. But Unionist leaders emerged independently in practically every county, including William B. Carter and J. P. T. Carter in Carter County, William Clift in Hamilton, and David Fry and George Kirk in Greene; and their importance should not be underestimated. Loyalists, in fact, established only three region-wide organizations, and only one of these, the Unionist Convention, was truly centralized.

The Unionist Convention was largely the concept of Knoxville loyalists. It met twice in 1861, planned but failed to meet a third time that same year, and gathered for the final time in 1864. Each meeting had a different purpose, but together they illustrate the flexibility of this organization. The first meeting, on May 30 through 31, brought 469 Unionists to Knoxville and culminated weeks of correspondence, organization, and mobilization. The primary purpose of the May meeting was to demonstrate Unionist solidarity, and delegates confined themselves to issuing a final, formal statement of the Unionist position. The second meeting of the convention, which brought 292 Unionists to Greeneville on June 17,

was quite different. Secession was now an established fact, and any deci-
sions that delegates made could have disastrous consequences. Unlike at
Knoxville, delegates at Greeneville engaged in serious, intense debate
over whether to defy the Confederacy openly or to submit, attempt to
win some concessions from the new government, and wait for Northern
aid. In the end the convention petitioned the state legislature to allow
East Tennessee to form a separate state and scheduled a third meeting for
August, a meeting whose purpose seems to have been to organize the new
state. The delegates at Greenville also established a secret Executive
Committee that was authorized to coordinate Unionist activities when
the full convention could not meet. The Unionist Convention, therefore, was flexible organization that could function as a party convention,
a committee of correspondence, and potentially a constitutional convention and a revolutionary committee.[10]

In addition to the convention, Unionists established two overlapping,
region-wide networks, one to secretly move recruits into Kentucky and one
to bring information back from the North and maintain contacts with
Union officers. Unionists were reluctant to discuss these organizations, even
well after the war was over, and most of the information concerning them
is anecdotal and fragmentary. But these networks, which became increasingly sophisticated as the war went on and which were linked with similar
organizations in western North Carolina and Middle Tennessee, seem to
have involved hundreds of persons at one time or another. The key figures
in the escape networks were the pilots, the men who guided parties of
recruits out of East Tennessee into Kentucky and took responsibility for
keeping them safe from Confederate patrols and natural hazards; but they
did not operate on their own. Women, children, older men, slaves, and free
blacks watched for Confederate troops, provided food, supplies, and directions, and operated ferries and safe houses. Similarly, while pilots played
an important role in the information network by bringing information
back from Kentucky, many women, as well as younger and older men, also
made regular trips to Kentucky to bring back letters and newspapers; and
Unionists appear to have had multiple means of distributing these securely
within their communities. Neither the escape nor the information network
had any central leadership, but they clearly had many links from county to
county and functioned effectively across the region.[11]

The primary Unionist military units, the home guard company and the guerrilla band, were both decentralized and were based on the county, village, or district. Home guard companies were official or quasi-official military organizations, essentially equivalent to militia units. In 1861 and 1862 Unionists, presumably acting on the assertion that they were operating as the true state of Tennessee, established these companies on their own authority. They then reconstituted most of these units in 1863 under a Federal order. The ostensible purpose of home guard companies was to maintain order and protect communities from Confederate troops and criminal bands, but in fact they played many different roles that varied from county to county. Home guards served as scouts, guides, and foragers for the Union army, guarded prisoners, skirmished with Confederate troops, and fought with secessionist partisans. Guerrilla bands, unlike home guard companies, claimed no official status; but in fact in 1861 and 1862 the two were essentially indistinguishable, and even after 1863 the differences were often very fine. Partisans bands in East Tennessee, as elsewhere, tended to be drawn from the same community or neighboring communities and to organize around either established leaders, such as county officials, or ordinary men who demonstrated a talent for this kind of fighting. Like home guard companies, guerrilla bands engaged in a variety of activities, including bushwhacking Confederate troops, assaulting and intimidating secessionists, stealing and destroying property, and occasionally raiding into neighboring states.

Unionist resistance activities throughout the war fell into three broad categories: service with the Federal army; intimidation of secessionists and Confederate officials; and harassment of the occupying Confederate troops. Within all these Unionists sought three clear, overlapping aims: to retain effective political and social control of their region; to see East Tennessee returned to Northern control as soon as possible; and to rid the region of as many secessionists as possible. In addition, Unionists had a more distant, less well defined aim, which was to create a government, either in Tennessee or within a new state of their own, that would protect their interests.

Despite all the attention given to the partisan war, far more Unionists actually chose to leave East Tennessee and serve with the Federal forces in the west rather than stay in East Tennessee and fight as guerrillas. Their

conclusion that they could make the greatest contribution to the
Confederate defeat by fighting as regular soldiers was almost certainly correct, for Unionists had no hope of expelling Confederate forces from East
Tennessee on their own. Of course, many who enlisted in the Federal
ranks hoped to return to East Tennessee within a few months, and they
were bitterly disappointed at repeated Northern delays in invading East
Tennessee. It is also true that, after the first Confederate Conscription
Act of 1862, it became more and more difficult for Unionists to avoid service; and increasingly they faced a choice between being drafted into the
Confederate army or volunteering with the Union. Both Confederate and
Union reports indicate that conscription greatly accelerated the Unionist
flight to Kentucky. But neither of these qualifications alters the fact that
a remarkable number of East Tennesseans risked imprisonment or execution, left their families at risk from Confederate soldiers and secessionist
guerrillas, and exposed their property to confiscation or destruction in
order to fight with the Federal army.

Determining the exact number of East Tennesseans who wore a blue
uniform is difficult, owing both to the incompleteness of service records
and to the fact that numerous loyalists enlisted in Kentucky, Indiana,
Illinois, or Ohio regiments and were not counted. But the best estimates
are that thirty thousand to thirty-five thousand East Tennessee Unionists
served with the Federal army at one time or another, a total that matches
the number of men who voted against secession in June 1861. Probably
over half of these entered the service before August 1863, when all East
Tennessee was occupied by Confederate forces. These thirty thousand
recruits represented a welcome, though not critical, addition to Union
forces in the West and certainly fulfilled one of Lincoln's hopes. More
important was the drain on the Confederacy, which needed every available recruit. Unionists not only denied the Confederacy at least thirty
thousand defenders, they also forced Southern commanders to divert several hundred more men to chase down draft evaders, patrol known routes
of escape, and skirmish with Unionist partisans. Again, these numbers
were not decisive, but they represented an additional burden on a fragile
nation that already suffered from too many weaknesses.[12]

Very few Unionists discussed in writing their decision to stay or go,
and the evidence is insufficient to determine whether those who remained
simply could not face leaving or whether they purposely determined to carry

on a second war at home. Whatever the case, Unionists who remained in East Tennessee to fight as partisans did possess clear military and political aims, and they were not mere brigands or psychopathic killers. At the same time, Unionist (and secessionist) bands were engaged in a desperate war. They were capable of extreme ruthlessness, cruelty, and destructiveness; and many did engage in theft, both as a means of punishment and as a way of sustaining their activities.

The clearest demonstration of Unionist aims occurred in Scott and Morgan Counties. In early 1862 Unionist partisans, in a clearly coordinated effort, killed at least half a dozen secessionists, assaulted numerous others, and burned several homes. They then threatened to mete out the same punishment to other active secessionists, forcing numerous Confederate families to flee to Kingston. Unionists also took complete control of the county government and courts and established large home guard units to defend against Confederate incursions and keep secessionists intimidated. When Major General Edmund Kirby Smith sent over one thousand troops to crush this open resistance, Unionists harassed their march all the way from Kingston, then threw up barricades at Huntsville and attempted to block the Confederate advance entirely. They failed, and Confederate troops killed a dozen partisans, arrested several leaders, foraged heavily, and attempted to break up Unionist organizations. But, while Unionists suffered from this and subsequent incursions, their political and military organizations remained largely intact, and Confederates did little more than temporarily interrupt their control.[13]

Scott and Morgan Counties had the advantage of being located in a remote area deep in the Cumberland Mountains and of having a population that was over 90 percent loyalist. Unionists in most other counties could not match these successes, and in places such as Knox and Hamilton Counties they had to settle for more limited aims. Even so, their intent and their tactics were essentially the same. In 1861 and 1862, for example, loyalists in Johnson and Greene Counties chased off several local officials, murdered a number of Confederate men, and forced many secessionist families to escape to North Carolina or Virginia for safety. Similarly, in 1864 Unionists in New Market publicly beat or whipped a number of Confederate sympathizers, threatened others, and again convinced many secessionist families to leave. And in practically every county in East Tennessee Unionist bands ambushed secessionists in their fields or on the roads, broke into homes at night to kill Confederate men and terrify their wives and children, burned barns, homes, and crops, and stole food, clothes, money, and valuables. The level of this violence, and the success of Unionists, ebbed and flowed during the war and depended on a range of factors, including the number of Confederate troops in the region, Southern policies toward East Tennessee, and the balance of the war in the western theater. Further, secessionists fought back with surprising ferocity and in some areas, particularly in southern East Tennessee, kept Unionists from achieving the complete domination that they sought.[14]

Even so, it is clear that throughout the war Unionists succeeded in retaining control of two-thirds to three-fourths of East Tennessee's thirty-one counties. In April 1862 Kirby Smith admitted that even after increased efforts under his command to arrest Unionist leaders and enforce conscription, Unionists still controlled twenty-five counties and kept secessionists there intimidated and subdued. In October 1862 Major General Sam Jones conceded that partisan fighting continued in every part of East Tennessee and admitted that the Confederacy was no closer to controlling the region than it had been a year ago. And by 1863 several Confederate officers had concluded that controlling East Tennessee politically was no longer a realistic aim and that it would be better to treat the region as enemy territory, exploit its resources as fully as possible, and draft or exile all military-age males.[15]

In addition to their war against secessionists, Unionists also waged a campaign of sabotage and harassment against Confederate troops in the region. They repeatedly cut telegraph lines, captured or destroyed supply wagons, occasionally derailed trains and burned cars, and made sporadic, though mostly unsuccessful, attempts to burn railroad bridges. In addition, Unionists bands hung on the fringes of Confederate camps to ambush small parties of soldiers going in or out, cut down trees to block roads used by Confederate troops, and bushwhacked Confederate couriers, foragers, recruiting officers, provost marshals, scouts, and small parties of troops. The heavily wooded, mountainous terrain of much of East Tennessee was perfectly suited to this type of fighting; and in many places Unionists could easily hide in the brush along the roads, fire on Confederate troops, and escape untouched. Unionist partisans did not pose a serious threat to Confederate military control, but they did kill or wound dozens of soldiers, force Confederates to travel in large parties, and significantly hamper Confederate supply and scouting operations.[16]

Finally, Unionist partisans provided various kinds of assistance to Federal troops in Kentucky and Tennessee. In 1861 and 1862 they furnished considerable information concerning Confederate troop movements and dispositions to Federal officers, and Kirby Smith complained that "East Tennessee [was] more difficult to operate in than the country of an acknowledged enemy." Loyalists also provided guides to the Army of the Ohio when it entered East Tennessee in September 1863, and when Confederate troops besieged Federal forces in Knoxville in November 1863 Unionists sent large amounts of food into the city. In addition, Unionist partisans scouted for Federal troops, provided detailed information about the roads and terrain, reported on the secessionist population, and occasionally fought alongside Federal troops. Finally, Unionists played a major role in carrying out Federal occupation policies. In September 1863 Major General Ambrose Burnside appointed Brigadier General Samuel P. Carter, cousin of William B. Carter and a successful cavalry officer, as Provost Marshal General of East Tennessee and gave him responsibility for enforcing occupation policies, maintaining order, administering the loyalty oath, and punishing dissent. In addition, a number of Unionists served as county provost marshals, and Federal officers provided arms and ammunition to home guard units and authorized them to assist the Provost Marshal's Office in maintaining order and enforcing the laws. Northern officials granted Unionists considerable latitude in implementing Federal occupation policies, while loyalists in turn relieved Federal forces of much of the burden of policing this region.[17]

Unionists, therefore, proved to be extremely helpful in the role of auxiliaries. On the other hand, all attempts at large-scale cooperation failed, with unfortunate results to both sides. The greatest disaster occurred near the beginning of the conflict. In October 1861 the Reverend William B. Carter, almost certainly in conjunction with other Unionist leaders, devised a plan to free East Tennessee from Confederate control before the year was out. Carter traveled to Washington, D.C., met with Lincoln, Major General George B. McClellan, and Secretary of War Simon Cameron, and proposed that once Federal forces were in position to enter East Tennessee, Unionists would burn every major bridge on the railroad line, thereby disrupting the movement of troops into and throughout East Tennessee. Federal troops could then enter the region with minimal opposition. McClellan and Cameron approved the proposal and gave Carter funds for his operation. After meeting with Sherman and Brigadier General George H. Thomas in Kentucky to finalize his plans, Carter returned to Tennessee and assembled his teams in complete secrecy. On the night of November 8 Unionists successfully burned five bridges, attempted but failed to destroy two others, and tore down telegraph lines in dozens of places. In addition, hundreds of armed Unionists turned out in practically every county in anticipation of the Federal invasion. Unionists, therefore, accomplished everything that Federal officers could have expected.

But the Federal army never appeared. Sherman, whose assessment of the extreme logistical difficulties that Federal forces would face in East Tennessee was sound, had never approved of the invasion plan, and he became increasingly pessimistic concerning the chances for success. On November 5 Sherman halted the Federal advance, and on November 8 he canceled the operation entirely. Sadly, news of this decision never reached Carter, and the result was that Unionists were left alone to face the wrath of the Confederate government. In the days following the bridge burnings Confederate troops broke up every Unionist camp, executed five suspected bridge-burners, summarily killed an undetermined number of others, arrested and imprisoned well over one thousand loyalists, and eventually sent two hundred of these to military prisons in the Deep South. Loyalist regiments waiting in Kentucky were in agony, and Johnson and Maynard, who had been marching with the army, threatened to take the East Tennessee troops and invade on their own. Unionists ultimately bowed to Sherman's decision, but they did not forget the costs.[18]

Conversely, Federal officers often found Unionist partisans to be weak allies. In 1862 Brigadier General George W. Morgan authorized William Clift, a prominent loyalist from Hamilton County who had fled to Kentucky, to organize a partisan regiment in Morgan and Scott Counties and harass Confederate troops stationed near the Kentucky border. Clift easily raised his forces, but he lacked the tactical skills to command a regiment. He had absolutely no success in disrupting Confederate movements or transportation, and in August Confederate forces scattered his troops, essentially ending his operations. Similarly, in 1864 Major

General John Schofield commissioned George Kirk, a highly successful pilot and guerrilla leader, to raise two regiments of mounted infantry in the border area of Tennessee and North Carolina. Schofield hoped that Kirk could weaken the Confederate hold on western North Carolina, but Kirk proved as inept at conventional operations as Clift, and he ended up using his regiments primarily to intimidate and plunder secessionists.[19]

Not all loyalists participated in the war against the Confederacy, of course, and a minority of East Tennessee Unionists eventually acquiesced in Confederate rule. The most spectacular capitulation was that of T. A. R. Nelson, one of the most influential voices in the campaign against secession and the leading advocate of open defiance in the summer of 1861. In August 1861 Unionists, in an act of deliberate defiance, elected Nelson, Horace Maynard, and George Bridges to the U.S. Congress. Immediately after the election Nelson attempted secretly to leave East Tennessee and reach Washington, D.C., but Confederate troops captured him in southwest Virginia and sent him to Richmond. There President Davis threatened him with charges of treason and imprisonment until the end of the war. For reasons that he never revealed, Nelson reached a written agreement with Davis to recognize the authority of the Confederate government and advise other Unionists to put down their arms. John Baxter believed that Nelson's observations in Richmond convinced him that the new nation was more firmly established and capable of survival than he had previously believed. Baxter had reached this same conclusion a few months earlier, and in August 1861 he ran unsuccessfully for a seat in the Confederate Congress. Nelson and Baxter, as well as Temple, John Netherland, Andrew Fleming, Connelly F. Trigg, and many other prominent Unionists, took a Confederate loyalty oath so that they could continue to practice law; and they avoided any open resistance activities after November 1861. Many ordinary Unionists took a similar oath in order to be able to secure salt or other critical goods and to acquire travel passports. Dozens of Unionist men, when captured by Confederate troops for draft evasion, chose to enlist in Confederate units rather than face imprisonment, though many also deserted at the first opportunity. And other Unionists withdrew from the conflict in order to avoid arrest or the confiscation of their property. Given the pressures that the Confederate government applied, however, the remarkable fact is not that some Unionists surrendered, but rather that so many remained unshaken and defiant.[20]

By 1865 East Tennessee Unionists could point to very real accomplishments. They had frustrated all Confederate attempts to break their solidarity and destroy their political and military organizations. They had retained political and social control of perhaps 75 percent of the region and forced hundreds of secessionists to leave the area. They had made significant contributions to the Federal occupation of this area. They had achieved a high level of visibility in the North and won a great deal of sympathy and support; and one of their own, Andrew Johnson, had been elected vice president. In the process, Unionists had assured themselves of a central role in the reconstruction of the state. The question that loyalists now faced was what they would do with their power, and whether they could translate their wartime victories into lasting political successes.

Sadly for Unionists, Reconstruction would prove to be a great disappointment, due to misjudgments, the character of their party, and national political realities over which they had no control. In 1861 East Tennessee Unionists, like West Virginians, had looked primarily to the formation of their own state, one that they would control and one that would protect their interests. But Confederate troops seized control of eastern Tennessee before loyalists could act, and East Tennessee, unlike West Virginia, lay beyond the reach of Federal forces in 1861. For the next two years, therefore, Unionists had to confine themselves to more limited aims. Curiously, though, when Northern forces did manage to seize most of East Tennessee in 1863 and early 1864, talk of a separate state seems not to have surfaced. Perhaps Unionists had developed larger aims by this time, or perhaps Northern officials discouraged plans for separation, wanting instead to restore the whole state of Tennessee to the Union. Whether Congress would have authorized such a step if Unionists had made the request cannot be answered, but dividing Tennessee as well as Virginia might have been unacceptable. But, whatever the reason, it is clear that by 1865 East Tennessee Unionists had determined to seize control of the entire state and reform it in line with the demands of Northern Republicans and their own interests. Tragically, within three years Unionists would find themselves permanently divided into radical and conservative factions, abandoned by powerful elements in the North, and fighting a hopeless political battle.

The division between radical and conservative Unionists was present at the beginning, as the 1861 Greenville Convention revealed. At
this meeting Unionists with more extreme views advocated a formal declaration of independence from the Confederacy, a proclamation that East
Tennessee would remain neutral in the coming conflict, and a warning
that if Confederate troops moved against the region Unionists would use
force to protect their independence and seek protection from the Federal
government. Radicals also looked to the formation of a separate state, in
cooperation with Unionist counties in Middle Tennessee and North
Carolina, which would remain a member of the Federal Union. But more
conservative loyalists argued that open defiance would not accomplish
any of their aims and would lead only to harsh repression. They instead
counseled restraint and patience and attempted to win concessions from
the Confederate government while waiting for Federal forces to rescue
them. Conservatives could not face the bloodshed and destruction that
open revolt would bring, but equally important they feared the notion of
revolution itself and the political and social changes that might result.
Conservative Unionists had opposed secession precisely because it was,
in their view, a revolutionary and illegal alteration of the established
political system that would bring vast disorder and suffering, lead to the
destruction of slavery, and perhaps have other cataclysmic results. Given
this view, they could not then turn around and themselves initiate a violent revolt against the new government. The severing of the American
Union deeply pained conservatives, but they preferred a separation that
might be temporary to the evils of revolt and internal warfare. Radical
Unionists, conversely, placed the preservation of the Union, and the
maintenance of their own liberties, ahead of almost every other issue and
were willing to risk the uncertainties of revolt. These differences brought
on a fierce debate at Greenville and left some radical Unionists permanently divided from their more cautious brothers. But at this point these
differences were not unbridgeable. Like radicals, conservative Unionists
also desired to establish, though through legal means, a separate state;
and they in fact petitioned the Tennessee legislature to authorize this
separation. Further, both factions realized that their ultimate deliverance
would have to come from the Federal government.[21]

By 1864 the differences between the two camps had broadened, and

hardened, considerably, as evidenced by the third and final meeting of
the Unionist Convention. In April 1864 Johnson, who had served as military governor of Tennessee since 1862, persuaded Nelson to reassemble
the convention at Knoxville. Johnson's attempts to rally Unionist support in Middle Tennessee had completely failed, and he had concluded
to look to East Tennessee for an endorsement of his policies and a base
for the establishment of a loyal government. But, though neither side
seems fully to have realized this fact, radicals and conservatives had grown
very far apart in the last three years, and the governor's hopes were disappointed. Johnson sought support primarily for his policy of disfran-
chising Confederate voters, but he also sought an endorsement of the
Lincoln administration's determination to end slavery and achieve a total
victory over the South. But conservatives found all these impossible to
stomach, and almost immediately radical and conservative Unionists
became locked in a furious, recriminatory, and futile debate. After two
days they adjourned, never to meet again; and on the following day
Unionist radicals staged their own convention to give Johnson the public endorsement that he still sought.[22]

The aims of conservatives had not necessarily changed since 1861,
and like radicals they would have welcomed the restoration of the Union
and the establishment of a loyal state government. At the same time, they
were appalled at the toll that the conflict had already taken. Conservatives
had concluded that the costs of continuing the war were too high, and
favored instead a negotiated peace, even if that meant permanent separation. Conservatives also believed that a number of the Lincoln administration's hard war policies, including the suspension of the writ of habeas
corpus and the confiscation of enemy property, exceeded the constitutional bounds of executive power and indicated a vengeful attitude toward
the South. But it was the Emancipation Proclamation that permanently
alienated many East Tennessee conservatives from the Lincoln administration. Many viewed slavery as a part of the natural order that no government should violate, and all believed that the act of depriving so many
Southerners of their slaves, without consent or compensation, was unconstitutional and could not be justified even on the grounds of military necessity. Conservatives found Johnson's attempts to deny the franchise to

Confederates an equally unacceptable denial of fundamental political rights.

In January 1865 Unionists from throughout Tennessee met in Nashville to initiate the formation of the new government. Most of these men were respected and influential figures, but they had not been elected in any way. It was expected, therefore, that this gathering would simply organize elections for delegates to a constitutional convention, which would then possess the clear authority to reorganize the state government. But the Unionists at Nashville were unwilling to trust this critical issue to an unpredictable electorate or to delay the restoration of the government. Therefore, they assumed to themselves the powers of a constitutional convention, repealed Tennessee's ordinance of secession, drew up an amendment ending slavery in the state, and scheduled elections for March 4. Brownlow won the governor's chair with no opposition, and the majority of legislators were in sympathy with his views.[23]

Now in control of the state, radical Unionists faced the issue of what kind of political system, and what kind society, they would try to create. Four related factors primarily shaped their views: the need for security, the necessity for the support of the North, the desire permanently to break the power of Tennessee's prewar elite, and the urge to punish secessionists. Radical Unionists were fully aware of their weaknesses and of the dangers that they faced. They knew that they were considerably outnumbered in the state, that they were viewed as traitors, and that a large number of Confederates would likely welcome an opportunity for revenge. Radical Unionists also understood that, in order to gain recognition, support, and perhaps military protection from the North, they would have to meet whatever reform requirements Congress and the president might set. Third, Unionists believed that the men who had led the state into secession had forfeited their right to represent the people, and they aimed to bar them from politics for as long as possible. They argued that Confederates themselves had forfeited the right to vote by their rebellion, and asserted that if secessionists regained the vote they would do everything possible to return the state to its antebellum condition and deny the North and Southern Unionists the rightful fruits of their victory. Finally, Unionists sought vengeance for the suffering that they had endured at the hands of Confederates. Radicals would not forget that Confederate troops and officials had hanged and shot Unionist partisans, expelled the families of leading Unionists from the state, hunted down hundreds of men and forced them into the army, harassed the wives and children of Unionist exiles, and confiscated and sold loyalist property; and they intended to exact payment for these and other grievances.

Brownlow was a poor executive, but he fully understood Unionist vulnerabilities, and he possessed the will to take whatever steps necessary to secure his government. Under his guidance the 1865 legislature quickly passed a series of laws that disfranchised ordinary Confederate voters for five years, barred Confederate officials from the polls for fifteen, and established strict requirements for Tennesseans to prove their loyalty and their right to vote. Legislators also approved the Thirteenth Amendment to the U.S. Constitution, nullified all acts passed by the Tennessee legislature in May 1861, and prohibited the wearing of a Confederate uniform. At the same time, East Tennessee Unionists filed thousands of suits against secessionists in the federal district court in Knoxville and in the county courts for treason, aiding and abetting the enemy, murder, unlawful arrests, theft, and destruction of property.[24]

Despite these laws, a considerable number of conservatives managed to vote in August 1865 and to win a number of local offices and legislative seats. Further, despite Unionist attempts at intimidation, Confederates in Middle and West Tennessee recovered faster than Unionists had hoped; and within a year they were threatening to sweep away the Brownlow government. In the spring of 1866, therefore, the legislature permanently barred all Confederate veterans and officeholders from voting and required all other applicants who were not Union veterans to take an extremely strict loyalty oath and secure testimony from two persons who were already entitled to vote. It also authorized Brownlow personally to appoint the voting registrars in each county, so that he could ensure that they would strictly implement the franchise laws. In case even this precaution failed, Brownlow was also given the power personally to examine the voting returns of each county and to annul the results in any county where he found substantial evidence of illegal voting. Finally, Brownlow was authorized to raise a state militia, which could include both black and white companies, to back up the authority of the registrars, protect the polls, and counter threats of violence from the Ku Klu Klan.[25]

The results of these policies were contradictory. On the one hand, they almost certainly extended the life of the Unionist government. Though the eastern counties guaranteed Tennessee a larger Unionist contingent than any other Confederate state, loyalists remained a minority. Unionists made strenuous efforts to expand their support in Middle and West Tennessee, but they could not overcome the bitterness left by the war. In a last bid to save their government, in 1867 radicals granted African Americans to right to vote, hold office, and sit on juries. But white Unionists failed to create an effective alliance with African Americans. Thus, the only way radicals could retain office was to ensure that only radicals voted. But the extreme measures that radicals employed drove away more and more supporters. Increasingly loyalists found it difficult to justify denying the vote to tens of thousands of citizens, and many viewed the granting of the franchise to African Americans as a dangerous alteration of the political system and an unacceptable move toward racial equality. Many loyalists eventually became willing to accept a Democratic/Confederate return to power rather than continue to subject the state to partisan violence and what they viewed as despotism.

At the same time, radicals found themselves once again abandoned by the North. Even though he had originally devised many of the policies that Brownlow was attempting to implement, after his assumption of the presidency Johnson had undergone a bizarre transformation; and he now insisted that the Confederate states return to the Union as quickly as possible and that virtually all citizens have their full political rights restored. Secessionists used presidential pardons from Johnson to protect themselves against Unionist lawsuits, and Johnson publicly criticized Brownlow's policies. Even more troubling was the loss of support in Congress. Even though radicals had taken all the steps that Congress could have expected, including the approval of the Fourteenth and Fifteenth Amendments, they now found Northern interest in their situation diminishing. Further, many Northerners criticized the continued disorder in Tennessee; and the pressure for the state to return to the Union without the taint of continued partisan fighting and political irregularities mounted.[26]

Thus East Tennessee Unionists were eventually forced into retreat. In 1868 Brownlow, who sensed that the end of his regime was near, persuaded the Tennessee legislature to send him to the U.S. Senate. The contest to replace him matched William B. Senter, an East Tennessee

Unionist who had once supported Brownlow's policies but had now turned conservative, against William B. Stokes, a former Federal officer and a radical from Middle Tennessee. Senter promised that if elected he would end disfranchisement and disband the militia, while Stokes pledged to continue the radical program. Tennessee voters elected Senter, as well as a legislature dominated by conservatives. By 1870 Democrats had reasserted control of the state, and East Tennessee loyalists had retreated to their region and their minority position.[27]

Thus, after eight years of great struggle, East Tennessee Unionists found themselves in a position little different from that which they had occupied in 1861. The Union was restored, of course, and loyalists took great pride in the contributions that they had made to the Northern victory and in their triumph over secession at home. Further, though the collapse of Reconstruction left radical Unionists in disarray, in the 1870s younger radicals such as Leonidas C. Houk transformed the loyalist party into a powerful Republican machine that dominated East Tennessee for the next several decades. Finally, radicals did alter the racial system in Tennessee, though they made these changes grudgingly and many were short-lived. Loyalists remained under the government that they cherished and retained power at home, and perhaps many were satisfied with those achievements.

At the same time, it is not clear that Unionists significantly altered their fate by rebelling or that their accomplishments matched their sacrifices. Federal forces would have occupied East Tennessee and triumphed in the war regardless of the activities of Unionists, though controlling East Tennessee would have been more difficult without their aid. Further, given the strength of the opposition Whig party before the war, East Tennessee likely would have embraced Republicanism regardless of whether Unionists had rebelled or remained passive, though without the appeal of shared suffering and victory Republicans might not have achieved quite so much strength. But East Tennessee possessed no more political power after the war than before, and neither radicals nor conservatives fit any better into the new national political alignment than the old. In the 1870s power shifted back to Middle Tennessee, and East Tennessee Republicans remained an alien minority in their state and in the Democratic South. At the same time, the Republican party was fundamentally a Northern institution, and despite their great loyalty East Tennesseans could not expect to receive substantial rewards or to be welcomed as equal partners. Conservative Unionists also found themselves adrift politically. Though they opposed most Republican policies, as former Whigs they had great difficulty with the prospect of voting Democratic, and the Democratic party was not particularly interested in welcoming them. Whether East Tennessee would have fared better as a separate state is an open question, but certainly by attempting to reconstruct the entire state, rather than forming a government of their own, Unionists lost the chance to transform their wartime sacrifices into lasting political changes.[28]

East Tennessee loyalists also probably did not benefit so much from their alliance with Northern forces in the war as they deserved. Federal officers who served in this area did understand the sacrifices that Unionists made and did acknowledge their contributions. They also provided a considerable quantity of arms and ammunition to Unionist home guard units and frequently overlooked the ongoing Unionist intimidation of secessionists. Further, thanks to the work of Brownlow, Johnson, and Maynard, the Northern public was quite aware of East Tennessee's struggle against the Confederacy; and when Unionists in 1864 appealed for aid to rebuild East Tennessee's shattered economy, Northern cities sent tens of thousands of dollars in response. But it is not clear that Congress, administration officials, or the public ever fully understood that nature and importance of the war that East Tennessee Unionists waged against secessionists, or the difficulties and dangers that they faced in attempting to reconstruct the state. Whether the North could have, or should have, saved the radical government in Tennessee is a debatable point; and certainly loyalists had their own purposes in taking on the task of Reconstruction. Nonetheless, it is also true that in Reconstruction, as in the bridge burnings of 1861, Northerners encouraged East Tennessee loyalists to take a grave risk, then left them without aid and allowed them to fail.[29]

The fate of Ben Knight in Jones County, Mississippi, must have resembled the end of this man being tracked by dogs and Confederate soldiers. FROM THRILLING ADVENTURES OF DANIEL ELLIS (1867).

All illustrations except "A family of defenseless civilians" and "Rebel bushwackers await a steamboat" were photographed by Gary Shepherd.

Yet another means of spreading terror within a community.
Rebels, in this instance, deal out justice to Unionists.
FROM *THRILLING ADVENTURES OF DANIEL ELLIS* (1867).

"A Confederate Volunteer" was the caption of this drawing
from *Harper's Monthly*, suggesting the source of friction between
Unionists and secessionists in places like Kinston, North Carolina.

A family of defenseless
civilians near Culpeper
Court House, Virginia.
LIBRARY OF CONGRESS.

A clandestine meeting of Tennessee Unionists
vowing to defend their community.
FROM *HARPER'S WEEKLY.*

This lynching scene depicts the fate of some Unionists in Tennessee who sought to escape Confederate conscription.

FROM *THRILLING ADVENTURES OF DANIEL ELLIS* (1867).

The ultimate
tragedy of home
front violence,
when revenge
left mothers and
children with
neither homes
nor providers.
*FROM THRILLING
ADVENTURES OF
DANIEL ELLIS*
(1867).

"Massacre of Fugitives" explains the slaughter in this scene as
Texas Unionists are cornered by Confederate cavalry.
FROM *HARPER'S MONTHLY*.

This band of
Federal counter-
guerrilla scouts
searches for their
quarry in the
rugged terrain
of Louisiana.
FROM *HARPER'S
WEEKLY.*

This band of Confederate sharpshooters could just as well have been
guerillas waiting to ambush the approaching riverboat.
FROM *HARPER'S WEEKLY.*

These refugees
have been driven
from home in the
vicinity of
Fayetteville,
Arkansas.

*FROM FRANK
LESLIE'S
ILLUSTRATED
NEWSPAPER.*

Both Unionists and Rebels formed home guards to police their neighborhoods. In this instance, a Confederate home guard near Vicksburg, Mississippi, checks the passes of local slaves. FROM FRANK LESLIE'S ILLUSTRATED NEWSPAPER.

"Refugees from Northern Missouri Entering St. Louis"
describes this scene, as depicted in *Harper's Weekly*.

Rebel bushwhackers await a steamboat in east Arkansas.
COURTESY STATE HISTORICAL SOCIETY OF MISSOURI, COLUMBIA.

# A People's War: Partisan Conflict in Tennessee and Kentucky

## B. Franklin Cooling

INTERNATIONAL SCHOLARS Stig Forster and Jorg Nagler have suggested that commencing with the American Revolution, the so-called "cabinet wars" of the eighteenth century gave way to "people's wars" of essentially three military types. The most radical form of people's war was guerrilla war, in which loose groups of armed civilians virtually without government control fought an irregular campaign against an invading regular army. A second type of people's war was fought with militia armies, in which citizens volunteered, often in large numbers, to fight for the interests of "their" state and by which they identified their own interests. Finally, say Forster and Nagler, people's war was consummated with conscript armies, in which the central government assumed the role of both organizer and leader via measures designed to coerce citizens into fighting for the state. All three of these war types could be found in Tennessee and Kentucky during the Civil War. In fact, they often blurred in defiance of easy interpretation.[1]

Forster and Nagler also note that people's war and the term "total war" enjoy some structural connections. One of those connectors was, in fact, irregular or guerrilla activity. Avowedly, all three forms of people's war engulfed Kentucky and Tennessee at one time or another. From Forts Henry and Donelson to Franklin and Nashville, the story of citizen armies battling head to toe is familiar; less so is the story of the so-called guerrilla conflict. But here, using the prism of guerrilla or irregular conflict, we can better understand the real meaning of the *civil* war that we commonly associate with this period. Anything but civil in the sense of military convention, this level of conflict linked war and society, major and minor personae, politics, economics, culture, and violence in a holistic manner far different from the conventional taxonomy of the Civil War.

People's warfare in Tennessee and Kentucky cannot be separated from but must be integrated with understandings of cause and character, campaigns and stratagems, and even gender and minorities. All of this and more—personal vendettas, family feuds, neighborhood hooliganism— constituted the real Civil War in these two states. Already imprecise contemporary use as well as subsequent literature and folklore have been further obfuscated by the modern semantics of "special," or unconventional, irregular warfare. From an organizational standpoint, this form of combat in Kentucky and Tennessee ranged across the spectrum. It incorporated line units, whether state volunteer or conscripted groups or equally authorized "partisan ranger" and home guard contingents, as well as headquarters-authorized groups and individuals. But, it also embraced poorly defined bands and individuals who broke off from authority and waged virtually uncontrolled mayhem, often without regard to allegiance or loyalty, much less legal controls of either the Confederacy or the Union.

Notwithstanding the blurring of distinctions, these irregulars, conventionally termed "guerrillas" or "partisans," often bore more homespun identities. Period synonyms included homemade Yankees, homespun Yankees, homemade tories, buggers, and jayhawkers, as well as bushwhackers, in the vernacular of the military and indigenous populace. Such impressions amplify why Union general William T. Sherman justifiably termed irregular warfare the most anarchical creation of the war, as at many points arson, murder, robbery, pillage, and other atrocities attended activities of the looser groups drawn from both sides. Later in the war, this people's conflict moved beyond prosecution of legitimate politico/military goals. Tennesseans and Kentuckians of this ilk aptly reflected a transition whereby formalized or organized violence, called war, became an uprising of people and became more closely identified with revolution.

Jill K. Garrett, one longtime student of guerrilla warfare in Tennessee, suggested that this was the only war ever known by most citizens of Kentucky and Tennessee. Prominent battles such as Shiloh, Perryville, or even Franklin and Nashville happened in "distant places." Irregular conflict, however, was in the citizens' midst, "and too often the citizenry found themselves the victims." She might have included participants as well! Richard Stone agreed in his study of the Kentucky militia, claiming that this kind of war "made combatants out of persons whose lives would not have been touched by routine operations." But, he also included raiders like John H. Morgan, Nathan Bedford Forrest, and other regular Confederate cavalry. Still, the contrast is apparent between such action and the episodic battles of the main armies as they affected the common man.[2]

Garrett too quickly postulated that the guerrilla war in this area of the Upper South was a war fought by desperate men as a "measure of retaliation against Federal depredation and occupation." To her, it appeared to have been a natural outgrowth of the conditions of the time and "proved also to be an outlet, in many cases, for man's inhumanity to man." Lost in her particular biases as a Southerner was recognition that nearly from the beginning irregular conflict embraced a myriad of causative factors, sometimes tangentially related to the Northern invasion or to reimposition of national law upon the seceded state. Such is the difficulty of separating myth and legend of a people's war still strongly felt in certain sectors of a tribal culture like the South. Yet, in the end, the leitmotif of both popular resistance and irregular warfare in Kentucky and Tennessee overtly related to the intrusion of central authority, whether Union or Confederate, via military-political-economic activity from 1861 to 1865.

The chronology of the war's events defines the interpretive pattern for analyzing irregular conflict in Kentucky and Tennessee. Such process suggests that this "people's contest" evolved from mere reaction/retaliation to Yankee invasion and occupation to a question of who would control a new order spawned by war. Noel Fisher suggests a somewhat similar paradigm for East Tennessee, but with popular opposition to Confederate, not Union, intrusion and occupation. We emerge then not only with a set-piece war of armies. We also uncover a festering cauldron in which the terms partisan, guerrilla, bushwacker, and irregular became indistinguishable from freedom fighter or bandit and, by implication, meaningless as differentials between legitimate and illegimate resistance. In the end, soldiers and citizens became disillusioned by such conflict which had amalgamated a popular uprising in self-defense when bona fide, constituted authority on either warring side failed to adequately protect them.[3]

Probably neither Unionists nor Confederates realized the transition of the conflict from formal to irregular activity in the heartland until the

late spring of 1862. In Kentucky and Tennessee, at least, certain signs of
this transition had already surfaced. Ulysses S. Grant claimed in his memoirs that the Confederate counteroffensive of Shiloh in April 1862 had
caused him to give up "all idea of saving the Union except by complete
conquest." Yet, soon after his twin victories at Forts Henry and Donelson
two months earlier, he had discerned the first signs of a citizen uprising
and had informed St. Louis headquarters that guerrilla bands were forming in his rear in western Kentucky.[4]

Random instances of secessionist or Unionist intimidation and violence, the actual mustering of irregular outfits for scouting and other
mobile duty, as well as stillborn proposals to organize such contingents
(even from free blacks) could be found in Tennessee in 1861. Yet, none
of this related to employing the guerrilla or partisan as a natural offspring
of the militia system before the spring of 1862. Therefore, in categorizing
the conflict in Kentucky and Tennessee as a people's war, we may conclude that it was the Federal winter/spring offensives of 1862 which
"opened the ball" (to use a soldier term of the period) or triggered various forms of irregular activity as well as the major regular theater campaigns. The first Yankees on Confederate soil spawned guerrilla warfare.
Moreover, the first Union moves toward pacification during occupation
mobilized citizen resistance.[5]

Sherman's own firsthand experience with "an aroused and hostile
population" as well as guerrillas had come as occupation commander of
Memphis in the second half of 1862 and as corps commander in the Army
of the Tennessee during the following year. This preparatory experience
metamorphosed his thinking and actions toward total war generally and
hard pacification in particular, according to Noel Fisher and others. A
similar process transformed the thinking of other senior Union leaders in
the West, leaders such as Grant, John Pope, Henry Halleck, and Rear
Admiral David Porter. All of them simply put into subsequent practice
what they gained through on-the-job experience with a more atavistic type
of warfare (to use John Keegan's term) in the greater Mississippi valley.
Thus, they so elevated to the high art of strategy a pragmatic solution to
problems of localized unwavering popular opposition. Here then was a
major contribution that irregular warfare in Tennessee and Kentucky made
to senior generalship and the art of war from 1861 to 1865.[6]

Guerrillas, as well as other irregulars, continued an active if rather dis-
jointed conflict behind advancing Union legions in the Deep South.
However, that conflict worried the generals less concerning Kentucky and
Tennessee than when Confederates rather effectively employed irregulars
together with regular raiding forces against their lines of communication
and other infrastructure targets. Guerrillas and partisans were left to the
responsibility of local garrisons or the military and civil governments in
the wake of the armies. Even here, however, independent irregulars helped
slow the pace of Union advance in 1862 and 1863 and at times proved to
be more effective inhibitors of the invaders' actions than Confederate cavalry or infantry.

Later, the Confederacy's uncoordinated efforts in this regard shifted
to more localized and politically focused activities against the occupation
forces (now viewed as oppressors of the civilian populace) as well as against
Unionist opposition and the newly liberated African-American population. Rebel generals thought their irregular contingents were off raising
volunteers, tracking down deserters and conscripts, and requisitioning or
capturing horses and provender while keeping Union garrisons off guard.
In reality, subordinate entrepreneurs in uniform were often merely conducting their very own vigilantism or quasi-wars for a variety of causes
known best to themselves.

Not that partisans were omitted from the formal warfare in Kentucky
and Tennessee. Joint teams of regular and irregular Confederates supported
major operations in the Upper South in the final eighteen months of the
war. Irregulars undoubtedly rode either with or in coordination with Forrest,
Morgan, and Adam R. Johnson or his successor, Hylan B. Lyon. When they
could be reined in, they actually served as a valuable reinforcement to the
ever-shrinking manpower pool for the Confederate mounted arm in the
West. But the disintegration of cohesion through casualties and attrition,
Union counterinsurgency programs, descent to brigandage and civil disruption for its own sake (often just to survive), and their altered human
and moral composition (with attendant loss of popular support) suggested
change. As the main war moved elsewhere, irregulars, more often than not,
were out of position to do the Confederacy the most good during its twi-
light hours.[7]

Irregular warfare in Kentucky and Tennessee might be periodized in the following manner. From secession through Grant's opening victories on the Tennessee and Cumberland Rivers can be considered a protean period with only the first murmurs of civil resistance and scattered organized resistance (apart from the main Confederate armies) to either Union or Confederate authority. The spring and summer of 1862 witnessed the rise of the partisan ranger concept in the wake of regular Confederate defeats and loss of territory. The full flowering of irregular warfare occupied a middle period from mid-1862 until sometime in 1864 as the main armies periodically traversed the region but Union occupation and reconstitution generally stagnated. The transition from successful irregular warfare to anarchic turbulence accompanied the waning year and a half of the active war but served as a prelude to the formal Reconstruction period via the banditry and lawlessness of the late 1864–1865 period. Cutting across this structured perspective, however, were all manner of changing faces and purposes for the irregulars' actions and their opponents' responses. What transpired then was a cycle of perpetration and retaliation that continued past Appomattox.

Intimidation, even violence, against dissidents accompanied the secession activities of 1861, thus setting the stage for future turbulence. The notion of raising irregular troops as part of Tennessee's military response emerged after that state left the Union in June 1861. Governor Isham G. Harris received proposals to raise such contingents (even "male free persons of color"), but little came either of those or any other variation on the theme that mobilization of uniformed military organizations was the proper response. Perhaps the need was not foreseen as yet. In any event, A. O. W. Lattern of Jackson thought, "If the people are armed, and have powder, ball and caps in their houses, ready for use, they will rise en masse and the whole country will be filled with armed men to repel the enemy at every point." No more "deadly and destructive antagonism" could be found to stop invaders, he advanced, with such "small expense to the state."[8]

At this point, white Southerners were interested in proving their mettle in uniform on the battlefield. Matters were disorganized enough in 1861. Avowed Kentucky neutrality generated its own type of uncertainty and confusion, and the question of popular dissent all across the Upper South kept both Washington and Richmond officials busy preparing responses. From eastern Appalachia and the north Alabama sand hills to Weakley and McNairy Counties in West Tennessee, even into that part of western Kentucky called the Jackson Purchase, national authorities wondered about people's loyalties. When Confederate authorities finally "violated" Bluegrass neutrality by pushing forward to Columbus on the Mississippi and Bowling Green on the Louisville and Nashville Railroad in September, the secessionist, the Unionist, and the uncommitted were all affected. Farmer L. C. Porter near Bowling Green would caustically term the Confederate occupation of the Green River country "the most absolute tyranny under the name of provisional government without even as much as consulting the people as to their wishes." Firearms confiscation, he decided, was nothing more than a means to thwart local civil resistance to Confederate authority, not the avowed ploy to help equip the Southern army.[9]

Invasion of northern Kentucky by Union troops from across the Ohio River provoked feelings among secessionists similar to those expressed by Porter. The die was thus cast in terms of popular dissidence, if not outright resistance. When Episcopal clergyman–soldier Leonidas Polk, commanding at Columbus, Kentucky, authorized one Len G. Paxon on November 5 to "raise guerrillas" for scouting duty, men responded from as far away as Clarksville, Tennessee. The following month, part of Colonel Nathan Bedford Forrest's Tennessee cavalry regiment killed a local Unionist named Scott near Marion, Kentucky. Scott had led a band "sworn to shoot Southern men from their houses and behind trees," claimed Forrest; and he had already lost several of his men to this group near Hopkinsville in mid-October.[10]

In Forrest's case, the Confederates thought they were "giving confidence to the Southern-rights men, and destroying the distorted ideas of Union men" who had anticipated violence from the Rebels. Such intimidation/protection, together with requisition (confiscation) of large quantities of livestock "under the auspices of the expedition," became trademarks of partisan operations over the succeeding three years. In fact, Forrest and Kentucky cavalier John Hunt Morgan provided the beginnings of formal independent mounted operations and scouting expeditions that eventually became a hallmark of Confederate operations behind Union lines. Unconventional warfare, psychological pressure, and foraging for supplies regardless of ownership attended such operations. Not without cause, perhaps, a Unionist shopkeeper "patronized" by Morgan's men at Harrington, in Bedford County, south of Murfreesboro, Tennessee, in early May 1862 termed these people mere felons.[11]

Still, authorities on both sides remained circumspect on how their regular troops should treat civilians. Official "rose-petal or kid-glove" policies enunciated in Washington notwithstanding, Richmond and regional Confederate authorities were less tolerant of dissent in places like East Tennessee. Nonetheless, professional military leaders on both sides sought to confine bloodshed to the battlefield and minimize both impact upon and reaction from any affected populace. Such an approach continued past the winter when Union forces advanced southward. After that there surfaced the first truly intense stirring of popular opposition and guerrilla warfare in Tennessee and Kentucky.

After his victory at Fort Donelson, Grant warned superiors about guerrillas forming behind his advancing columns on the Tennessee and Cumberland Rivers and dispatched a counterinsurgency contingent to Paris in West Tennessee to eliminate secessionist intimidation and nurture reported Unionism which the Union navy professed to have uncovered along the Tennessee all the way to north Alabama. Federal invasion, battlefield success, occupation of territory, and confiscation/destruction of "secessionist" property (including ad hoc freeing of slaves, seen by the soldiers as affecting the enemy war effort) produced understandable popular reaction. Even closet Unionist Southerners protested the heavy hand of blue-coated soldiers toward persons and property everywhere south of the Ohio River. Such developments held larger implications for irregular activity as time passed.[12]

Moreover, Grant's first victories caused a Confederate military retreat all the way to north Alabama and northern Mississippi and shattered the image of Confederate invincibility throughout the western theater. Vaunted chieftains like Albert Sidney Johnston proved incapable of preserving Southern territorial integrity. Confederate authority could no longer protect property or guarantee the region's citizens peace, liberty, and prosperity. Confidence in Southern generals and their armies crumpled, although hope for renewal never completely left the hearts and minds of the populace. For now, however, people searched for some approach to

defend themselves. What surfaced were raiders of the Morgan stripe and
something styled a partisan ranger corps.

The bloody two-day repulse at Shiloh in April and repeated Confederate setbacks elsewhere produced reaction in Richmond with wide ram-
ifications for irregular as well as regular military activities. For one thing,
the Confederate Congress passed the first conscription law in America. In
addition, after lengthy debate, they also authorized the recruitment of special "Bands of Partisan Rangers." Before this time, President Jefferson Davis
and other officials had been opposed to such independent contingents.
Then, the gloom of battlefield defeat was offset by exploits of mounted cava-
liers like Morgan in Kentucky and Tennessee, Turner Ashby in Virginia,
and Jeff Thompson in Missouri. True, manpower was needed for the regular service, hence conscription. But "Morgan fever" gripped a young nation
struggling to find heroes and a way to defend hearth and home. Partisan
warfare in the tradition of honorable ancestors from the Revolution, as well
as civilian dissatisfaction with the West Pointers' organized war, fueled public enthusiasm.[13]

Whether by companies, battalions, or regiments of infantry or cavalry, rangers could be received into the regular Confederate forces, operate under army regulations, and gain the same pay, rations, and quarters
as other soldiers. In addition, they might also secure rewards for arms and
supplies captured from the enemy. Best of all, from the individual ranger's
perspective, they were on their own where the lure of independent glory,
freedom of action, and closeness to home neighborhoods appealed to many
young Southern swains, especially when the alternative was the carnage
pen of the conventional battlefield. Confederate senators protested that
the partisan corps would impact upon implementing conscription, a valid
fear as it turned out, since Southerners abhorred the perceived abridge-
ment of civil liberties implied by conscription. Nevertheless, they voted
the partisan corps into law on April 21, 1862. As transmitted by army general orders, the Confederate War Department seemingly substituted the
partisan idea for outright guerrilla service.[14]

The partisan corps suggested a middle ground between the West
Pointers' war and the completely freewheeling guerrilla. Partisans could be
a sort of auxiliary—a home-based guard and recruiting pool—for the regular Confederate cavalry, especially as they passed through a locale on some

special mission. Of course, the element of freebootery or brigandage that lurked beneath the veneer of this grassroots fervor escaped many people in 1862. It would take several years of experience to elicit such recognition.

For the moment, popular image easily lifted middle-class businessman John Hunt Morgan to the position of aristocratic knight of the Bluegrass, although nobody did the same with the rougher-hewn, slave-trading West Tennessean Bedford Forrest. But both images served well in gaining adherents among brethren in their respective corners of the Upper South. The partisans were but a slight of hand between Confederate gray and ramshackle guerrilla hue. Yet what was uppermost in the spring of 1862 was the need for action. And men like Forrest, Morgan, and their partisan auxiliaries offered positive action against Yankees who sought to profane Southern soil.[15]

Over the next year and a half, partisan warfare combined with the mounted raiding strategy of the Confederate military in the West and dislocated operational as well as occupation plans of the Federals in the region. Legends were born of lightning-like mounted strikes against railroads and river transport, supply bases and occupation garrisons. Moreover, while less successfully coordinated with the abortive three-pronged counteroffensive conducted by West Pointers like Braxton Bragg, Edmund Kirby Smith, Earl Van Dorn, and Sterling Price in 1862, as well as the later counteroffensive lurch of John Bell Hood to Middle Tennessee in late 1864, the irregulars nevertheless contributed to another dimension of war and society. They provided what Richard Gildrie has termed an effective "defense of a rural society, predominantly of small farmers, threatened by invasion and internal opposition from slaves and Unionist 'Tories.'" Moreover, says Stephen Ash, this fact conveyed not only for Kentucky and Tennessee but all over the Confederacy.[16]

Irregular warfare and citizen opposition became the centerpiece of Confederate resistance to the Federal and Republican revolution in Kentucky and Tennessee. Even the slightest signal of Unionism or presence of Federal authority and programs triggered irregular activity. As a consequence, Union officials came down hard. Brigadier General Jeremiah T. Boyle, commander of the Kentucky department, for instance, decreed on June 1, 1862, "[W]hen damage shall be done to the person or property of loyal citizens by marauding bands of guerrillas, the disloyal of the neighborhood will be held responsible, and a military commission [will be] appointed to assess damages and enforce compensation."[17]

With Union armies poised along the line of northern Mississippi and north Alabama by the late summer of 1862, demonstrations of a militia war waged by irregulars and civil resistance behind and around the invaders held omens for the future conflict in the region. Let the enemy at every advance "meet with a deadly volley from every thicket," was the exiled Memphis *Appeal* editor's prescription. Every rifle and shotgun should be trained on the advancing hordes of Yankees so that any further step they make southward "is made with hazard to themselves," he thundered. It was within the power of the citizens of the country "by a judicious and well organized system of ambuscades and guerrilla warfare, to harass, terrify and hold the enemy at bay," he decided. Here then was the doctrine of armed citizenry in defense of home and civil liberties against tyrannical enemy in the absence of its organized army of the state. Little wonder then that this spokesman could boast, "A people determined to be free will submit to any sacrifice and cannot be conquered."[18]

And so it appeared, as the flame of Confederate resistance sparked anew. Differences between regular forces, partisan rangers, guerrillas, and civil resistance melded from this point on in Tennessee and Kentucky. It is not always clear even now as to whether a particular combatant was legitimately partisan or guerrilla, bushwacker or jayhawk. Subsequent depredations committed in the name of the Union or the Confederacy by armed men in various garb, either afoot or mounted and under varied conditions, became indistinct to press observers and public officials (military and civil) as well as to the citizenry — either Unionist or secessionist by persuasion. Outlawry and brigandage by deserters, freebooters, bushwhackers, or jayhawkers — all titles that became increasingly indistinguishable from one another and from the partisan/guerrilla — broke down finely constructed legal walls as the war progressed.

Efforts by all authorities (Washington and Richmond, state and local civil, or regular Union and Confederate military) to control violence foundered upon the pillage, murder, and physical destruction of property. Assuredly, it never approached the levels of atrocity found in Missouri and Kansas, although the Fort Pillow massacre in 1864 equaled the sack of Lawrence on the road to Michael Fellman's edge of nihilism. Each side blamed the other and then freely committed the same transgression. By November 1863, Confederate secretary of war James A. Seddon wrote to President Jefferson Davis that the anticipated advantages of a partisan ranger corps had been "very partially realized." Their methods had produced only "license, depredations, [and] grave mischiefs." Their opportunities for profit from their captures as well as the lax bonds of discipline rendered them pariahs in the view of line soldiers. In Seddon's view, they had "come to be regarded as more formidable and destructive to our own people than to the enemy." The partisans had moved beyond the regulars' control, but another fifteen months would pass before the government ended the partisan experiment.[19]

What began in the summer and fall of 1862 as activity against legitimate military targets quickly spawned Federal retaliation. This retaliation was directed, in turn, against the guerrillas' own support base, which comprised the habitats and family groups of the predominantly rural farmers in arms. Resistance in the cities was more passive, there being no urban guerrilla warfare of note to prompt Union response. This is not to say that residents of Nashville, Memphis, and other urban areas did not feel just as oppressed by blue uniforms as their country cousins. Their opposition could be just as spirited if less violent. But outlying rail lines, steamboats, patrols and couriers, bridge guard posts, and subsistence expeditions were the favorite targets of raiders and irregulars. Authorities (whether regular Union army garrisons, Unionist militia, home guards, or loyalist farmers protecting hearth and home) reacted in both cases. Counterinsurgency, pacification, eviction, exile, confiscation of property, physical destruction, and the hated Oath of Allegiance to the United States all became part of the Union tool kit for enforcing submission. The first stages of national Reconstruction—along with military government, martial law, suspension of the writ of habeas corpus, carefully manipulated elections, and the controlled restoration of trade and commerce—formed part of the "New Order." All of this produced an ugly turn to the conflict in Kentucky and Tennessee, with political and personal feuds, mayhem, and unbridled violence not only against authority but against any difference of opinion randomly expressed in the course of daily life.[20]

In an area fought over for three long years, the symbol of resistance fighter offered hope to Southern patriots. Raiders like Morgan, Forrest,

Frank Armstrong, and others combined with local partisan chieftains to provide the only positive Confederate response to the relentless presence and advance of the Union enemy. The September 1862 capture of Clarksville, Tennessee, and its Yankee garrison by partisan commands under Tom Woodward and Adam Rankin Johnson ranked as high in favor with the local secessionist populace as Forrest's similar taking of Murfreesboro that same month. While the names of irregulars would be legion, key figures began to surface to the delight of the homefront, figures such as Woodward, Johnson, Robert M. Martin, and Alonzo Napier in western Kentucky, and Jacob Biffle, Alexander Duval, Frank McNairy, Duncan Cooper, Dick McCann, and Thomas J. Williams in Middle Tennessee. The infamous Champ Ferguson held sway to the east, closer to the Cumberland Mountains. There were countless others, including the legendary Jack Hinson, who wrought an individual vendetta against Federal soldiers in the lower Cumberland and Tennessee River region. Some guerrillas slipped in and out of that way of life from their regular army assignments under the guise of going home to collect stragglers, deserters, and draft dodgers.

Colonel John M. Hughs from the Twenty-fifth Tennessee Infantry was an example of this latter category. From the autumn of 1863 into the spring of 1864, Hughs prowled the Cumberland Mountains on independent assignment collaring stragglers. But he then employed these malingerers to hunt "the Union tories," who "were becoming very troublesome" in robbing and murdering citizens and soldiers, rather than immediately returning them to the army. One of his protagonists was the infamous "Tinker Dave" Beatty, leader of Unionist bushwhackers in the region. Never popular with his superiors in the regular forces, Hughs was brought back into normal Confederate ranks in time for the Petersburg, Virginia, campaign.[21]

Still, Hughs could claim that his command ranged from 85 to 300 men on any given occasion and that they had "destroyed for the enemy over half a million dollars' worth of Government stores, besides capturing and destroying 3,000 or 4,000 stands of small-arms." Hughs extravagantly reported tying down 5,000 to 8,000 Federal troops while inflicting casualties of 400 killed and from 600 to 750 captured and paroled. More realistically, he also noted, "[O]ur presence afforded protection to a large section of country against the depredations of the gangs of robbers and bushwhackers, who had become a scourge to the Southern citizens." Ironically, that was precisely what Tinker Dave Beatty and irregulars on the opposite side were also claiming and contradicted Secretary Seddon's opinion that Southern irregulars were threats to the civilian sector.[22]

Hardly unified in organization, program, or purpose, irregulars on both sides in Kentucky and Tennessee emitted a sort of common portrait as the war progressed. They hated with a passion and acted with vehemence. Whatever their degree of previous association with regular units, they continued to claim validity and legality in their irregular incarnation. As children of their age and regional way of life, they were mindful of their assumed responsibilities for conveying a sort of oversight of law, order, and governance to communities, protecting women and children, keeping displaced blacks in subordination, and intimidating or otherwise persecuting those wavering in loyalty. In some ways, the irregulars of both sides seemed not unlike youth in any era. These quasi-legitimate warriors were striking out at authority, convention, and social or economic constraints, as well as the frustrations of life's passage. Many may have been psychopathically violent, yet violence has always been an ingredient in American life, stoked by that streak of independence that beats in every American breast. This said, much remains to be discovered about motivational behavior and the guerrillas of Kentucky and Tennessee.[23]

Union response quite naturally exacerbated the highly inflammable situation. At first, local commanders strictly adhered to dictums from Washington, directives that projected a large loyal population in the South that had been misled by secessionists into separation. Of course, field commanders and their soldiers quickly learned otherwise. In fact, the men in the ranks and their immediate leaders were the first to discover that Southern Unionism was largely myth, that the Washington-prescribed policy for treating Southern people and property kindly did not lessen opposition or win allegiance or even acquiescence from most Southerners in town or country except under duress. The men in blue uncovered precisely what Ash has conveyed by his catchy phrase "sharks in an angry sea"—guerrillas and the hostile Upper South population as part and parcel of a resistant whole. And so it wasn't long before the Union army moved toward "hard war" virtually by default.[24]

Union authorities could do little but react to what was largely beyond their control. Tolerance, permissiveness, and even protection of the civil populace leading to reconciliation did not work under official "rose water" policy. Soon, loyalty oaths, confiscation and destruction of property, imprisonment, exile, and even some executions (for questionable acts conveniently labeled espionage) replaced the policy of lenience. In turn, various forms of punishment and intimidation only further inflamed the situation as Union occupation progressed. But notwithstanding over a century and a quarter of Southern complaint (popular and even academic) concerning Yankee barbarity and repression, harshness of policy and action, and brutality, one fact is clear. Union counterinsurgency policies and practices eventually ferreted out enough guerrillas for destruction. Pacification and occupation activities overawed a large enough segment of the populace. The end result was to reduce the potency of irregular warfare.

Like so many other things about the Federal conduct of the war, its pacification or counterinsurgency campaign in Kentucky and Tennessee was apparently just enough to get the job done. In a sense, it was the old saw about the Union simply overwhelming the Confederacy with more resources. Decapitating the command and control elements of the guerrilla bands and relentlessly pursuing gangs and individuals even into their own sanctuaries were among the methods. Raising counterforce Unionist home guards (who fought brutality with brutality) also proved effective over time. The emergence of accomplished counterinsurgency units helped turn the tide.

Federal authorities established their own counterinsurgency infrastructure. Occupied cities and towns provided command centers, bases of operation, strategic hamlets, and concentration points for effecting pacification of population and control of guerrillas. Federal authorities utilized former Confederate positions such as Columbus, Kentucky, Fort Henry, and a newly constructed Fort Donelson, adjacent to the Confederate fort of that name, as control points on the rivers. They protected supply routes and provided staging areas for counterguerrilla missions into the interior. Such points also served as recruiting stations for black units to be used as construction battalions, railroad guards, and garrisons in the antiguerrilla campaign.[25]

Irregulars occasionally gained the upper hand by capturing isolated

Federal bases or controlling a neighborhood. The Federals often relin-
quished a position when the partisan/raider threat subsided or as forces
were needed elsewhere. The situation was always very fluid. But here lay
the rub. Without concerted, determined, and permanent success at
reestablishing Confederate control over the Upper South, the transitory
and uncoordinated activities of Confederate raiders, partisans, and guerrillas promised only fleeting success and fame.

Even the Union navy assisted with pacification as part of joint operations in the western theater. Gunboats not only convoyed supply boats for
armies and garrisons but also conducted riverine counterinsurgency patrols
and provided landing parties for destroying guerrilla nests like Palmyra,
Tennessee, on the Cumberland on April 5, 1863. Here was replication of
Sherman's own directed obliteration of the town of Randolph on the
Mississippi the previous September as retaliation for guerrilla interdiction
of that river. Both operations, whether conducted by sailors or soldiers, were
done systematically, without remorse or pity. Modern-day Romans such as
Sherman and navy commander Leroy Fitch, as well as the lowliest Yankee
soldier or Jack Tar, conducted counterguerrilla war with a goal of leaving
only the salted earth of Carthage as a monument to superior force.[26]

Southern resistance in the western theater, as well as in Virginia,
prompted Union codification of the rules of engagement, known as
"Lieber's Code," which went to the field on April 24, 1863, as General
Order No. 100. While careful perusal of the ten section, 157 article document probably lay beyond the capability (much less interest) of most
Union field soldiers, this document posited a code of conduct toward
unarmed citizens, guerrillas and partisans, property, and the like. Still,
the nuances of the law escaped most of the frontline participants' appre-
ciation of guerrilla war. The new rules took the sternest tone (a far cry
from the previous "rose water" approach) toward not only punishment
but also the definition of irregulars. By this time, from top to bottom, the
Union army regarded Upper South civilians as farmers by day and bushwhackers by night.[27]

The unremitting cancer of irregular activity on the Tennessee and
Kentucky home front became onerous to all parties (excepting the guer-
rillas, perhaps) by 1864 and 1865. Not that citizens necessarily embraced
Union policies and programs, particularly those regarding African

Americans (always an anathema in slave-holding, if Unionist, Kentucky). Nor had Union counterinsurgency and pacification succeeded in substituting reconstruction and peace for war. Nevertheless, few citizens could abide guerrilla lawlessness as a continuing part of their daily lives. So with irregular warfare no longer serving the policy purposes of either side in winning the people's hearts and minds, the Confederate Congress repealed the Partisan Ranger Act on February 17, 1864. Moreover, Confederate field forces needed manpower in their fight for survival, not a variety of free-ranging, independent, wanna-be great captains operating seemingly without purpose. Forrest pointed this fact out to superiors in March 1865 when he proposed drawing the various independent operators in Kentucky and Tennessee into his own fast-depleting ranks. Thus could he rid the region of "deserters and break up the bands of lawless men who not only rob[bed] the citizens themselves, but whose presence in the country [gave] a pretext to Federal authority for oppressing the people."[28]

As for guerrilla warfare itself, in the words of Kentucky historian Hunter B. Whitesell, "In the East, Lee condemned it. In the West, Forrest damned it." Both soldiers defined the Confederacy's fight for independence and survival by service in the regular ranks. For other leaders such as Forrest in the month before Appomattox, it was a pragmatic matter of desertion, not desertion to home but to lawlessness. And Forrest saw this as good for no one. Not only a sure sign of the collapse of the Confederate war effort, these deserters and conscription evaders represented the state of society in war torn Tennessee and Kentucky. Even Confederate authorities recognized now that "their acts of lawlessness and crime" had undercut their cause. Still, Whitesell suggested wryly, neither Forrest nor many postwar writers of the Lost Cause could see that "from the cold perspective of history" the turbulent conditions in Kentucky, created to a great extent by guerrilla warfare, actually benefited the Confederacy in the final analysis. Did not Kentucky, during Reconstruction, "become the standard bearer for the states of the old Confederacy?" Whitesell posited.[29]

Ironically, it was the arch-guerrilla himself who may have had the final word respecting Kentucky and Tennessee. Hunted like a wild beast for his depredations west of the Mississippi, William Clarke Quantrill transferred his activities to a still turbulent Kentucky in January 1865. Here the unsettled climate might have provided him cover and camouflage. But, perhaps by joining his notorious Bluegrass counterpart Sue Mundy (Captain Jerome Clarke) on several forays, even Quantrill was finally rooted out of his hideout near Bloomfield on May 10. The veteran new Federal commander in Kentucky, Major General John M. Palmer, employed Unionist guerrilla chief Edwin Terrill of Spencer County to complete the job. Wounded and captured, Quantrill died in a Louisville military prison hospital on June 6. It may have seemed an appropriate capstone to the saga of guerrilla warfare in wartime Kentucky and Tennessee.[30]

Scholarly analysis aside, guerrilla warfare in Kentucky and Tennessee was simply a bloody, disruptive business for everyone involved in it. Worthington Davis, writing his *Camp-fire Chats of the Civil War* in 1887 as a veteran campaigner of the war in Tennessee and Kentucky, captured the regular's view of the issue. Focusing on bushwhackers, he declared it to be beneath the dignity of the "Society for the Preservation of Unpublished History" to bestow any panegyric on this brand of combatant. Still, noted Davis, they were a part of the war, "just as vermin were part of prison pens."[31]

The bushwacker was not a soldier but a cowardly, contemptible individual who never carried on hostilities unless he was unopposed, observed Davis. Around the flanks of armies on the march and in camp, he could be found peddling various goods to the soldiers during the day and at night lying in ambush to kill some unwary victim simply for the plunder. A bushwacker was similar to the guerrilla, observed Davis, "except that he sometimes had a smooth side to his character, which would permit him to walk among the soldiers in daylight and acquire such information as would aid his despicable designs at night." He never grew bold like the guerrilla, but "generally perambulated alone in thickets and obscure places, invariably keeping near a safe retreat." His marksmanship was good, as many a poor sentinel "who went forth to die in the front ranks of a great battle in the war" found instead an "unprovoked and untimely demise at the instance of a bushwacker's musket," with nothing but the quiet stars to "witness the atrocity."[32]

A civilian's view came from Logan County, Kentucky, preacher and farmer George Dick Browder. Just before Christmas 1863, Browder jotted in his private journal how a Unionist neighbor had survived a robber band

and had promptly filed a bill for five thousand dollars in reimbursement under a military order calling for secessionist neighbors to pay such damages. This assessment was two or three times the value of the Unionists's property, Browder thought, "but if it were only a part of the value it [was] unjust and oppressive to require people to pay it who knew nothing of the raid and had no connection with it." Although Southern in sympathy, Browder consistently referred to the bandits and thieves, not guerrillas, roaming his area of Kentucky. On September 2, 1864, he noted that many people were in Russellville paying their assessments. He railed, "[T]he best & purest, most honorable, peaceable and quiet men in our country are by that act classed with horse thieves & house burners and made to pay for what they never did." The proceeds went into the collectors' pockets at three or four times in excess of the value of the losses in his view. On April 26, 1865, he wrote of guerrillas derailing a train near Russellville; "it [was] a terrible piece of wickedness." Yet, one of Browder's old school chums and neighbors was the notorious Tom Morrow, who harassed southern Logan County throughout the war.[33]

Guerrilla warfare in Kentucky and Tennessee can be studied through many different prisms. William T. Sherman, sharing his views on this matter with his friend and naval colleague David Porter in the autumn of 1863, suggested that he was not "going to bother [him]self about guerrillas and citizens" as long as they could not "do [Union] main arteries harm." Admitting that his own men were "full of the idea that all the people [were] secesh, and would as leave plunder and kill all as not," he believed that until "the Confederacy [was] shaken to the center," Union forces should not bother with "attempts to reconcile people and patch up civil governments." Our duty, stated Sherman prophetically, "is to strike and break up the large armies of the Confederacy, which once broken and defeated, the smaller bands will soon be as obnoxious to the people of the South as to us."[34]

Posterity still must refine the retrospective meaning of this war within a war, but there can be no mistaking the central issue. It was the people's conflict, not the major battles, that caused the passage toward total war for leaders, soldiers, and civilians. Indeed, here was a large part of the legacy of the Civil War in Kentucky and Tennessee. The ultimate irony for this author came with a small packet of Civil War paper memorabilia obtained at a Maryland auction. It contained five pieces of innocuous paper currency—state and local bank bills from Georgia and Michigan as well as Confederate and Union notes. Accompanying these relics was a notarized statement that they had belonged to John H. Hart, who had farmed on Youngers Creek near Elizabethtown, the county seat of Hardin County, Kentucky. Living in a border state, read the note, with numerous bands of partisans of both sides operating in the area, the settlers on Youngers Creek received frequent visits. Hart had kept this currency as "souvenirs of the 'payments' he received for feed and livestock taken by the partisans of both sides." Perhaps the irregulars were not bandits after all. Here, at least, was one victim who could look back with sardonic humor concerning his very personal experience with Civil War guerrillas in Kentucky and Tennessee.[35]

# The Limits of Dissent and Loyalty in Texas

## David Paul Smith

IN MARCH 1862, the newly appointed commander of the Sub-Military District of the Rio Grande, Colonel Henry Eustace McCulloch, reported his discovery of a "considerable under-current at work through this country against our cause."[1] He was convinced that Unionists in his district were trying to depreciate Confederate currency by charging outrageous prices to those paying in the new Confederate currency and by demanding cash sales with no credit. Loyal Confederates in the region gathered in a mass meeting in San Antonio to declare the death penalty for those who persisted in undermining state or Confederate warrants, notes, or bonds. The citizens were further alarmed when McCulloch discovered that approximately seventy-five settlers of German descent had organized a militia, well armed with rifles and pistols, supposedly to uphold the Unionist stand taken by the large number of German settlers who were part of the south Texas population.[2]

Two and one-half years later the same McCulloch, now a brigadier general in charge of the widespread Northern Sub-District of Texas, commanded a region rife with Unionist plots and with a bloody history of dissent and reprisals. Faced with large gangs of deserters, mixed with those avoiding conscription, McCulloch's patience was nearly at an end: "Extend pardon to all that you believe come in voluntarily, arrest all others alive wherever found and let them all understand that they must go to the army and stay obedient [to] the Country or be killed."[3] Five weeks later, the commander of the Trans-Mississippi Confederacy, General Edmund Kirby

Smith, ordered McCulloch to show no mercy to those who failed to do their duty to their country: "You will, of course, use every exertion to effect their extermination as soon as possible."[4]

Such was Texas, a state almost wholly "behind the lines." There was little of the type of guerrilla activity associated with Missouri or Virginia, or any other place where Confederates, partisans, or irregulars by any name operated behind Union army lines. In Texas the Union invaders for a while hung precariously to a strip along the south Texas coast and up the Rio Grande a ways, or to Galveston Island for a short time. In every Texan's mind, however, was the fear of imminent invasion in force, perhaps by way of Louisiana or by Federal forces coming from Arkansas or the Indian Territory. As the war progressed into 1862, with serious Confederate reversals at Shiloh and New Orleans, intolerance against Unionists increased and intensified with utter ruthlessness in some quarters until the war's last days. A search for order in a society with a vigilante or militant tradition came face to face with what every generation of Americans has confronted in time of war—security versus individual freedoms. The clash would be especially trying in any society that attempted to observe democratic practices.[5]

It was apparent from secession's first days that Unionist sentiment in the state would not fade from the scene. The most famous citizen of Texas, Governor Sam Houston, was removed from office on March 16, 1861, for refusing to take an oath of allegiance to the Confederacy. An Ordinance of Secession had been passed earlier, on February 1, but the people voted in a referendum on secession three weeks later. In an election marred by irregularities, secession was approved by a three to one vote, and just 18 out of 122 counties rejected secession. These 18 counties were in two general groups, centering on counties with heavy German population in south-central Texas and in counties along the Red River in north Texas.

Many, although certainly not all, of the German families opposed secession and the Confederacy; and after the Confederacy's first conscription law in early 1862 many of the German Texans refused to serve. Hundreds of them joined a Union Loyal League and formed minutemen companies which defended equally against Comanches and Confederate conscription officers. Henry McCulloch closed the Mexican border after he learned that many of the Germans were headed for the other side of the Rio Grande to evade conscription, and he recommended that martial law be declared.[6] Not long afterward, the commander of the Western Subdistrict of Texas, Hamilton P. Bee, declared six German counties to be in rebellion; and a force of soldiers under Captain James Duff was sent to the counties between Fredericksburg and San Antonio to enforce conscription. When Duff learned that a small force of men from the German companies was headed for the Rio Grande he took his contingent of nearly one hundred rangers to intercept. The resulting Battle of the Nueces, on August 10, 1862, was a bloodbath in which more than thirty Germans were killed and nearly that many wounded, while Duff lost two killed and eighteen wounded.[7] The hostility that arose in the area in these early months of the war would continue to cause difficulties for Confederate authorities throughout the war.

In 1861, while most eyes in the state looked to the coast for a threat of Federal invasion, state officials also listened to the cries of frontier settlers to provide for protection against raids by Comanches, Kiowas, and Apaches. The frontier, throughout the previous decade, had advanced approximately ten miles per year. By 1861 the frontier line ran from a point on the Red River just east of present day Wichita Falls to near Eagle Pass on the Rio Grande. Anything northwest of that line, particularly in the unorganized area of the state in the Texas Panhandle, was simply known as Comancheria, land of the Comanches. Henry McCulloch formed a mounted regiment to protect what Texans called the Indian frontier, from the Red River to south of the Concho, northwest of San Antonio. The one thousand men who rode with Henry McCulloch in April 1861 were part of the First Regiment, Texas Mounted Rifles, the first regiment mustered into Confederate service in Texas. They occupied the frontier forts on the northwest frontier which had been previously occupied by United States soldiers, and they guarded the frontier until the following spring.[8]

The state legislature, knowing that the enlistment of the Mounted Rifles was to expire in April, wanted to ensure that a body of rangers remained on the frontier to offer protection to the citizens who lived in the forty frontier counties, which had recorded an 1860 population of nearly forty-five thousand. The legislature, in December 1861, authorized the formation of the Frontier Regiment, a state funded regiment, to take the place of the Mounted Rifles. The new regiment was offered by the state to Confederate service, but Jefferson Davis would not stipulate that it be required to remain in service on the Texas frontier, so for the next two years the state struggled to finance it.[9] The Frontier Regiment had mixed success in guarding the Indian frontier, until the arrival of a new colonel, James Ebenezer McCord, in early 1863. In the late summer of 1863, however, the regiment faced another problem never before encountered by any body of Texas rangers on the frontier: the job of policing the frontier counties for deserters and for those avoiding conscription. This seemingly secondary role for the regiment quickly expanded as the problem escalated among state and Confederate forces across the entire frontier. Even the omnipresent Indian menace receded in importance as attention turned to deserters, disaffection, and concomitant problems.

To tell the story of the attempt by authorities to quell the rising tide of dissent against Confederate laws of impressment, taxation, and conscription among an increasingly alienated population, it is necessary to begin with the single most controversial act of violence and vigilantism in the state's four years of Civil War: the Great Hanging at Gainesville.[10] In the late summer of 1862 word came to north Texas of a planned invasion of Texas by Jayhawkers, abolitionists, and their Indian allies, by way of Fort Cobb in Indian Territory. The impending invasion turned out to be nothing more than rumors and tall tales, but the rumors spread, and their effect on the state of mind of the populace created a crisis in northern Texas during the fall of 1862. Since the first months of the war, Unionist sentiment in the region of Texas between Dallas and the Red River had been strong, particularly in the counties of Cooke, Denton, Wise, and Collin.

As early as January 15, 1861, settlers circulated a document that called for northern Texas to form a separate state and remain in the Union. Disaffection intensified with opposition to Confederate conscription laws passed in April and September of 1862. In north Texas, discontent centered in Cooke County; and it was here, during the excitement of the supposed invasion, that the "conspiracy of the Peace Party" took place. Internal turmoil led to murder, mass hangings, and a cloud of unrest that plagued this portion of the state until the war's end.[11] The forces and attitudes that fostered the Peace Party conspiracy and subsequently the Great Hanging at Gainesville were bound together by the prevalent anti-secessionist or ambivalent feelings of citizens who owned no slaves and had few ties to the social and economic system of slavery, other than the ideology of racism, which was instilled with growing frequency into every argument for secession on the eve of the war by pro-slavery writers and speakers. For so many, morale declined from the opening months of the war. Bitter feelings were further engendered by the demand for conformity by outspoken secessionists who controlled the military.[12]

In the midst of rumors of a possible invasion from Indian Territory, evidence was uncovered in Gainesville, evidence that pointed to a Unionist plot to seize militia arsenals in north Texas to facilitate the invasion. Initially, this Peace Party or Union League organization consisted of men with Unionist sympathies who secretly banded together to discuss political views with others of similar inclination. Members swore oaths to remain loyal to the United States Constitution and often communicated with secret signs, handshakes, and passwords, while leaders of the organization boasted of thousands of members and sympathizers in the region. Their activities allegedly included the accumulation of arms and ammunition that might aid a Union invasion of Texas, and it was said that Cooke County members established communication with Jayhawkers to the north.[13]

Local state and Confederate authorities acted, and at daybreak on October 1, 1862, widespread arrests were carried out. By noon, more than seventy men had been seized and were confined in Gainesville. Although most in the town probably did not favor hanging as a solution, the followers of James G. Bourland were intent on rooting out and ending dissent. Bourland, a local slave holder and former state senator, was provost marshal of the area, chief enforcer of the conscription laws.[14] Later called "the Hangman of Texas," one of his peers called him "a good fighter and a good hater."[15] Two years later Bourland wrote, "I think that 27 years in Texas, and a part of the time was helping hang and whip rascals out of the country, surely ought to give me some ideas of Mankind."[16]

Over the next ten days, while a citizens court tried the leaders of the Peace Party and took testimony, nearly eighty more prisoners joined those already in custody. In the first week seven men, alleged leaders of the Peace Party plot, were condemned and hanged; but a growing and restless mob called for more. When word leaked that the court would probably hang no one else, the mob sent word that they demanded twenty prisoners be hanged or they would would kill everyone in the makeshift prison. The citizens court then turned over the names of fourteen men to the waiting crowd, and they were hanged in two groups, three on October 12 and the rest on the following day.[17]

The breakup of the citizens court and the deaths of the twenty-one men brought but a lull to the grisly activity going on in Gainesville. On October 16, Colonel William C. Young was murdered, an act that once more generated hysteria of more Unionist plots; this led to further arrests and more executions. A reorganized jury began new trials, even of some men formerly acquitted. Nearly sixty prisoners were released finally, but nineteen more men were condemned. On Sunday morning, October 19, the executions began; and the nineteen were hanged, two per hour, throughout the rest of the day. At the same time, five men were condemned in similar fashion in nearby Wise County. Only after this three-week blood-bath did state and Confederate courts step in to halt the hangings.[18]

The animosity, of course, could not be ended so easily. These acts of October left a mark on the northwest frontier of Texas, a mark that lin-gered for the duration of the war. Not surprisingly, this part of Texas became, in the last two years of the war, a sanctuary for Confederate desert-ers, renegades, active Union sympathizers, and draft dodgers. They were to find covert sympathy from those whose anti-Confederate feelings crys-tallized during these days of October in 1862. These circumstances even altered the nature of the military defense of the region. Frontier defense now came to mean the protection of frontier settlers from foes as ruthless as the enemy, that is, each other. Any discussion of the defense of north Texas and the northwest frontier must take into consideration the increas-ingly complex dilemmas that forced civil and military authorities to deal with the internal problems of desertion and resistance to conscription, as well as the ever-present Indian raids and threat of Federal invasion.

Until war's end, this part of Texas would remain the number one prob-lem area of the state, and until the spring of 1863 the region remained under command of officers some three hundred miles away in Houston. The situa-tion changed when the Northern Sub-District of Texas was formed on May 30, 1863. It was under the temporary command of Smith P. Bankhead through August, then Brigadier General Henry McCulloch took command, with headquarters in Bonham, Fannin County. He would remain until the fall of the Confederacy. Earlier, Governor Francis Lubbock had notified General Smith in Shreveport of the need to coordinate the protection of the northwest frontier from the ravages of Indian attacks; and now he congratulated McCulloch, glad that he was now "in charge of the Indian frontier."[19] For the most part, the state government and frontier settlers viewed the creation of the new subdistrict primarily as a means to best combat the problem of Indian raids and only secondarily to resolve the desertion-conscription dilemma. General John Bankhead Magruder, commander of the District of Texas, and General Kirby Smith rarely saw it that way. Their correspondence did not mention the Indian menace, but the men and women who lived on the northwest frontier were never able to forget it. McCulloch's command represented to Confederate officials a way to coordinate the defense of northeast Texas against possible Federal offensives, to enforce Confederate conscription laws, and to control a growing disaffection among the civil population of the Red River counties. In fact, one of the first works to chronicle the role of Texas in the war stated simply that McCulloch's object in taking command of the Northern Sub-District was to ensure "by either forcible or pacific efforts to get men out of what was called 'Jernigan's thicket,' which had been made a place of refuge by deserters and others that avoided conscription."[20]

McCulloch began immediately to confront the conscription-desertion dilemma, a problem that never subsided and that came to dominate his administration of the subdistrict. The problem was a serious one. The great numbers of men who hid out in the "brush" in the Northern Sub-District threatened the integrity of the entire region.[21] Estimates of armed men in the brush range upward to three thousand. Many of these were absent from Confederate and Texas commands stationed in the area, or mixed with those avoiding conscription, and were joined by hundreds who had straggled in from surrounding units in Louisiana, Arkansas, and Indian Territory. In an attempt to entice these men back to their commands General Smith granted a "general pardon of amnesty" to all officers and soldiers in the Trans-Mississippi Department who willingly returned to duty by September 30, 1863.[22]

After only a few days on the job McCulloch reported that he had received a number of pleas from loyal citizens in the area, urging him "to take steps to arrest deserters and conscripts that have gone into the brush in large numbers. These men live off the property and produce of the people near their camps, and are a terror to the country about them."[23] McCulloch and his aides, along with prominent citizens who were Unionists in the secession crisis of 1860–61 but who now supported the Confederacy, all attempted to persuade the men "by kind, and gentle means" to report for duty.[24] McCulloch, however, left no doubt that the men were going to come in one way or the other. He preferred it to be a peaceful transition, but informed his staff that military power would be used if results were not quickly seen: ". . . and when driven to that—any hope of pardon and reconciliation ceases, and that I will hunt them down as the enemies of my Country, and her people, that I will send an armed force to take them dead or alive. Tell them I offer them peace, pardon, and friendship, and if they refuse, warn them of the consequences."[25] General Smith's advice to McCulloch was terse: "The deserters must be arrested and brought back to their commands or exterminated. The question now is whether they or we shall control."[26]

By late October of 1863 McCulloch estimated that over one thousand deserters remained in the brush in northern Texas, most of them located in the counties which voted against secession in 1861. He estimated that the area bounded by Bonham, Dallas, and Gainesville harbored three armed camps of deserters, over two hundred men strong in each, who regularly patrolled roads leading to their encampments.[27] One group, estimated at nearly five hundred strong, was under the leadership of a "desperate character" named Henry Boren, who, McCulloch later learned from an informant, planned to seize Bonham and "wipe out secession in this part of Texas."[28] It was now, in the fall of 1863, that troops were urgently needed on the northwestern frontier to guard against an increasing Indian threat, troops that could not be sent because McCulloch considered the deserter problem to be more serious.

In October McCulloch received reinforcements, the most controversial unit to ever serve in Texas during the war. A band of Confederate guerrillas under the notorious William Clarke Quantrill crossed the Red River at Colbert's Ferry and established winter camp along Mineral Springs Creek about fifteen miles northwest of Sherman, Texas, approximately forty-five miles from McCulloch's headquarters. This winter camp was necessary, in part, for Quantrill's men to escape retribution for two of their recent affairs, their infamous sack of Lawrence in August and their near annihilation of General James G. Blunt's headquarters escort.[29] Some of Quantrill's men preceded him into Bonham on Friday, October 23, and made a grand entrance into town. About two hundred of them, "all young, fine looking, well disposed," rode around the square in Bonham in celebration, displaying Blunt's captured headquarters flag.[30] Their reputation preceded them. McCulloch had heard about the Lawrence raid and probably the Baxter Springs incident, and he voiced his own opinions about Quantrill and his manner of combat: "I do not know as much about his mode of warfare as others seem to know; but, from all I can learn, it is but little, if at all, removed from that of the wildest savage. I appreciate his services, and am anxious to have them; but certainly we cannot, as a Christian people, sanction a savage, inhuman warfare, in which men are to be shot down like dogs, after throwing down their arms and holding up their hands supplicating for mercy."[31]

From his comfortable perch in Shreveport, General Smith ordered McCulloch to keep Quantrill's men together to collect stragglers and deserters, and referred to McCulloch's new reinforcements as "bold, fearless men . . . under very fair discipline. They are composed, I understand, in a measure of the very best class of Missourians."[32] It was probably sometime in the first week of November that McCulloch authorized Quantrill to hunt down those in the brush, but then just to arrest them, not kill them. Quantrill later said he learned that many of those in the brush planned to turn themselves in, then planned to desert to the Federals, so he took action on his own. He and his men captured only a few of those in the brush, and killed several, whereupon McCulloch quickly pulled him off such duty and sent him to report to Kirby Smith's headquarters. Smith merely agreed with Quantrill, then recommended to McCulloch that "the only thing to be done now is to go vigorously to work, and kill or capture all those who refuse to come in . . . the ringleaders should have no quarter."[33] But McCulloch had other plans. He pulled Quantrill and his men off such duty and sent them chasing Comanches. At least it got Quantrill's men away from the populated areas for a short while.

McCulloch had not heard the last of Quantrill and his men. During the winter they made a general nuisance of themselves by occasionally

shooting up the town of Sherman and providing little assistance in rounding up deserters. Stories of plunder and robberies by Quantrill's men filtered into Bonham for some time, but when murder became commonly
attributed to them, McCulloch determined to act. He reported to General
Magruder that he planned to arrest Quantrill and his men and send them
to either Houston or Shreveport: "They regard the life of a man less than
you would that of a sheep-killing dog. I regard them but one shade better
than highwaymen, and the community believe that they have committed
all the robberies that have been committed about here for some time."[34]
McCulloch requested that Quantrill report to his headquarters, where he
dispatched nearly three hundred state and Confederate troops to arrest the
guerrilla leader and his men. Quantrill reported on March 28, 1864, and
his subsequent celebrated escape led he and his men to flee for the Red
River. The troops sent after Quantrill outnumbered his force by three to
one, but they were unsuccessful in pursuit, probably more out of reluctance
to press the issue with men of Quantrill's reputation than an inability to
overtake them. McCulloch observed, "I have not had troops that had the
moral and physical courage to arrest and disarm them."[35]

By the end of 1863 McCulloch must have felt the land tightening
around him like a fist. In frustration he requested a transfer to field command. In a harsh letter to Magruder, he tried to point out the real situation
in his part of Texas, a situation that stemmed from the deserters still in the
brush. He bitterly wrote that the best thing for the country would be to kill
them—as traitors they deserved death. In recent weeks, McCulloch
reported a dozen deserters killed and severely wounded, some by his men
when trying to arrest them, but most by bushwhackers. In addition, he
added, "almost one-fourth of this population ought to be taken up for aiding and assisting deserters . . . and [for] disloyal expressions and acts." "I
have never been in a country," he wrote, "where the people were so perfectly worthless and cowardly as here."[36] Colonel James Bourland, now
commanding the Confederate Border Regiment, guarding the northwest
frontier of the state and patrolling both sides of the Red River, was reporting the same thing, particularly assaults and robberies against "secessionists." One enrolling officer and former sheriff of Wise County reported, "It
is generally believed that we are on the very eve of an insurrection, and

that the secession portion of our population are daily in great danger of being jayhawked."[37]

If the most egregious acts of dissent and repression occurred in the Northern Sub-District, suffering and lawlessness were no strangers to other locales as well, particularly along the entire length of the frontier. The legislature, now determined to transfer the Frontier Regiment to Confederate service, even if it might be ordered away from the frontier, also provided, once again, for another force to be in place to provide frontier protection. Thus was born the Frontier Organization, created in December of 1863. The act divided the fifty-nine frontier counties of Texas into three frontier districts and declared that all persons liable for military service who were actual residents of the frontier counties were to be enrolled and organized into companies. Approximately four thousand men were enrolled in the organization by spring and put on a rotation basis so that one-fourth of them would be in the saddle at any one time.[38] These counties represented an area approximately the size of the state of North Carolina.

Major George B. Erath took command of the Second Frontier District headquarters at Gatesville. While his attention went immediately to the problems of the increasingly active Indians and white renegades in the western part of his district, he requested, and obtained, provost guard companies for constant duty in the capture and guard of deserters. The units were necessary, he said, if he was to "drive rascalls [sic] and torys [sic] from the country."[39] During an inspection tour of his district Erath learned of the low morale of the citizens of the region, and he heard much criticism of the government. He ordered his men to root out some sixty to seventy deserters who seemed to be causing the trouble. It took three weeks and three companies to do the work, but more than one hundred men were taken into custody. Just as he quelled those troubles in Lampasas County, rumors swirled of some three hundred Jayhawkers who were soon to rendezvous along the San Saba River. This force, however, seemed intent on heading westward to California, and in any event Erath did not have the manpower to overtake them.[40]

In the spring of 1864, a string of incidents occurred in the recently formed Third Frontier District in south Texas. After a series of murders,

robberies, and outrages committed west of San Antonio, crimes attributed
to soldiers of the state's Frontier Organization and the Frontier Regiment,
the commander of the district, Major James Hunter, arrested seven men.
One of those taken was the captain of Company A of the Frontier
Regiment. After jailing the men in Fredericksburg, Hunter wrote to the
governor and requested that the prisoners be moved to Austin or San
Antonio, lest a rescue attempt be made. Hunter miscalculated. Less than
two weeks later some two hundred armed men rode into Fredericksburg
and overcame the twelve-man guard stationed at the jail. With no intention of freeing the men inside, the mob pushed their way into the stone
jail and opened fire upon the prisoners. They killed one instantly and
wounded four others critically, two of whom died the next day.[41] All this
occurred not long after a bold band of renegades left the vicinity but
vowed to return and to "have the frontier in a blaze before any troops
[could] get there."[42]

The district, plagued by Indian attacks on the west and lawlessness
from within, soon acquired a commander to replace Hunter. John D.
McAdoo arrived at his headquarters in Fredericksburg on June 23 to take
command. A report he later filed described conditions as he found them:
"I found almost the entire population of a large portion of the District
laboring under the greatest excitement. Within a few months, twenty
men had perished by violence. Some had been waylaid and shot; others
taken from their homes at the dead hour of midnight and hung, and their
houses robbed; and some had been mobbed and murdered in jail and in
irons. No man felt secure—even at home. The Indians seemed to be the
least talked of, the least thought of, and the least dreaded of all the evils
that threatened and afflicted the Frontier."[43] Under McAdoo the morale
of the Third Frontier District improved visibly, due largely to the efficient
work done by the troops under his command. By autumn the companies
of his district, by extraordinary effort, captured or drove to cover many of
the gangs that previously terrorized the countryside. Soon, the recent outrages became scarce occurrences.

More than two hundred miles to the north, the weary people of the
Northern Sub-District of Texas simply tried to endure. An officer reported:
"Any amount of deserters in the Country yet. Our scouts are bringing them
in every day, and occasionally shooting one."[44] As morale sank, Con-

federate and state authorities hardened themselves to ever more repressive measures to root out the disloyalists. McCulloch described the extent of disaffection to Governor Pendleton Murrah: "I can assure you that there is a large disloyal element here constantly at work in the army to get men out and keep them out of service. There are untrue men in every command made up of men from this section of country. No man can know and understand the condition of this country unless he was in it to see for himself . . . and I will save the country or go down with it."[45] Now, in the spring of 1864, echoes of the "Peace Conspiracy" and the Great Hanging hysteria revisited north Texas. This lesser-known story is called simply the "Frontier Conspiracy" of 1864.

The commander of the First Frontier District was Major William Quayle, headquartered in Decatur in Wise County. On Sunday, April 10, one of Major Quayle's captains, James M. Luckey, made some disturbing revelations. He disclosed that he was secretly working for the overthrow of the Confederacy and that he had organized some three hundred men of the Frontier Organization and the Frontier Regiment, all ready to be moved to the western limits of the First Frontier District to initiate communications with Federals in Indian Territory and ready to aid a Union invasion of north Texas.[46] When General McCulloch learned of the plot, he prudently began making plans just in case the information was accurate, but in a manner so as not to cause alarm. No doubt reminded of Colonel Bourland's zeal in stamping out disloyalty in Cooke County in 1862, McCulloch did not want a repeat performance of that bloodbath on his hands. He instructed the Confederate troops of Bourland's command not to precipitate action in the First Frontier District unless Quayle requested aid.[47] McCulloch suggested to Quayle that he take careful steps in gathering proof of guilt before the ringleaders and their men should be arrested. If the investigation showed substantial evidence of treason, McCulloch proclaimed, "[P]ounce on them and kill or capture the whole of them and better kill than capture them."[48]

In one sense, at least, the conditions in which this Frontier Conspiracy took place resembled the situation of 1862. Then, the Peace Conspiracy took place in the midst of rumors of a Federal invasion, only now they were not rumors; Union forces were converging on Texas through Arkansas and Louisiana. The state and Confederate forces who set out to break up the conspiracy did so in the belief that the conspirators, if left unchecked, would soon be aiding Union troops in the region. McCulloch authorized Colonel Bourland to direct the arrests of the men in question and to send them immediately to General Magruder in Houston. Bourland was primed and ready for action. As the operation was about to be launched, Bourland's parting shot to Quayle was, "Major, you must manage this affair in the same way we did in Cooke [County]."[49]

As the target date for the arrests drew near, the security lapse that inevitably accompanies such missions enabled a large number of those implicated to escape, and they eventually joined either the Federals or deserters in the brush. As the arrests began taking place, primarily in the counties of Parker, Wise, and Jack, many of the populace envisioned a repeat of the hangings of 1862. A "stampede" took place in Wise County when the rumor went out that Confederate troops were arresting every-one who voted "the Union Ticket" and who had opposed secession in 1861. Many of them fled to the interior of the state and as far away as Mexico.[50]

With so many other similarities to the Peace Conspiracy of 1862 it is conspicuous that the mass executions of those days did not occur again in 1864. But the northwest frontier of Texas had suffered too many hardships, had seen too much misfortune and death. The mood of the populace to take action was no longer there as before. No Union army had ravaged the land, but a war weariness lay upon this portion of the Confederacy. The call to fight intangible rumors of conspiracy no longer moved the people.

Even with the turbulent Frontier Conspiracy at an end, military lead-ers and ordinary men and women in the Northern Sub-District found no respite. With both state and Confederate forces sweeping the countryside for deserters, and for those who would aid them, at least more men now began to turn themselves in to Quayle's state forces. Whenever his men procured any deserters they were required to send them directly to Colonel Bourland's headquarters in Gainesville, whereupon the colonel would then send them to General McCulloch in Bonham. Complaints mounted against Bourland and his men. Since early in 1864, charges abounded that Bourland's men often murdered some of their prisoners, not in the act of capturing them, but after they were taken and under guard. A muster roll for a First Frontier District company records tersely: "Ransom Graves, age

27, taken by Col. Bourland's men and killed, April 25."[51] So many reports
filtered into McCulloch's office that when word came of a series of murders in May and June McCulloch sent a strong reprimand to Bourland
informing him of complaints about the cold-blooded murder of prisoners:
"There is no one in the land more anxious than I am to rid the country of
such men as by their actions deserve death, but I cannot in any manner
agree to make myself Judge Jury and Court Martial to decide their cases
and execute them without trial and if such things have been done let them
occur no more."[52] The decisive factor was when Bourland's own men prepared court-martial proceedings against him, charging that he "ordered,
permitted, or connived" in the murder of prisoners. Twenty-eight men of
the Border Regiment signed the list of specifications, including five of his
captains. No trial was ever held, but the leverage of such charges, combined with McCulloch's strict accounting for future deaths of prisoners,
ended the practice.[53]

As 1864 came to a close, supporters of the Confederacy, as well as their
neighbors who prayed only for war's end, girded themselves for the last blast
of winter, with still little relief of any kind in sight. Beset by the collapse of
Confederate purchasing power, the civilian population on the frontier and
within the interior was forced to bear inflated prices for goods, army
impressment, and a tax in kind on their produce. For those who lived near
the frontier, there was constant threat of attack or raids by outlaws, marauding deserters, and Indians, as well as the threat of invasion by the U.S.
Army. Homesickness, lack of pay, the hardships of camp life, and news of
Confederate military reverses east of the Mississippi River all contributed
to erode discipline among the soldiers and deepen the despair of the people.
All these factors complicated the already fragile social fabric of a people at
war and contributed to the decline of civilian morale that continued
unabated from the war's first months.

By April of 1865, in Texas as well as throughout the Trans-Mississippi
Confederacy, chaos seemed the order of the day. Desertions increased and
gangs of stragglers and fugitives terrorized the Texas countryside, forcing
Governor Murrah to call out draft-exempt volunteers to police the state.
By the last week of May, discipline in the hard-pressed Northern Sub-
District completely broke down. Unionists and Confederates alike, embit-
tered by their shared experiences, escalated the violence that would

continue in many parts of the region for years after the war.[54] Deserters
and renegades committed robberies in the countryside and threatened
towns with pillage. Special targets were officers who had worked to
enforce Confederate laws by the harshest of methods. In some ways, and
to many Texans, it was a war in which the enemy's armies were farthest
from the mind, when just surviving your neighbor's wrath or treachery
seemed victory enough.

In North Texas, General Henry McCulloch gave his last command
and concluded his service with a predictable end. Two days after learning of the surrender of the army of the Trans-Mississippi he spoke as the
last voice of Confederate authority in the region. He instructed the men
of the Frontier Organization and volunteer militia groups to maintain
patrols against Indian raids until relieved by the United States cavalry.
Then, accompanied by twenty-seven men as an armed escort to protect
him from retaliation by deserters who vowed to kill him, and by a mob
who tried to stop him, McCulloch left Bonham.[55]

If disorder seemed pervasive at the Confederacy's end, it only fore-
shadowed a society soon awash in violence during the days of Reconstruction. Texas was settled by Southerners who brought a code with them
which taught every man to right his own wrongs, but even militant
Southerners of antebellum days were stunned by what befell Texas during the Civil War and Reconstruction. The social chaos and political
hatreds of the Civil War, coupled with the persecution of freed slaves and
Union men in the years immediately following, contributed to lead Texas
to the nation's highest homicide rate by 1870. Texas sheriffs reported
4,425 crimes during the six years following the Civil War and only 588
arrests. Governor E. J. Davis proclaimed Texas a state filled with desperate characters, estimated seven or eight hundred homicides a year in the
state, and created a state police force in 1870 that arrested forty-four murderers and felons during its first month.[56] Most of the violence and lawlessness concentrated in central and northern Texas. In the region in and
near Cooke County Unionists looked forward to the return of Federal
authority and vindication for those who had been victimized in the
Gainesville hanging and subsequent violence. They received little relief,
as ex-Confederates intimidated those who had opposed them and crimes
and atrocities abounded. It was evidence from northern Texas, where

homicides rose dramatically in 1866 and 1867, that helped persuade Congress of the necessity for military reconstruction.[57]

The limits of dissent were put to severe test in Texas, as its leaders wrestled with the problems faced by most nations at war before and since: how to deal with disaffection and how to distinguish between varying shades of dissent, patriotism, and growing war weariness. To deal with such factors in the context of a naturally violent frontier society required herculean efforts, and even those were in vain. From early in the war, when a large portion of the state became the Trans-Mississippi's haven for deserters, bushwhackers, and renegades, hatreds were inflamed, hatreds that spilled over into the postwar years and lingered in smoldering partisanship for decades. In a South where violence was common during Reconstruction, nowhere was it more pervasive and deadly than in Texas. It was but another legacy of civil war.

# "Out of Stinking Distance": The Guerrilla War in Louisiana

## Donald S. Frazier

LOUISIANA, with its position on the Mississippi and abundance of close terrain and unpopulated prairies, had a long tradition of rural lawlessness in the antebellum period, a problem which reasserted itself as guerrilla warfare during the Civil War. Indeed, during the colonial period, smuggling became a major industry in the region, promoting lawlessness and extralegal traditions that permeated the culture. When the United States purchased Louisiana in 1803, the smuggling base at Barataria came to epitomize, for U.S. officials, the casual attitude toward the law held by many people in the acquired territory. After the abolition of the African slave trade, Louisiana became a leading haven for scofflaws who continued a healthy traffic in human property from the Caribbean and West Africa.[1]

Amid this long tradition of relaxed attitudes toward law and regulation, ethnic, racial, and economic strife among Louisiana's diverse population helped to accentuate the problem. Francophone Acadians distrusted incoming Anglo-Celtic settlers, while other ethnic enclaves, including the Germans of the Lac Des Allemands region and the various free black communities of the Louisiana hinterland, remained insular and wary. The agricultural exploitation of the state heightened these divisions, accelerated by the aggressive and energetic cotton culture of the lower South, whose newly rich entrepreneurs advanced into the northern reaches of the state and eclipsed in power and numbers the population that had lived

there for generations. The fabulously opulent and factory-like sugar operations of southern Louisiana brought wealth and prosperity to the region,
but this wealth, too, did not flow evenly to many of the people who witnessed this new immigration. Before long, Louisiana emerged as a balkan-
ized state, with Anglo-Celtic Southerners dominating the red lands of the
north, while foreign and newcomer capitalists controlled the wealth of the
sugar parishes, leaving many of the poorer French-speaking population
searching to accommodate the strangers while clinging to their traditional,
and somewhat xenophobic, culture. By 1861, Louisiana was a land of
blurred loyalties and simmering animosities.

   Louisiana's guerrilla war came about as a process of evolution. Secession
created an opening for legitimizing lawlessness already active in the society. Union occupation fractured and fragmented the ties binding the population together. Union policies, especially confiscation and conscription,
provided the fuel that kept the fires of private civil wars burning. The slide
into guerrilla chaos began in April 1862 with the arrival of the Yankees, a
radical blow to the status quo. The Confederate government of Louisiana
fled before the advance of Flag Officer David Glasgow Farragut's gunboats,
while the infantry of General Benjamin Butler seized and controlled New
Orleans, the most important economic site in the state. Together, these
hammer blows of the Union war effort threatened Louisiana's interior with
the twin plagues of anarchy and, increasingly, famine, as traditional agriculture and lines of market exchange broke down.

   Rapid emancipation added to the combustible human fuel in the
Louisiana furnace. "Freedom meant freedom to starve," one Confederate
soldier noted upon discovery of a particularly pitiful group of freedmen. The
same conditions that pinched the more established residents of Louisiana
punished newly free blacks, leading them to a life of abject dependence on
U.S. largess or to a life of depredation and predatory raiding.[2]

   U.S. war planners knew that a firm clutch on lands west of the
Mississippi remained vital to controlling the course of that river. The Red
River, that great divide of Louisiana culture, also divided the Louisiana
west bank into distinct strategic zones. Southwest Louisiana, that area
from New Orleans to the rust-colored Red, fell into a number of easily
discerned avenues along the great Atchafalaya Basin. This forty-mile-
wide swamp harbored numerous streams and bayous that mingled and

twined around the Atchafalaya River, which in turned connected the Red River to the Gulf of Mexico more than one hundred miles away. Few places in its interior lay above the surrounding waters. Dry land lay between the Atchafalya Basin and the Mississippi River to the east, and Bayou Teche to the west. An added feature was Bayou Lafourche, which had at one time been the main channel of the Mississippi. It left the Father of Waters at Donaldsonville and proceeded south by southeast to the Gulf of Mexico while the Mississippi made its great turn to the east toward New Orleans. The lands bordering Bayou Lafourche composed the so-called Lafourche District, an area known for huge mansions and fabulous wealth.

Control of the Louisiana bank of the Mississippi, however, would come with terrible baggage. While the highly prized acres of the Lafourche District would provide a great supply of livestock, commodities, and labor, the land marginal to the surrounding swamps would provide safe haven for guerrillas. An occupying Federal army would have to secure their gains west of the river by an aggressive counterinsurgency policy that encompassed the great Atchafalaya Basin south of Red River.

Northeast Louisiana, too, seemed custom-made for insurgent operations. North of Red River lay another zone of tangled waterways. As though a northern extension of the Atchafalaya, the mouth of the Black River entered the Red near its junction with the Mississippi. To follow it upstream meant a torturous sixty-mile trip around tight bends, with the Tensas breaking off to the east to create a twenty-five-mile-wide strip of swamps and cotton fields on the Mississippi's western littoral. A few miles further on lay the first high ground, at Harrisonburg, followed shortly by the junction of the river's great branches, the navigable Ouachita coursing generally north by west through Monroe, and the smaller feeder streams that composed the Beouf drainage system to the east.

Croplands bordering the Mississippi would provide useful materials of war to the Federals, but the maze of bayous in the Tensas and Black River systems also housed a hundred different refuges for guerrillas. With a lower population density, however, this area could not support as large a number of combatants as other parts of the state.

The geography of Louisiana suggested obvious strategies for Yankee and Rebel alike. The Federal invaders realized quickly that the Atchafalaya

Basin and Tensas River Basin would serve as a natural no-man's-land. Everything east of that point was within reach of the U.S. Navy or its landing parties. To the west southwest lay the Attakapas Prairies, while central and northern Louisiana were covered with red hills and piney woods. The keys to controlling the strategic areas bordering the Mississippi and Bayou Lafourche were the tenuous strips of arable land along the major streams which, generally speaking, all ran north to south. The potential gain made the effort worthwhile, since these same acres were among the most valuable on earth. Huge plantations lay side by side for miles on end, and millions of dollars in agricultural commodities had flowed yearly from Louisiana in happier times. Cattle and horses abounded, as did other forms of wealth, including some 21,500 slaves in the Lafourche District alone. To Confederates, only a determined defense by a sizable force would keep these treasures in Southern hands. Barring that, mounted troops might, through the use of frequent raids, keep the enemy from gaining much benefit from its conquests. As events unfolded, the Rebel government could provide neither men nor the resolution to hold the rich west bank of the Mississippi. In the face of this reality, and given the divided nature of the state, many of its citizens looked to position themselves to best advantage given the new realities.

When the Yankee warships first made their appearance in the spring of 1862, the urgency and alarm along the shore, especially west of the river, betrayed just how totally unprepared the Pelican State was for this invasion. Confederate planners had divided the state three ways, with the Florida parishes east of Baton Rouge administered from Jackson, Mississippi, the sugar parishes and Acadiana north to Alexandria served from Houston, and the northern parishes aligned with the army headquarters in Little Rock. This placed all of Louisiana west of the Mississippi at the fringes of their respective military districts. Far from the centers of command, men and materiel had been siphoned away until literally none remained beside an unmotivated militia. The citizens of Louisiana, thus unprotected, lay at the mercy of the Union invaders.

As a result, planters in the western parishes faced difficult choices. As long-time supporters of Whig politics, the sugar growers of southern Louisiana saw the arrival of the Yankees as a event not necessarily to be embraced, but potentially far short of the disaster bewailed by their pro-

Confederate neighbors. Many shrewd businessmen sought immediate contact with U.S. troops to safeguard their plantations and to guarantee a market for their crops. Instead of burning their cotton and wetting their sugar,
they cached it away to await events. Many, however, trusted neither the
Union invaders nor their neighbors and made plans to evacuate. Others,
defiant in the face of a grave situation, clung to their property, quietly con-
fident and secretly hopeful that someone would come to their rescue.[3]

The nature of the Union presence in Louisiana revealed itself quickly.
On May 28, as Union troops arrived in front of Baton Rouge, Confederate
partisans fired at a boat party coming ashore. Incensed, Farragut ordered
the big guns of U.S.S. *Hartford* and U.S.S. *Kennebec* to shell the town.
The panicked residents of the surrendered city fled the maelstrom, which
killed a woman and caused two other citizens to fall into the river and
drown.[4]

Elisa Bragg, the wife of one of the Confederacy's rising generals,
Braxton Bragg, saw war firsthand as the Hoosiers of the Twenty-first
Indiana passed by her farm near the town of Thibodaux. "A detachment
came [to town] searching for arms and ammunition," she wrote to her
warrior husband. "They brought a cannon, but said it would be unnecessary as they could have taken the town with brickbats." After obtaining
keys to the public buildings, the U.S. troops conducted their search, found
nothing of importance, and then promised to return. "They say they will
return in a little while to seize cattle," she wrote. Ominously, though, Mrs.
Bragg described an even more immediate concern: "We can get nothing
from [New Orleans], and no place is provided with provisions. The house-
holds have no supplies." For civilians in this new war zone, a host of
troubles loomed, not the least of which might be famine.[5]

Butler, like Farragut, believed that military necessity required a firm
hand in the region; and he moved to control as much of Louisiana as he
could, as rapidly as he could, to exploit the region's momentary defenselessness. Despite occasional raids by Rebel partisans, the few hundred
Union troops patrolling along the Opelousas Railroad proved to be
adequate for its defense. When required, the bluecoat infantry made forays
to break up gatherings of Louisiana militia; but aside from a few skirmishes, the summer of 1862 would pass without serious challenge to the
tightening Union control.[6]

Uncontested occupation favored Butler, who also harbored a sincere love of profit. With the aid of his brother, Andrew, the general began scheming to plunder the state. Within weeks, the two were speculating heavily in rum, sugar, salt, cotton, and even Texas beef cattle, employing soldiers and sailors to carry contraband of war to New Orleans for auction. Loyal planters, with the judicious application of bribes, sent their goods to the city and into Union lines without fear.[7]

On July 12, President Abraham Lincoln signed the Confiscation Act, greatly expanding the Butler boys' ability to plunder. Already hip deep in semi-legal trade with loyal planters, they could now target the homes and real estate of Confederate soldiers as forfeitures to the Republic. Unionists—including many of Butler's cronies—spent the summer occupying these seized and abandoned plantations, paying freed slaves a wage to continue raising crops which were in turn sold in New Orleans and shipped by sea to the North. The middlemen in this traffic made money by shepherding and safeguarding these war-rare commodities to eager Yankee merchants and factory owners. In Louisiana, this meant U.S. troops guarded the workers on government plantations, and the Butler brothers used their position and access to siphon profits.[8]

The crafty Butler was also careful to cultivate allies and punish enemies. The poor and destitute in the newly occupied areas received food and clothing seized from Confederate sympathizers. By this stratagem, the Union occupiers began to enjoy the support of a newly beholden constituency. With the looting mood upon the land, the discipline of the Union troops in southern Louisiana eroded as everyone sampled the spoils of war. Field officers, with the tacit approval of Butler and the Confiscation Act, helped themselves to furniture, silverware, art, and valuables while the rank and file worked over livestock, crops, and anything not under guard. For many Federal troops, the abundance of sugar and rum was bewildering and delightful. Despite laws and orders issued to stop the plundering, the destruction in Louisiana proceeded at a steadily accelerating pace.[9]

Governor Thomas O. Moore of Louisiana, shocked at the enemy occupation of his state, took the initiative to rally resistance to the invasion. With his government forced west of the Mississippi by early May, Moore authorized the creation of two new training camps, one at Monroe in northeastern Louisiana, and the other near Opelousas. This town would also serve as the new state capital. In the absence of Confederate troops west of the Mississippi, Moore began raising partisan ranger companies— semi-irregulars exempted from conscription into regular volunteer units— to keep the Yankees at bay until reinforcements could arrive. On June 14, he also activated two thousand militia; they only haphazardly answered his call. All of the newly constituted military units west of the river faced extreme shortages of uniforms, camp equipment, and weapons, for all of the war materiel saved from New Orleans, it seemed, had been seized for the defense of Vicksburg. In addition, Confederate officers in Little Rock had appropriated all military property in Alexandria. Moore demanded better support from the Confederate government, requesting that officers be sent from Virginia to organize and drill his ragged troops. In the mean-time, he ordered detachments of these untrained levies to guard the mouth of the Red River and to patrol the Mississippi.[10]

In early summer, Moore sent Lieutenant Colonel Valsin Fournet's Tenth "Yellow Jacket" Battalion of Louisiana infantry, a duly constituted Confederate unit, but full of conscripts, into the Lafourche District in an attempt to rally its militia. The Confederates succeeded in bloodying Union troops in a few heated gun battles and ambushes, but failed to gain the much-needed confidence of the locals. On June 25, one local militia captain rode to see if Fournet's troops would remain along the Lafourche long enough to rally his men. "[Fournet] stated that he was ordered to come here for five or six days and expected the Malitia [sic] to be drawn out of the parishes to keep this country free from the enemy," related the officer. In fact, the Tenth Louisiana Battalion was actively preparing to evacuate the region. The militia captain's spirits plummeted as he explained to the Confederate leader the severe shortages of weapons, ammunition, and sup-plies: "I stated . . . that it would be impossible to get out the Malitia here without a force." Unmoved, Fournet withdrew his troops back into the Attakapas country, reporting to his superiors that the militia had refused to cooperate.[11] Three days later, the commander of the St. James Parish militia regiment reinforced this perception by writing, "[I]t is in my opin-ion entirely impracticable to attempt any thing. . . . We are as completely under control of the Federal forces as [New Orleans] itself."[12]

Moore's attempt at military strategy continued to backfire. Without a shred of Confederate support, the militia commanders were insubordinate, oftentimes making their own policy and countermanding orders from the governor. Very soon the leading citizens of the Lafourche District, especially those along the Mississippi River, made clear to the Confederate leadership that without a substantial infusion of weapons and troops, the militia would stay home. "It would be unwise to invite by a vain display of our meager resources, the attack of a ruthless enemy who would not hesitate to spread desolation over our land and deprive our women and children of shelters," declared Colonel W. W. Pugh of the Assumption Parish Regiment. "If our militia is to be called into active service, there should be a supporting force of sufficient magnitude to give it . . . the semblance of a successful resistance. . . . There is a serious doubt, whether the militia as a body can be brought into active service without aid of a sustaining force from some other quarter."[13]

Governor Moore answered this stand by dispatching two mounted companies of irregulars to Donaldsonville. Refusing in turn to follow directives of militia officers, these raiders took positions along the Mississippi and harassed passing gunboats. These troops also began to plunder anyone considered to be lukewarm to the Confederacy, driving some of their fellow Louisianans to the invaders for refuge. Fearing Federal retribution, the mayor of Donaldsonville begged the Confederates to stop their activities in the area. Partisan Captain James A. McWaters simply replied that he would take it under advisement with the governor.[14]

As feared, Union forces brooked no resistance. When McWaters's gunmen began firing at navy vessels from the vicinity of Donaldsonville in mid-July, Admiral Farragut simply stated, "Every time my boats are fired upon, I will burn a portion of your town."[15] On August 9, with the attacks continuing, he made good on the warning and shelled the town before sending ashore troops to enhance the destruction.

A worse fate befell Baton Rouge that same week. After Confederates under John C. Breckinridge unsuccessfully attempted to retake the town on August 5, General Butler ordered the town destroyed and his exposed garrison withdrawn to New Orleans to protect that city. Within a week, the town had been sacked as soldiers cut down its massive shade trees, plundered its homes, and crated up its art for shipment to New Orleans and ultimately points north. A third of its homes lay burned. This terrorism had its desired effect.[16]

Based on the Union reaction to guerrilla activities, militia officers west of the river moved to curtail Rebel activities. By mid-August, militia troops arrested McWaters and another partisan captain in response to what they considered irresponsible behavior. This event got Moore's attention, which in turn restrained his aggressive yet ineffective military operations in favor of regaining the support of the Lafourche citizens. He banned illicit trade with Union-controlled areas. He then began organizing relief drives to help the indigent—especially soldiers' families. Later, Moore promoted Confederate associations to encourage patriotism and a sense of loyalty to the Rebel cause. Eventually, all of his work would begin to have an effect as the situation in southwestern Louisiana stabilized. Still, in Moore's opinion, the Confederacy was reacting slowly to a crisis that would surely get out of hand.[17]

In Richmond, the impact of the fall of New Orleans, while a body blow to Confederate dreams of independence, had dissipated with distance and time. More immediate dangers lay to the east, a few dozen miles from the city. Union General George B. McClellan, in command of the ballooning Army of the Potomac, began his march down the peninsula that May, driving back Confederate forces under Joseph E. Johnston. The Battle of Seven Pines, followed quickly by news of determined fighting in the Shenandoah and later by the savagery of the Seven Days, distracted Confederate leadership. President Jefferson Davis and Secretary of War George W. Randolph, consumed with events nearby, took until late summer to react to the calamity on the Mississippi.[18]

The government asked General P. G. T. Beauregard to comment as to the feasibility of recapturing New Orleans. "Of course I should be both proud and happy to drive from my native state the abolitionists who are now desecrating its soil," the Creole veteran had replied. "We can retake New Orleans but we cannot hold it without subjecting it to destruction . . . and its destruction would be attended with a degree of human misery frightful to contemplate, without a proper return of evil to the enemy." The famously ambitious hero of Manassas and Shiloh declined to endorse an offensive against Butler. Recapturing New Orleans, he replied, "would not even give us the command of a single foot of ground along the Mississippi, much less the river itself; hence, why make the sacrifice?"[19]

This answer satisfied Jefferson Davis, but not Randolph. Besides creating the Confederate District of Louisiana on August 20 out of the parishes west of the great river, Randolph's only other available solution was to dispatch any spare troops he could find to this arena of war. He also sent a talented officer, Richard Taylor.[20]

Taylor arrived and stabilized the situation by removing Louisiana's militia regiments from their home parishes, clearly establishing an identifying line between friend and foe. Confederate sympathizers of service age in the Pelican State would henceforth be serving with the army, farther east. Men in their prime left lurking near home would be obvious conscription dodgers or, more simply, foes, and subject to Rebel justice. By doing so, Taylor advanced a pet theory that soldiers fought best the farther away they were from home, and he intended to defend Louisiana with troops from Texas. When the militia, reporting to the general's orders, headed to conscription camps and, ultimately, the armies in Tennessee and Virginia, their numbers were noticeably smaller than indicated on muster rolls. The new policy had simply prompted many militiamen to hide out in an attempt to escape the Rebel snare or take the loyalty oath in Union-held areas.[21]

Taylor had little time to complete this process before a Federal offensive gobbled up more of the state. In the last months of 1862, a Union offensive under General Godfrey Weitzel overran the Lafourche District, establishing a garrisoned and defined presence in the region while driving Taylor's army west of the Atchafalaya Basin. The Lafourche District militias still on hand scattered or returned to their homes while the Federals claimed victory and declared the region pacified.[22]

The nature of the Union occupation quickly revealed itself to the indecisive citizens of occupied Louisiana. With Confederate control of riparian Louisiana broken, the philosophical agents of the Union war effort sought to implement their vision of a postwar South. The labor system, obviously doomed, had to be reconstructed. Confiscated plantations also needed to be brought back into production. Until such a new order could be imposed, though, former slaves found themselves displaced and homeless, often in want of the basic necessities. Poor whites and others found themselves competing with semi-lawless groups of displaced peoples, coupled with skulking conscripts, and further burdened by Yankee depredations into increasing levels of despair and panic. Union battlefield successes also shook hundreds of reluctant Rebels loose from their organized commands, sending them into the swamps and out on prairies to fend for themselves as they tried to wait out the war.[23]

Union planners proposed several solutions for these problems. To reinvigorate the agricultural bounty of Louisiana, confiscated plantations would be leased by the government to contracting operators, most of whom were from the North. The labor issue remained a larger challenge. Ultimately, former slaves would be turned into wage laborers on government-owned plantations or put into the army—an experiment in its infancy in late 1862. The junction of these agricultural and military concerns began a process of social engineering that had far-reaching implications for the population of Louisiana.[24]

In December 1862, General Nathaniel P. Banks assumed command of the Department of the Gulf, including southern Louisiana, and laid ambitious plans for the subjugation of the state. Under orders to act in concert with the Union efforts to control the Mississippi, Banks received a large amount of discretion as to what this meant in practical terms. Dedicated to the idea of emancipated labor and inspired by a New England reformist impulse, the new department commander saw Louisiana west of the Mississippi as a suitable laboratory for his views on a new South. He also realized that, in the parishes west of the Atchafalaya, a wealth of plunder awaited a successful invading army. As Banks formulated his strategy, his attention focused on a sweep up Bayou Teche to Alexandria, and from there to coordinate with the Federals further north.

General Ulysses S. Grant led the army with which Banks was to cooperate. Already in control of the riparian parishes of northeastern Louisiana, this force struggled to find a route around Vicksburg. Establishing a fortified line between Lake Providence and Milliken's Bend, some thirty thousand U.S. soldiers marched through this low country in a move that, in March and April 1863, would ultimately bypass the Rebel citadel all together. For this detour to succeed, however, the West Bank had to be held secure against any Confederate threat.

Banks saw to that. His campaign in April and May scattered Taylor's Rebels in two directions. The Confederate commander fell back to Natchitoches with part of his command, while most of the newly arrived Texans made a dash for the Sabine River, where they regrouped at Niblett's Bluff. Banks's columns paused in the country around Washington and Opelousas where the level of their plundering reached new heights. Even

Union officers reported disgust at the actions of their commands. After having decided not to turn west toward Texas, Banks restarted his offensive to
the north and captured, then burned, Alexandria. Convinced that Grant
did not need his help, the commander of the Department of the Gulf
instead turned southeast toward Port Hudson, which he besieged starting
in late May.[25]

The Union strategy would succeed. Just weeks before, the Confederacy
had placed the Trans-Mississippi under the command of Edmund Kirby
Smith. He, and his most capable subordinate, Taylor, proved unable to
counter both enemy threats in Louisiana. Instead, the Rebels in Louisiana
found themselves scattered and on the defensive. In the end, both enemy
juggernauts snared the Mississippi River strongholds and starved the Rebels
into submission.

West of the river, Kirby Smith's lack of imagination manifested itself.
Instead of shepherding all of his department's resources against either
Banks or Grant, he allowed his forces to be committed piecemeal. As a
result, the actions of Taylor's little army, and other Texas reinforcements
that arrived that summer, proved to be of little value. In late June and early
July, Taylor's command did manage successfully to invade the Lafourche
District, disrupting the activities at Union plantations and conscript camps
but failing to effect Banks's strategy. In the end, this brave showing came
to naught as Taylor withdrew his forces back across the Atchafalaya, aban-
doning the region for good.

During the campaigns of the summer of 1863, Union observers
claimed to see guerrillas everywhere, when in fact most were regularly
enlisted members of Confederate regiments. Naval planners leveled most
of the charges against the South's use of such "uncivilized" warfare, but
their observations tended to confuse the actions of mounted troops atop
the river levee with those of actual guerrillas. To respond to this threat,
the navy created the Marine Brigade, designed to act as a counterguerrilla
unit for operation in southeastern Arkansas and northeastern Louisiana.
Largely ineffective, this special unit instead turned to informal tactics of
their own as they plundered the countryside. There were guerrillas operating in Louisiana, and more would do so in the coming months, but to a
steamboat skipper dodging bullets in his pilot house, all hostile snipers
looked and acted like guerrillas, no matter what their unit affiliation.

The summer of 1863 revealed much about the way war would be fought in Louisiana in the future. The passage of armies, the breakdown of order and society, and the availability of disaffected manpower resurrected guerrilla bands and made them increasingly bold. The terrain along the Mississippi made the deployment of large bodies of troops there risky and subject to being cut off by Union troops aboard transports, so guerrilla-style tactics became especially useful. Small groups of men on hit-and-run attacks added to the frustration of Union planners, especially those in the navy; but the lack of discipline among these raiders also led to depredations against civilians. Before long, no one was safe in the war-ravaged parishes, no matter their politics. For those who gloried in the role, Louisiana became a haven for guerrillas, even attracting the disciples of William Clark Quantrill from Missouri to the Tensas River region.

Down south, in Acadiana, the problem of undisciplined and unaffiliated bands began to plague Confederate planners as well. West of Washington, a sizable band of jayhawkers plundered the neighborhood, keeping the home guard at bay. Politicians and soldiers alike identified most of the perpetrators as skulking conscripts, deserters, or free blacks. Estimated at more than three hundred men, under the command of a Cajun named Carrier, locals called these raiders "the clan," and identified them as pro-Union jayhawkers. Whoever they were, Louisiana civil authorities asked Taylor and his soldiers to intervene.

He ordered two companies of Texas cavalry to rendezvous with the local home guard and attempt to flush out the guerrillas. "The outrageous acts of the conscripts, deserters, and free Negroes who inhabit the region . . . came to the knowledge of the 'powers that be,'" wrote Texan private William Howell of the Fifth Texas Cavalry. "There is quite a number . . . who have taken to the woods and bottoms and evaded the enrolling officers, and declared it to be their intention not to fight for either Federal or Confederate governments." This soldier—and his comrades—were not buying the jayhawker's declaration of neutrality. When Union troops had been in the area, these same ruffians had served as guides in exchange, rumors said, for permission to plunder their pro-Southern neighbors. "This clan formed an alliance with the 'rail-splitters' minions," the Texan reported, "to . . . murder alike citizen and soldier."[26]

The sweep occurred on the night of August 8. Numbering about seventy-five men, the Confederates moved west from Washington at 5 P.M. under the command of Captain J. A. A. West of Taylor's staff. When

they arrived at Bayou Mallet, the troops broke into three parties with lists
of houses to search and persons to capture. At each targeted house, soldiers surrounded the building while a storming party broke in and
searched the dwelling. Soon, captures were made. "Thus we hunt conscripts," wrote Howell, "visiting a man's house at the hour of midnight
and in some instances we took them away." Often, the people seized had
families on hand to witness the violence. "The women in some cases
appeared much grieved, and cried and begged at an awful rate, when their
husbands, fathers, and brothers were taken away," the Texan continued.
Most, he contemptuously noted, spoke only French: "As we could not
'Parly Francais,' their wails amounted to nothing at all." By morning, the
Texans rounded up a dozen men described as "deserters from the army"
or "liable to conscription." Home guards escorted the men to Opelousas
for imprisonment and trial.[27]

On August 9, the guerrillas retaliated. A party of around fifty mounted
jayhawkers emerged from the woods and surprised a group of Texans
scrounging for breakfast at the home of two free blacks in the area. The
Texans, many of whom were sleeping off the night's weariness, thought
nothing of the approach of the guerrillas, assuming they were friends.
Several of the Texans mounted up to exchange greetings with the new-
comers, only to be met by shotgun blasts. Private J. W. Watkins of the
Fifth Texas Cavalry, napping at the time of the attack, wrote, "I got up
when the firing commenced." Confused, milling soldiers surrounded him.
"Our officers were still calling out 'not to shoot, they are our men.' [So]
I wasn't in a hurry." Not until a wounded comrade rode up did Watkins
learn the gravity of the situation. "I . . . found his thigh broken just above
the knee. [The jayhawkers] commenced a cross-fire on me about that
time," he added, "I thought it best to get out of there." Watkins and the
rest of the Rebels mounted and fled, heading for the open prairies and the
safety of their compatriots. When Captain West had concentrated his
troops, he ordered them to stand fast in the open country until the whereabouts of the enemy could be determined. That afternoon, the Second
Louisiana Cavalry and the remainder of the Fifth Texas Cavalry arrived
to reinforce the mission. These horse soldiers received new orders, according to Howell, to "scour the woods and country for miles around, and to
shoot every man connected with the clan."[28]

The nearly three hundred Texas and Louisiana troops formed a long line of battle the following day and headed into the woods, "driving for them as if for deer." That evening, August 10, the Confederates surprised a large number of the clan in their camps and immediately opened fire. "Most of them fled," Howell remembered, "while two or three stood up [and] fired." Two more Texans fell wounded, one mortally. The Confederate riders lunged ahead and rounded up four of the guerrillas and marked them for death. "The family of one of them came to take leave of him a few minutes before he was led out to be shot, and it was truly an unpleasant scene," Howell wrote. "Methinks I can hear that woman and her children's cries to this moment." Private Watkins, who had come close to being killed, was more callous. "As soon as we captured them," he wrote home to his wife, "we walked them out of stinking distance and shot them."[29]

Texans in Louisiana, based on their recent experience battling the clan, cautioned their countrymen to stay at home. "I am writing this for the purpose of informing the citizens of Texas, who may intend travelling from Niblett's Bluff to the eastward, of the state of affairs existing in this portion of the state," Howell wrote. "After the late punishment inflicted on the conscripts, consider it very unsafe for small parties to travel alone."[30]

In fact, the punitive expedition had broken the back of the clan and, after an offer of amnesty, many Confederate deserters and conscripts turned themselves in. Even so, a renewed Federal offensive would have an even greater chilling effect on guerrilla activities in southwestern Louisiana. General Banks, urged to make a lodgment in Texas, planned a two-pronged invasion of that state from his enclaves along the Mississippi and the Lafourche District. In September, Texans successfully fended off an invasion of their coast at Sabine Pass and checked Union advances east of the Atchafalaya. Banks responded by driving up Bayou Teche, retracing his route of April and May, driving the Rebels before him, but again halting near Washington, Louisiana. After remaining idle for several weeks, and losing a few pitched skirmishes to Brigadier General Tom Green's Texans, Banks withdrew to New Iberia and put his men into camps for the winter. The presence, then, of sizable armies in the neighborhood discouraged unconventional warriors from emerging from their lairs.[31]

In the meantime, though, the harsh, yearlong Union occupation began to reap its bitter harvest. Surprisingly, many Louisianans who took the oath of loyalty to the Union subsequently took up arms against the United States as members of guerrilla bands. Espousal of the Federal cause did not exempt them from confiscation as was hoped. Texan W. L. Robards, reporting on what he was seeing in Louisiana, wrote a note to the Houston newspaper: "You may tell Union men, if there be any in Texas, [that] Union sentiment will avail them nothing with Yankees." Having campaigned in the Lafourche District during the summer of 1863, the soldier was shocked at conditions there after nine months of Union control. If a plantation owner "whipped a Negro," Robards wrote, "his testimony was sufficient to convict and send the master to Fort Jackson." Whites, he reported, were kept under constant surveillance. "A white man can go no where without a pass; a Negro was permitted to go and come when he pleased." Many of these loyal planters began having second thoughts about their allegiance to the Union, especially when commissary officers pressed their supplies and livestock for the good of the army. "It is a remarkable fact," Robards continued, "that Union men suffer most in loss of property. They respect the man who is ready to fight for his country, or do all in his power to help the cause, while they detest the cringing sycophant."[32]

Those taking the oath of loyalty to the Union had another cause to regret their decision as well. These men became subject to conscription, much as their former slaves had become. Starting in 1863, Federal officers began ordering white Louisianans, both those who had taken the oath of loyalty and some who had simply been paroled from the Confederate army, into Federal service under the laws of the Conscription Act. Those who had desired to remain neutral in the war, for whatever motivation, now had to choose. For some, this meant heading into the backcountry and joining the growing number of guerrillas gathering in remote camps and secret hideouts.[33]

The following spring, 1864, Banks tried again to finish the job in Louisiana and to turn west against Texas. This time accompanied by a sizable fleet, he ordered a two-pronged invasion toward Alexandria from the Mississippi and up the Teche, to act in concert with an advance from Arkansas. After the Louisiana elements united in the center of the state, the army and navy would proceed up the Red River to Shreveport where, if all went well, they would join the Arkansas column. This campaign stalled after Confederates under Taylor stopped the Federal advance at Mansfield and Pleasant Hill on April 8–9, then pursued them back to Alexandria. By early May, Banks and his army retreated, leaving the Rebels in control of a plundered and war-ravaged state.

As in previous years, this passage of large armies left chaos in its wake. The same allegations regarding guerrillas were leveled against Texans operating against Union shipping, but records reveal that mostly these troops were duly enlisted Confederate soldiers. By the end of the summer, 1864, the old battle lines of the previous year fell back into place, but the large armies had moved on to other fields. The absence of large armies left the arena to nasty little contests instead of great battles. The new combatants, instead of the veteran regiments of Banks and Taylor, were freed blacks serving as plantation guards, various small, white garrisons of detachments and battalions, and guerrillas who were busy settling the scores of the previous years.

In the sugar parishes, now the backwater of the Trans-Mississippi, guerrilla warfare flared with a hot intensity, and bands of partisans multiplied throughout the region. The majority of these irregulars in the Lafourche District, for instance, displayed, if not pro-Southern proclivities, certainly anti-Yankee sentiment. Most were sixteen- to twenty-year-old Acadians from the backcountry of the Atchafalaya Basin, but with a fair number of other Louisiana men representing the broad economic and ethnic spectrum of its population. These raiders, in true guerrilla fashion, lived off the generosity of their neighbors, slept in safe houses, and preyed upon the Unionist planters and merchants against whom they nursed prewar grudges. Included in this mix were detachments of regular Confederate units, including the Second Louisiana Cavalry, which numbered many of Moore's old partisan ranger companies in its ranks. In addition, Taylor authorized the organization of two more mounted regiments, the Seventh and Eighth Cavalries, filling them with pardoned conscripts who had turned themselves in after Captain West's raid near Washington. They were formed to combat jayhawkers in the Teche and Attakapas country; Taylor had in essence decided to use guerrillas to hunt guerrillas—or Yankees—as the situation dictated. East of the Atchafalaya, the newly constituted Fifth Louisiana Cavalry used unconventional tactics in its operations near the junction of the Red and Mississippi Rivers and points south. Another band, led by an Arkansas captain, H. U. M. C. Brown, had served as partisans in other theaters of the war but had relocated their operations to the woods and swamps of Louisiana, as had a partisan named Williams. While these new formations usually acted independently, they occasionally served as part of larger Confederate operations in the area, and their knowledge of the back roads and byways of Louisiana served their cause well.[34]

These irregulars gave Union commanders in the area fits. Even as Banks was marshalling his forces for the Red River Campaign of 1864, Rebel partisans infiltrated into supposedly safe Union enclaves to create havoc. Thibodaux, especially its merchants in contact with Union contractors, suffered repeated attacks as arsonists burned stores and stocks with increasing regularity. When Union patrols moved into the countryside, snipers harried their movements. Eventually, the tempo and severity of these attacks led Federal leaders to launch campaigns to seek out and destroy the guerrilla strongholds. On most such occasions, the insurgents fled after only token resistance; but the bluecoats netted few prisoners and saw their frustrations mount as the guerrilla menace remained unabated. Oftentimes, the partisans would follow close on the heels of these Union probes with campaigns of their own, carrying away livestock and torching the homes of Union families.[35]

These raids and retaliations fueled a deepening bitterness, which led to a bloody autumn in 1864. Union war planners decided that a cordon of fortified towns and villages would provide an effective tool for countering Rebel incursions, and established garrisons at key positions up and down Bayou Lafourche. At first, expeditions launched from these strategic strongholds—aided by local guides—drove away the guerrillas and made impressive gains in returning stability to the region. These raids succeeded in destroying houses and caches of food, but failed to break down the guerrilla's ability to move swiftly and with surprise. Within weeks, the ephemeral enemy had returned. By winter the partisans had caged the Union troops in their fortified towns and enclaves, leading the Rebels to grow bolder still. In January 1865, a series of clashes between Union forces and guerrillas around Donaldsonville and Plaquemine illustrated just how badly out of hand the problem had become as the Third

Rhode Island Cavalry and Eighteenth U.S. Colored Infantry limped back into those towns, obviously roughed up. By February, Brigadier General Robert A. Cameron, the Union commander of the Lafourche District, decided that the conventional approach had not worked: "If we pursue them with cavalry, they take to their canoes and small boats. If we undertake to cut them off with a gun-boat, they run into a chain of smaller bayous where a gun-boat cannot follow." Cameron reorganized his command to increase their effectiveness as a counterguerrilla force.[36]

As the war wound down, time ran out for the Rebels. In early April, Cameron's strike force finally caught and scattered Captain William A. Whitaker's band of partisans operating out of the Atchafalaya Basin. Upon receiving word that one hundred Rebels, spearheaded by Company C, Seventh Louisiana Cavalry, were heading into the Lafourche District, Cameron formed a trap to block the guerrilla's approach and to cut off their retreat. Several hundred men from the Ninety-third U.S. Colored Infantry, the Sixteenth Indiana Mounted Infantry, the Seventy-fifth U.S. Colored Troops, the First Louisiana Cavalry (U.S.), the Third Rhode Island Cavalry, and the Eleventh U.S. Colored Heavy Artillery succeeded in surprising Whitaker's men deep in the Atchafalaya swamps. In two days of fighting, Union troops captured or killed one out of five of the partisans and drove the rest away. Next, Cameron's men turned their attention to Brown, and by mid-May, managed to wound him and scatter his forces for good. On May 27, Federals surprised Omer Boudreaux's detachment of Company C, Seventh Louisiana, capturing one and wounding the guerrilla chief in a fight south of Houma.[37]

The fall of Boudreaux effectively ended the Civil War phase of the guerrilla war in the Pelican State. Of course, murder and plundering relating to the war continued in Louisiana, just under a different designation and at a reduced level. The violence that had wracked western Louisiana from 1861 to 1865 had many faces and many antecedents, and peace between North and South would never solve them all. In most general histories of the Civil War, this theater of conflict is often dismissed as irrelevant; and most military treatments, in fact, close out the war in Louisiana with the end of the Red River Campaign in the early summer of 1864. As has been demonstrated, however, men, women, and children died and suffered all the same until the closing moments of the national struggle. Reconstruction violence in Louisiana, like that of other Trans-Mississippi states, has been categorized by historians as a separate phenomenon from its Civil War counterpart. Most likely, though, they are more closely related.

Louisiana proved to be a near perfect incubator for guerrilla warfare. Its geography and society certainly contributed to the nature of the warfare. The passing of armies, rampant looting, Reconstruction policies, and white and black conscription helped to breed bitterness that accelerated this irregular war into a bitter and bloody struggle. This shadow war, though, like guerrilla activity in the rest of the Confederacy, remains an imperfectly known story.

# Bushwhackers, Provosts, and Tories: The Guerrilla War in Arkansas

## Robert R. Mackey

T HE CIVIL WAR in Arkansas had two dimensions, a conventional conflict between the organized military forces of the Union and Confederacy and a brutal guerrilla struggle that involved all levels of
Arkansas society, from the occupying Federal troops to freed slaves. The
conventional conflict absorbed most of the resources and manpower, and
it was the main focus of the military organizations on both sides. Yet
Arkansas became a backwater of the conventional war after the 1862 battles
of Pea Ridge and Prairie Grove, a sideshow that occasionally supported the
great campaigns of the war, such as the 1863 Vicksburg campaign, but
which never matched the strategic significance of the battlefields in
Virginia or Tennessee. Instead, the war in Arkansas was a conflict of a thousand skirmishes between regular and irregular forces and between the irregulars themselves.

The dilemma faced by Confederate leaders in both Little Rock and
Richmond in the dark days of early 1862 led them to turn to guerrilla warfare. The sixteen-thousand-man Army of the West, the main Confederate
field army in the Trans-Mississippi District, under the command of Major
General Earl Van Dorn, disintegrated after its defeat at the battle of Pea
Ridge in March 1862. So, as the Federal Army of the Southwest, commanded by Major General Samuel R. Curtis, marched across southern

Missouri and reentered northern Arkansas on April 29, only a handful of poorly armed state militia units remained to defend the state. Van Dorn had even stripped the state arsenals before he left, taking the few remaining military supplies and thus preventing the raising of new forces. The defenselessness of the state led Governor Henry M. Rector to threaten President Jefferson Davis with secession from the Confederacy and a negotiated peace with the Union. Davis, finally realizing the critical situation in Arkansas, named General Thomas C. Hindman as Van Dorn's successor. Hindman, a prominent politician in the state before the war, had little military experience, but he was energetic and wholly devoted to the Rebel cause.[1]

Desperate to turn back the Federal advance into Arkansas, Hindman resorted to organized guerrilla warfare. On June 17, 1862, he issued General Order No. 17, which called for the raising of independent guerrilla companies from men not subject to conscription. At the same time, all able-bodied males ages fifteen to forty-five were drafted to form his new Army of Arkansas. Hindman clearly saw the formation of this conventional field army as the main effort, with the independent companies serving in auxiliary roles. He and his officers expended little effort and sparse resources in organizing and arming the guerrillas. Hindman hoped that by permitting Arkansans to serve in their own districts and to organize as they saw fit, he could field additional men against the Northern juggernaut. In reality, he and the other Confederate leaders gave Arkansans carte blanche to fight the war without interference from the military or government and encouraged the spread of uncontrolled partisan units who owed loyalty to neither side.[2]

Federal commanders in Arkansas formulated several contrasting policies over the next three years as they struggled to deal with the guerrilla menace. Their first reaction was to pursue an antiguerrilla strategy aimed at killing guerrillas who attacked their invading columns. Very soon, however, they adopted a more elaborate two-tiered strategy aimed at cutting the guerrillas' logistical system by destroying the property of suspected supporters and, through aggressive offensive operations, eliminating irregular units.

The first tier of this strategy was retributive burning. When guerrillas fired on Union forces, local residents were held accountable for the attacks, and their homes and farms became forfeit. Federal troops would loot, then burn, the property of suspected guerrilla sympathizers. When guerrillas fired upon the forage trains of Colonel William Weer near King's River (east of Fayetteville), he ordered his subordinates to "proceed to said neighborhood [and] destroy every house and farm, &c., owned by secessionists, together with their property that cannot be made available to the army." Weer even ordered his men to "bring away the women and children to this place [the town of Carrollton, Arkansas, between Yellville and Fayetteville]," presumably as hostages against further guerrilla attacks.[3]

The second tier of their strategy required Union commanders to use mounted infantry or cavalry to catch and destroy the roving bands. Yet in Arkansas a lack of suitable mounts prevented a substantial expansion of cavalry units, many of which possessed enough horses for only half their men.[4] The wear and tear on these horses exacerbated the shortage, so that, beginning in the winter of 1863–64, the Federals limited most patrols to areas ten to fifteen miles around their major posts. Few statewide cavalry expeditions occurred until the last months of the war.[5]

Despite some Federal success with this policy, the quick-moving guerrilla bands still preyed upon small outposts, isolated detachments, foraging parties, and Arkansas Unionists. This realization—made worse by the political pressure to establish a loyal government in Arkansas by late 1863—produced yet another approach to combating guerrilla warfare, based on the assets available to the Federal army in Arkansas and the inventiveness of individual commanders.[6] The Union army needed a greater mix of counterinsurgency and pacification to eliminate guerrilla units and their base of popular support. The original direct attack on guerrillas remained a possible option, but Federal authorities came to recognize that it would not suffice to eliminate the guerrilla bands themselves, and that to target civilians was barbaric as well as ineffective, serving mainly to reinforce Confederate propaganda that portrayed all Northern soldiers as uncontrolled jayhawkers.[7]

Consequently, the Federals instituted four additional programs to counter guerrilla warfare and restore loyal civil government in the backcountry: a provost marshal enforcement system, expanded use of riverine assets (gunboats and ship-borne ground forces), recruitment of Arkansas

Unionists for counterguerrilla operations, and the development of fortified farm colonies.

The Union provost marshal system served to reestablish law and order
in occupied areas, gather intelligence on guerrillas, administer loyalty
oaths, and reinforce the legitimacy of the United States government in
Arkansas. The system duplicated one previously established in guerrilla-
infested areas of Missouri, especially in areas where the civilian legal structure had collapsed. The system would eventually play a major role in the
political reconstruction of Arkansas as it worked closely with the
Freedman's Bureau and became the clearinghouse for amnesty requests by
ex-Confederates. Interestingly, the Confederates had used a similar system to police their own guerrillas when they still controlled the state.

The Union provost marshal organization in Arkansas, typical of most
military police forces in the Civil War, consisted of officers and men drawn
from infantry units in the state and placed on detached duty with the Army
of Arkansas provost marshal general, Lieutenant Colonel John L. Chandler,
formerly the commander of the Seventh Missouri Cavalry.[8] Colonel
Chandler divided Arkansas into four districts, three under district provost
marshal generals (officers holding the rank of captain) and one under
his direct command. The Frontier District, based at Fort Smith, covered
the state's western counties and Indian Territory (modern Oklahoma).
Northeast Arkansas District and East Arkansas District, operating out of
Batesville and Helena, respectively, covered Union-occupied Arkansas
from the north-central region to the Louisiana border. The Central
Arkansas District, commanded by Colonel Chandler, included Little Rock
and the surrounding counties. The district provosts marshal maintained a
substantially smaller staff than the department's provost marshal general,
without secret service or military prison sections. Weekly reports flowing
from district to state level kept Colonel Chandler advised of the state of
his far-flung command.

Chandler saw his mission as twofold. His primary set of goals included
the "general police of the army and of the towns and country occupied, the
arrest of stragglers and deserters and forwarding them to their Regiments,
the suppressing of brawls, bawdy houses, drunkenness and disorderly conduct." These missions provided the regimental commanders and the commanding general with the discipline needed to keep their forces effective.

His second objective, tied directly to the guerrilla war, was the "arrest of spies, smugglers, *disloyal and dangerous persons,* carrying [out] sentences including execution," and the "enforcement of orders [and] redressing complaints of citizens against soldiers or others." Chandler's office also issued passes to merchants operating within the Federal lines, seized contraband property, and administered loyalty oaths, although these were generally considered ineffective in rehabilitating die-hard Confederates. As one observer noted, "[A]n oath never made a loyal good citizen out of a rebel anymore than a penitentiary makes an honest man."[9]

The guerrillas, living on the margins of Arkansas society, had little use for Yankee passes or oaths. When Union forces captured and tried Charles Hauptmann, a member of "Lt. Blackburn's detachment of the Rebel Army," for guerrilla activities in October 1863, they discovered that he was a paroled prisoner of war. The Federals sentenced him to six months at hard labor for "violation of the oath of allegiance." Corruption within the Department of Arkansas and the provost marshal general's office exacerbated the problem. During a congressional inquiry of the Army of Arkansas in 1864, the chief investigator, Brigadier General John W. Davidson, described the ease with which a Rebel sympathizer could acquire a pass through Federal lines from the provost marshal's office. He cited the capture of a furloughed Confederate soldier who had acquired a pass, from Major General Frederick Steele's provost marshal, that allowed him "to pass in and out of our lines *at will* for thirty days." Since bureaucratic measures had little effect, the Federals adapted other means available to the provost marshal general to inhibit guerrilla operations.[10]

The Federals possessed one asset that proved useful in providing needed intelligence on guerrillas, the provost marshal's "Secret Service" branch. Its members scoured the countryside to gather information about both guerrillas and regular Confederate forces. They also served as an internal affairs bureau within the Army of Arkansas, but it was their intelligence-gathering mission that proved most useful to field commanders. Although some officers accused the agents of providing poor or old information, even going so far as to accuse them of disloyalty, the network of spies often gave the Federals vital data in the war against the guerrillas.[11]

The final element in the administrative network that aided the counterguerrilla campaign was the military prison system operated by the provost marshal general and the judge advocate general's office, both of which played a critical role in pacifying the state. For the average Arkansan, Federal military law represented the only working legal system in the Yankee-occupied territories. For the guerrillas, the U. S. Army judges, lawyers, and constables provided the sole recourse to summary execution by Federals in the field. The fate of guerrillas captured by Union forces was virtually preordained when Union commanders from Washington to St. Louis issued standing orders for their men to execute surrendered or captured irregulars. Many units followed these orders to the letter. Sergeant Charles O. Musser, Twenty-ninth Iowa Infantry Regiment, in a letter to his family in June 1863, described the fate of seventeen guerrillas captured by Federal cavalry near La Grange, fifteen miles north of Helena. "They started towards town [Helena] with them [the guerrillas], going through some thick timber," he explained. "They [the infantry scouts accompanying the cavalry] mysteriously disappeared one by one, and when they got to the lines there were no prisoners with them. About that time, the cavalry scouts came up and asked where their butternuts was. [T]hey replied, '[T]hey got away in the brush just after you left us,' and winked to the cavalry. [T]hey all had a good laugh over the fun, as they called it, said that no guerrillas should ever enter our lines alive. *So you can guess the way the guerrillas escaped that time.*"[12]

However, the Federal commanders in Arkansas apparently disregarded the orders of their higher commanders on numerous occasions. Although Union officers carried out executions of captured guerrillas in accordance with the instructions of the War Department when Federal forces entered the state in 1862, as time passed, and as the support of the local populace became more important to the occupying army, executions became less frequent. Inventively interpreting military law, Union commanders in Arkansas avoided wholesale executions while still obeying the orders prescribed by the War Department. Beginning in the fall of 1863, men convicted of "Being a Guerrilla" were sentenced to death under General Order No. 30, which stated that anyone found guilty by a military court-martial of guerrilla activities would "suffer death, according to the usages of nations, by sentence of a military commission." Following the sentence of death, and its subsequent reporting to the command at St. Louis, the commanding general would commute the sentence to "Hard Labor for the

Duration of the War" for cases only involving membership in a guerrilla band. If the accused committed any violent crime, such as rape or murder, while a member of an irregular unit, the death sentence was carried out.[13]

Confining guerrillas to hard labor for the duration of the war allowed Federal officers to treat irregulars as prisoners of war despite their orders. The extent of the cover-up of the imprisonment of Arkansas guerrillas is unknown. Interestingly, the departmental provost marshal's office reclassified prisoner categories about the same time as leniency was granted to the guerrillas, adding a new category, "citizens arrested for violation of the laws of war," to the rolls at the Little Rock Federal military penitentiary. The number of prisoners in this class began to increase, and despite the wishes of field soldiers who wanted the guerrillas summarily shot, the provost marshal's record reflects increasing leniency toward guerrilla prisoners. By February 1865, the military prison at Little Rock reported 313 prisoners of war, 22 "political citizens," 70 Federal soldiers, and 8 Federal citizens on their muster rolls. When the prisoners of war were sent to New Orleans, Louisiana, for eventual transfer to the prison camp at Elmira, New York, no "political citizens"—that is, suspected guerrillas—were listed on the manifest, nor were they mentioned in monthly reports to St. Louis. Federal commanders in Arkansas managed to keep their secret until the end of the war, when they released the "political citizens" without fanfare.[14]

The use of riverine forces by the Federals, much like the implementation of the provost marshal system, was not new. From the beginning of the conflict, Union leaders recognized the necessity of controlling the rivers around and inside the state. In addition to the obvious strategic advantage of controlling the Mississippi, the lack of roads in the Trans-Mississippi made rivers the only dependable routes for Federal forces. As Northerners realized that guerrillas could threaten the river supply lines, they organized units to fight on water. By combining the massive firepower of gunboats and specialized landing forces, the Federals had a deadly combination of mobility and firepower. River-based forces would be central to antiguerrilla operations along the Mississippi and Arkansas Rivers, especially in 1862 and 1863.

The most famous of these riverine forces, the Mississippi Marine Brigade, operated primarily along the Mississippi River in support of

Ulysses S. Grant's 1862–1863 campaign. Flag Officer David D. Porter, commanding the Mississippi Squadron, asked the Navy Department for "a force of marines to be carried in suitable vessels accompanying the gunboats and to be landed at points where parties of guerrillas were wont to assemble." Since the Navy Department lacked U. S. Marines for the mission, the War Department organized the Mississippi Marine Brigade for service on the river, naming Brigadier General Alfred W. Ellet, a man with little military background but much political pull, to command the unit.[15]

As Ellet began recruiting in November 1862, he made his first mistake as commander. Since the Marine Brigade did not belong to any single state, enlistment provided no extra cash, in contrast to enlistments in state-sponsored units. Seeking to fill his unit to capacity, Ellet scoured army hospitals in the Midwest, advertising "Soldiering Made Easy!" and "No long, hard marches, camping without tents or food, or carrying heavy knapsacks, but good comfortable quarters, and good facilities for cooking at all times." Consequently, Ellet found himself commanding a group of soldiers who were ill disciplined, medically unfit, lazy, or incompetent, a poor beginning for a mission that demanded competent, elite troops. Despite recruiting difficulties, Ellet's Marine Brigade began operations in Tennessee before moving down the Mississippi to assist Grant's drive on Vicksburg.[16]

The unit comprised mounted infantry, cavalry, and artillery units, a combined-arms team of twelve hundred men capable of independent operations. Its fleet of transports, eight in all, carried the unit and served as floating barracks, mess hall, and hospital. Five steamers, six coal barges, and three steam tugs provided logistical support for Ellet's small navy. Supported by the gunboats of the Ram Fleet, the Marine Brigade seriously threatened guerrilla units along the Mississippi. Ellet later modified the transports with ramps, winches, and booms that allowed rapid debarking of horses and cannon and partially negated the guerrillas' speed advantage. Although the unit's manpower and ample supplies and equipment were sufficient to meet any guerrilla threat along the Mississippi River, supplies and men did not guarantee victory.[17]

The Marine Brigade, like other riverine forces along the Mississippi, resorted extensively to retributive burning to punish citizens who aided the guerrillas. For instance, the brigade's report for May through June 1863 reads thus: ". . . a party of rebels being discovered 35 miles north of there [Helena, Arkansas] returned May 24th and disembarked—had a close engagement with 800 rebels who fled leaving their dead & wounded. Burned the town of Austin [Mississippi], that had harbored the guerrillas and refused to give information." An Arkansas guerrilla leader, Captain J. H. McGehee, used Hopefield, Arkansas, as a base from which to destroy numerous steam tugs, steamboats, and flatboats between Helena and Memphis. When the Union squadron discovered that McGehee operated out of Hopefield, Major General Stephen A. Hurlbut, the commander of the Sixteenth Corps stationed at Memphis, ordered that town burned also; but the attacks on Yankee vessels continued.[18]

The destruction of guerrilla hideouts along the river infuriated the local population, who responded by providing even more support to the irregulars. William W. Heartsill, a Confederate prisoner of war en route to a prison camp, wrote in January 1863, "On the west bank of the Mississippi, extending from the mouth of White river to this point [Helena, Arkansas], evidence innumerable WHY WE SHOULD love the 'Glorious Union,' no less than FIVE HUNDRED blackened walls and lone chimneys are standing as monuments to departed civilized warfare." Grant and Major General William T. Sherman attempted to mitigate the wanton destruction by issuing orders to burn only the homes and property of known Southern sympathizers. Their charge put the burden of determining the loyalty of homeowners on company officers and sergeants who lacked detailed knowledge of the local populace. Consequently, the lower-echelon commanders continued to order their men to destroy entire towns despite protestations of loyalty by the citizenry.[19]

Unhappily for the Union, the Marine Brigade failed to cure the guerrilla plague. The weaknesses in the brigade began at the highest levels of command. Instead of concentrating solely on the elimination of guerrilla bands, Admiral Porter and other Union commanders constantly shunted the unit up and down the river, preventing its officers and men from becoming familiar with the populace and terrain. For example, during the siege of Vicksburg, guerrilla attacks along the river reached their highest point since the beginning of the war. Porter detached Ellet's force to assist in reducing Richmond, Louisiana, in conjunction with a land attack by Brigadier General Joseph A. Mower's First Division, Sixteenth Corps, an operation that had nothing to do with stopping the guerrilla menace.

A second hindrance, a problem of interservice rivalry and personality conflict, arose between General Ellet and Admiral Porter. Porter, who
wanted to enfold the Ram Fleet and Ellet's transports into his Mississippi
Squadron, disliked Ellet from the beginning, calling him "adverse to har-
monious action . . . [and] determined to assume authority and disregard
my orders." The admiral insisted that either the War Department merge
Ellet's brigade with Grant's Army of the Tennessee or turn it over to naval
control. Secretary of the Navy Gideon Welles denied Porter's request,
but his decision left the question of who commanded the unit unan-
swered. Porter responded by sending the brigade to the Tennessee River,
far away from him, his squadron, and, perversely, the guerrillas infesting
the banks of the Mississippi.[20]

A third major defect in the Marine Brigade stemmed from Ellet's poor
recruiting practices and weak leadership; this is what led to the eventual
disbandment of the unit. Beginning in late 1863, the poor quality of Ellet's
men became evident as many soldiers plundered locales along the river.

Many cases of misbehavior by Ellet's men became known to the
Federal command, but despite Porter's warnings to Ellet, the brigade continued to pillage. After the 1864 Red River Campaign, the Marine Brigade
"stopped at every landing . . . on its way out of Red River, solely for the
purpose of pillaging and the destruction of private property." A Louisiana
Unionist claimed that the brigade stole or destroyed twenty thousand dollars worth of property on his plantation. One Union commander reported,
"Marine Brigade has done more toward embittering them [the people along
the river] toward our cause than any movement yet made under the auspices of the Navy." By late 1864, Union commanders, tired of the
Mississippi Marine Brigade's activities, disbanded the unit ended the experiment in combined-arms riverine counterguerrilla warfare.[21]

In contrast to the failure of the Marine Brigade, one of the greatest
successes in the Federal war against Arkansas guerrillas was the raising of
indigenous forces for counterguerrilla operations. As the conventional
war moved east, the bulk of Northern forces shifted to more strategically
important battlefronts. Consequently, the war in Arkansas fell to locally
raised loyalist units. Arkansas Unionists responded to the call for volunteers by providing nearly ten thousand men for the Federal army, all of
whom served within the state. Union commanders quickly realized that

their detailed knowledge of Arkansas's terrain and people suited them perfectly for use in counterguerrilla units.

Arkansans began joining Union units at the beginning of the war, but not until 1862 was the First Arkansas Cavalry Volunteers formed at Springfield, Missouri. From 1862 to 1865, Arkansas provided four cavalry regiments, two light-artillery batteries, and eight infantry regiments to the Union cause. Poor combat performance against regular Confederate forces, especially that of the First Arkansas Cavalry at the battle of Prairie Grove, on December 7, 1862, led some Federal commanders to argue that the Arkansas Unionists should only be used for static depot guards. Luckily for its commander, Colonel M. La Rue Harrison, the men later fought well against regular Confederate forces and guerrillas, despite chronic shortages of horses and equipment.[22]

The First Arkansas Cavalry became the primary counterguerrilla unit in the northern part of the state. Its record, like those of other Unionist regiments, surpassed regular Federal units in fighting guerrillas, perhaps due to the intense hatred between Confederate irregulars and the "Mountain Tories." Sergeant Musser, of the Twenty-ninth Iowa, wrote, "[T]hey [Arkansas Unionists] are already doing good service as Scouts. [T]hey are acquainted with the country and Know who are loyal and who are not." He added that the Unionists "brought in a good many Guerrillas and bushwhackers." Their efficiency soon made them particular targets of Rebel guerrillas. Colonel Harrison reported in April 1864 that "Lyon's gang, 22 strong," approached his "corral-keepers near Prairie Grove, and killed every man, 9 in number." Witnesses later stated that the guerrillas approached the corral dressed in Federal uniforms and executed those attempting to surrender.[23]

The guerrillas took whatever actions they could to hamper the First Arkansas's ability to fight them. When the guerrillas discovered that the Federals lacked horses, they raided the regiment's lightly guarded mules, killing three men and escaping with the herd. Harrison lamented that "the moment the alarm was given two columns were started in pursuit, but being mostly dismounted, could not overtake [the guerrillas]." As his aggressive patrolling kept the irregulars constantly on the run, a degree of hatred approaching a blood feud grew between the First Arkansas Cavalry and partisan bands. The 180-man bushwhacker company of

Captain William "Buck" Brown raised the black flag against Harrison's troopers, signifing that no quarter would be given to captured Federals. In May 1864, the Union cavalrymen found a note from another guerrilla captain, J. W. Cooper; it read, "We will kill all men who pass this road [between Fayetteville and Yellville] and woe be to the man that takes down this [black] flag." The personal and vicious war between the Unionists and bushwhackers added a new dimension of cruelty and destruction to the guerrilla war.[24]

From mid-1864 to April 1865, Harrison's Arkansas cavalrymen fought bushwhackers on a daily basis and distinguished themselves in engagements with Confederate regulars during Sterling Price's Missouri expedition in the fall of 1864. Paradoxically, Price's defeat created further problems for Harrison, as large numbers of isolated Rebel detachments, including deserters and stragglers, joined local bushwhacking companies in northern Arkansas. Federal forces responded by withdrawing from many garrisoned towns in northeast Arkansas, including Jacksonport and Batesville. Harrison, however, stood his ground by increasing cavalry patrols between Yellville and Fayetteville, fortifying Fayetteville, recruiting and arming additional men, and setting ambushes for Confederate regulars and guerrilla bands.[25]

Harrison continued to fight guerrillas by direct means. Learning that the irregulars used gristmills as meeting places, he organized and launched an incendiary expedition in late August 1864. Despite explicit orders from the department commander to protect the buildings, the Federal horsemen destroyed three large mills in the region before returning to Fayetteville. During the foray, Harrison heated the feud between his men and the guerrilla companies by destroying the mill owned by his nemesis, Buck Brown. Harrison wrote that the "disabling of mills cause[d] more writhing among bushwhackers than any other mode of attack," although he also acknowledged that the bushwhackers still "threatened to stay and fight . . . on boiled acorns."[26]

The Union's lack of success against the guerrillas, using what looked like twentieth-century "search and destroy" tactics, became visible throughout the fall of 1864 as the guerrilla war forced many residents of northwest Arkansas from their farms. Their departure reduced supplies of fodder for the mounts of the First Arkansas as well as fresh food for the troopers. Confederate refugees moved to Texas, while those loyal to the Union fled to Missouri. The linked problems of guerrillas and the abandonment of farmland led Harrison to develop one of the most original army programs implemented in the Civil War, a system of fortified farm colonies. Closely resembling the "strategic hamlets" of the mid-twentieth century, these colonies protected Unionist farmers from the guerrillas and allowed Federal military units to resume their aggressive counterguerrilla operations in the spring of 1865.

Harrison determined that farmers would only return to their fields if he protected them from bushwhackers, an impossible task in view of his manpower shortage. Instead, he proposed a four-point plan for establishing "fortified colonies," or small farm villages capable of self-defense. Initially, an armed home guard company of fifty loyal Unionists, the core of each colony's population, moved with their families to a defensible location chosen by Harrison. The guardsmen then built a small earthen fort or wooden blockhouse large enough to shelter the colony's population against attack. Each man received a parcel of land based on the vote of the community, which had "nothing in common except common defense and obedience to law." All persons living within ten miles of the colony were expected to join the program or leave. If joining the colony, citizens had to swear loyalty to the United States, agree to obey the laws and orders of the nearest Federal military post, and acknowledge the reconstructed Unionist government of Arkansas.[27]

By Christmas Day, 1864, Harrison had six colonies in operation with eight more in various stages of construction. The scheme benefited the Federal cause in three ways. First, the exodus of Unionist refugees from Fayetteville to the colonies freed the First Arkansas Cavalry from guarding and supplying them. The colonies had much to offer the refugees, many of whom had lived in the region before the war. For example, the Union Valley colony, near Prairie Grove, possessed a blacksmith shop, a wagon shop, a church, and a free public school, in addition to free farmland. Second, the colonies provided increased supplies for the Federal cavalry. Union Valley, for example, pledged to send a thousand tons of hay to the regiment that spring. Most importantly, the blockhouses provided

way stations for cavalry patrols throughout the region, allowing the First
Arkansas to police the territory between the colonies and lower their
response time to guerrilla attacks.[28]

Harrison's fortified colonies became models for other Federal commanders in Arkansas. Around Batesville, Colonel Hans Mattson organized
farm colonies for "self-protection, to encourage agriculture and commerce
and to assist the citizens in restoring civil government." At Pine Bluff, ex-
slaves formed a colony that included one of the first schools for freedmen
in the state. The social benefits of the farm colonies were completely secondary to the Federals, whose main goal was to separate the guerrillas from
the civil population. The success of the fortified colony program allowed
Harrison to destroy the insurgency in northwest Arkansas. Large guerrilla
units splintered into smaller parties of brigands that either had to flee the
area or risk being destroyed by the home guards of the farm colonies. The
major guerrilla companies, like Buck Brown's, became victims of Harrison's
two-pronged approach of pacification and counterguerrilla operations.
During a patrol between colonies, Harrison's men killed Brown and several
of his men and dispersed the band. Between February 1 and March 20, 1865,
they went on to kill over one hundred bushwhackers in northern Arkansas,
their biggest tally since the war began.[29]

Federal forces managed to bring the guerrilla war under control by
April 1865 through a combination of conventional military tactics, fortified towns, and innovative concepts of pacification and counterinsurgency.
Other solutions, such as the river-based Mississippi Marine Brigade, fell
short of their potential due to mismanagement or ignorance of guerrilla
warfare by their senior commanders. Arkansas Union regiments, such as
Harrison's First Cavalry, played a critical role in eliminating the effectiveness of the Confederate guerrillas. Unlike their fellow Union soldiers,
the Arkansans had the same knowledge of the countryside and populace
as the guerrillas; this offset the ability of the partisans to meld into the
populace at will. The integration of pro-Union Arkansans, farm colonies,
superior logistics, riverine mobility, and military law enforcement proved
a deadly combination that limited the ability of Rebel partisans to roam
freely.

Ultimately, then, Rebel irregulars accomplished little in Arkansas.
They failed to hinder the Union's military occupation of the state or its

political reconstruction. They never won a major battle or played a significant role in supporting the conventional Confederate war. Their impact on the war was psychological, not military, intended to keep the flame of rebellion alive inside Federal lines. Yet they failed even there. By 1865, their ravages, along with a Federal policy of retribution, had all but depopulated the state north of the Arkansas River, and some communities in the southern half of the state became ghost towns. Organized in order to save the state from invasion, Arkansas's guerrillas ended the war being hunted by Federal soldiers and Unionists and feared and hated by their neighbors and friends.[30]

# Inside Wars: The Cultural Crisis of Warfare and the Values of Ordinary People

## Michael Fellman

*The reaches opened up before us and closed behind, as if the forest had stepped leisurely across the water to bar the way for our return. We penetrated deeper and deeper into the heart of darkness. . . . We were wanderers on a prehistoric earth, on an earth that wore the aspect of an unknown planet. We could have fancied ourselves the first of men taking possession of an accursed inheritance, to be subdued at the cost of profound anguish and of excessive toil. . . . The earth seemed unearthly. We are accustomed to look upon the shackled form of a conquered monster, but there—there you could look at a thing monstrous and free. It was unearthly, the men were—No, they were not inhuman. Well, you know, that was the worst of it—this suspicion of their not being inhuman. . . . What thrilled you was just the thought of their humanity—like yours—the thought of your remote kinship with this wild and passionate uproar. . . . What was there after all? Joy, fear, sorrow, devotion, valour, rage— who can tell?—but truth—truth stripped of its cloak of time.*

—JOSEPH CONRAD

WHEN WRITING *Inside War*, I approached the cataclysm of the Civil War not by depicting waving flags at grand battles, but by exploring the most inglorious and brutal arena of guerrilla conflict, in Missouri, a place where civilians as well as soldiers, women as well as men were sucked into a general catastrophe which became immediately personal. Not only did thousands of ordinary people as well as the better off write and save the diaries and letters in which they gave witness to what they knew to be the hugest experience of their lives, during the conflict they went to the nearest military outpost to make depositions amounting to oral histories of shattering events, giving the depositions within hours or days of pro-Confederate guerrilla attacks upon them. Union provost marshals took down this testimony verbatim, and the victims then signed, about 20 percent with an X. After the war these records were shipped to Washington, where they remained unread in the National Archives, because, until recently, cultural historians have ignored the meanings of war and because military historians, among the most conventional of elitist historians, have remained indifferent to war as a cultural event.[1]

I shall never forget the powerful impact those depositions had on me when first I uncovered them in the National Archives. The faded red ribbons which I was untying had, I knew, last been touched by the Union provost marshal who had packed them off to Washington at the end of the war. The stories which poured out to me, their first reader in over a century, were filled with horrible events and primal emotions.

Consider, for example, the story of Mary Hall, who, in the middle of the night on May 18, 1865, was awakened at her bedside by a group of guerrillas. They demanded she light a candle and then took it to set fire to her children's clothing, shoving the clothes under the bed where her three youngest children were sleeping. Hall stated: "I caught the clothes they were burning and threw them in the fire place. One of them says, 'God damn you let them; if you don't I will burn up the house.' I answered, 'They will burn just as well where they are and will give more light.'" They then went to the bed of Hall's eighteen-year-old son and demanded his pistol. He said he had traded it for a watch and added, "'Its hanging by the glass though some of you have it—as I do not see it.' One of the guerrillas said, 'God damn him. Shoot him.' I thought they would shoot him and knocked up the pistol several times, injuring my shoulder by so doing," Hall reported. "They finally succeeded in shooting him in the head killing him instantly. I was screaming and entreating them all the time to spare his life. After they killed him one of them says, 'Shut your God Damn mouth or I will blow a hole through your head.' . . . All this time my niece, 16 years of age, was lying in the bed. One of the guerrillas stood by the bedside and as she made an effort to rise ordered her to lie still saying one woman was enough at a time. After they had killed my son and plundered the house one of the guerrillas ordered me out of the house and shut the door. The door had scarcely closed before I heard my niece scream and say 'Lord Aunt Mary run here to me.' I started and as I reached the door my niece who had succeeded in effecting her escape from the men came rushing out. I says, 'Let the poor girl alone, you have done enough.' . . . I do not think they effected their designs on her."[2]

Such invasions of civilian homes were carried out by Union troops as well as by guerrillas. Although often less fatal than the attack on Mary Hall, such raids frequently included not only assaults on persons and things, but also orgies of destructive acting out, symbolic crusades against communal values and the emotional structures of the victims.

In February 1863, M. G. Singleton, a wealthy Centralia farmer of known Southern sympathies, reported the attack of twenty Union militiamen who had come calling for dinner. His wife, who had her two nieces as company, refused to serve the men. The militia commander then flew into a rage and demanded to be fed, and the troops commenced ransacking the house, "all the time using the most profane and vulgar language" in order to offend the women. Singleton reported: "One fellow danced jambone with the heels of his boots on the carpet in my wife's chamber till he cut it through. They had thrown their overcoats and a gun on her bed, which she quietly removed—placing the coats on a chair and set the gun up by the side of the bed—when one of them threw them on again and called on the rest to pile on their guns—and then jumped on the bed and rolled over it—took the pillows threw them down on the floor, sat and then stamped them under his feet." After they had dined, two armed Negroes who accompanied them ate "the family dinner" and then took a pan of bread dough and threw it on the kitchen floor.[3]

In their reports, Hall and Singleton expressed moral outrage and a desire for justice. Through less official channels they also may well have demanded revenge as the appropriate response to such assaults.

Just as horrifying was the response of going dead emotionally due to such assaults. Dr. J. F. Snyder heard from a friend in Boliver in the summer of 1864: "Times are about as usual in this county. Occasionally we hear of a man being shot or a horse stolen. No houses have been burnt recently. Recently we have begun to think times tolerably quiet. Old Man Staley was shot a few days ago, since has died." During the same summer, J. N. Woods coolly wrote from Newton County, "[T]hings are in such a commotion here & if no one is killed we think it is not of much interest."[4]

At least some of the men inflicting such misery could step back from their anger and open themselves to fellow feeling. They could be at least somewhat aware that the soldier in them was acting ( and failing to react emotionally), in a dehumanizing manner which would have been unacceptable to their peacetime selves. "We had quite a hunt last night," Illinois cavalry lieutenant Sardius Smith recorded in his diary in May 1862. "Having heard that a notorious secesh by the name of Jackson was in the neighborhood . . . we started after dark to his house[, h]aving taken our sabres off our belts, and taking only our pistols." His company stealthily surrounded the house, only to find that the guerrillas had fled like dogs. At this point, Smith broke the narrative line in his diary and made an analysis of what had changed inside him during the war: "We are getting quite hardened to this kind of thing and I can go into a house with a pistol in my hand, with a smile on my face, speak politely to the ladies, ask where there [sic] men are in order that I may shoot them . . . with as much grace as though I was making a call for friendship sake."[5]

Most often furious and vengeful, fighters and civilians sporadically reasserted a sense of their own humanity and that of others. They also observed that the ferocity of war could destroy both the mind and the soul. Seeing the shell of a victim, and at some level vicariously identifying with her or with him, they could sense the depths of damage which guerrilla war inflicted. On July 30, 1863, at a refugee camp in the Ozarks, the Reverend Francis Springer wrote, "A wild man . . . was seen descending the adjacent hill densely covered with trees. He seems an apparition suddenly revealed. He is barefoot, hatless, scratched with briars & with no covering for his nakedness but a coarse dark gray homespun blanket over his shoulders and reaching halfway down his thighs. . . . His countenance is expressive of extreme dejection. [Since his arrival] he refuses conversation, takes but little food, & seems alike careless of the attention of friends & the threats of foes. His constant posture from morning until night is sitting or crouched on the floor of the guard house."[6]

Not compassion but rage and savage destruction were the norms, often manifested physically as well as psychologically, sometimes including torture and mutilation as well as murder. In June 1862, near Warrensburg, following a nighttime skirmish, Major Emory S. Foster found two of his soldiers "stripped of their clothing and horribly mutilated, one of them with more than a dozen revolver-balls in his body and his head frightfully broken and mangled." On September 29, 1864, at Centralia, Bloody Bill Anderson's gang pulled twenty-four unarmed Union recruits off a train they had stopped. A Union colonel later reported, "Most of them were beaten over the head, seventeen of them were scalped, and one had his privates cut off and placed in his mouth. Every man was shot in the head. One man had his nose cut off."[7]

Not only did some men mutilate bodies, other men exalted over the mangled corpses of their enemies. After Alfred Bolan, the terror of southeastern Missouri who boasted of killing forty Union men, was slaughtered in 1863 by a Union spy who beat him repeatedly over the head with a broken plowshare, Bolan's body was placed on display at the nearest Union outpost. "I went to see the murdered murderer," Iowa infantryman Timothy Phillips wrote in his diary. "His hair was all matted with blood and [blood was] clotted over his face, rendering him an object of disgust and horror. Yet there were hundreds of men who gloated over him. . . . There had perished a monster, a man of blood, of every crime, who had no mercy for others and had died a death of violence, and today hundreds gaze upon his unnatural carcass and exult that his prowess is at an end."[8]

Such exaltation over the destruction of the ogre, and violence against the enemy in general, could be comprehended within the most sacred value structure of the Evangelical Christian culture, in which all factions of these warriors had been bred. Union sergeant Sherman Bodwell, a Congregational Sunday-school teacher originally from Connecticut, hated the fetid animality of his guerrilla enemy, of the sort he found clinging to a hidden camp upon which his men stumbled one day in October 1863. "There seems to be something of the deathlike brooding over these camps. Always hidden where hardly more than a horse track points the way, in heavy timber and creek bottoms, offal lying about, cooking utensils, cast off clothing . . . the very air seems thick with the clime with which so lately they seethed." When his unit surprised two of these animals, Bodwell's major "brought one down" with a pistol shot; and Bodwell stood by as Lieutenant Reese finished him off with a pistol shot "just back of the eye & he was with his judge with all his imperfections on his head." Bodwell later regretted that he had not gazed on the countenance of his enemy at the moment of the fatal shot, to see the direction in which his soul had flown; but he was reassured when the lieutenant told him that the guerrilla had "intentionally raised his hand to protect himself and an ashy paleness overspread his face, as when a cloud passes over the sun."

Two years later, on the day he was mustered out of the army, Bodwell concluded his war diary by thanking the Holy Spirit for remaining with him and his men throughout the war. "So ends my service, in all three and a half years filled with tokens of loving kindness of Him who granted me the privilege of standing in my lot . . . on every march and in every engagement. [For] the loving, comforting, strengthening of the Holy Spirit, even when I have been most unfaithful and forgetful of my Christian obligation, I can never, I feel, be grateful enough."[9] Bodwell's war had been a sacred crusade—the children of light obliterating the children of darkness. Reaffirmed through war making, his Christian conscience was clear.

When I first confronted these terrible stories I was emotionally overwhelmed. Nothing in my peaceful lifetime experiences had prepared me to really comprehend such havoc. The documents were physically filthy, and so I washed my hands about once an hour; I also took a lot of walks on the hot Washington streets. Indeed, I literally could not write about this cultural catastrophe for over a year. My first response was that war is hell and people are shits, which did not amount to anything approaching an analysis. I needed to develop explanatory devices which were emotionally distancing, but not so distancing as to bleed away and thus violate the urgency of these people's experiences and reactions. Neither did I wish to eliminate my compassion for them. I also wished to avoid the breast-beating attractive to too many Americans writing their history, the perversely patriotic lament that America is the most violent society ever. Nor did I wish to affirm the belief, so dearly held by many on the Atlantic seaboard and beyond the sea, that the American West and South were filled with cultural primitives. Neither did I wish to create a grand theory of inhumanity, nor a typology of incidents, nor a set of categories in which to count up and statistically render such crimes. For me the point of analysis of such events was not to reduce them to the cool scholarly calculus, but rather to walk right through the maelstrom, senses alert, while using reasoned arguments to sort out some of the powerful issues. If I did not want to fall into the Scylla of grand theory, neither did I want to drown in the data, the naive empiricist Charybdis still so common to historians. But most urgently I did not want to ignore or downplay the horror—which is something many Civil War historians seem to accomplish.

At the most general level, in order to confront rather than avoid such historical dirty work, I developed for myself a sensibility (rather less than a theory) of the multiple capacities of humans: Under varying circumstances, especially extreme ones, within our common humanity, each of us can be both creative and destructive, both a hater and a lover. Wartime killing, destruction, mutilation, and all, must be seen most honestly not as inhuman and antisocial acts, but as human and social ones. Destructiveness is not necessarily exclusive—the same humans can also be creative and caring. And those of us who have not been tested must remain skeptical agnostics about our own moral potential and the categories by which we would render judgment on both victims and victimizers.

The very best book on many of these issues was written in 1959 by a World War II veteran, the philosopher J. Glenn Gray—*The Warriors: Reflections on Men in Battle*.[10] Gray suggests that during combat, the most common means of maintaining and balancing these dual capacities of creativity and destructiveness is to intensify love within one's cohort, in part by rejecting the common humanity of all those alien others who are attacking one's own people. Seeking to broaden the meanings of Gray's construction, I learned a great deal from those working on white colonial attitudes toward the Indians, learning especially from Richard Slotkin and James Axtell, and from Nicholas Canney on the even earlier set of anti-Irish attitudes developed by the English as they colonized the northern six counties of Ireland, a process which, Canney argues, prepared them to greet the Indians.[11]

Under extreme duress, many Missourians collapsed or panicked and fled; others carried on through a process which the social psychiatrist Robert Jay Lifton terms "doubling."[12] With this careful word, Lifton wishes to avoid the reductionism implied by the term "character splitting," with its overtones of the psychosis of schizophrenia. Ordinary people, Lifton suggests, *add on* a persona (or multiple personas, I would think) to deal with extreme circumstances, while at the same time seeking somehow to preserve the core values of the earlier self. I developed the argument that the "soldier me" was added on to the "peaceful citizen me," and, when this doubled persona became especially hard to maintain, that it was the "not me" emptied of conscience who was acting, only out of dire necessity, a kind of zombie alternative self acting at variance with the "real me" of normal times.

Elsewhere in his work, Lifton discusses "psychic numbing"—turning off emotionally under an unmanageable overload, a kind of death in life, which occurs further along the character-doubling spectrum, at the very end of which lies the human ability to commit atrocities.[13] My ability to come to grips with such gruesome actions was helped by the essays of several psychiatrists treating returned Vietnam War veterans, psychiatrists who have written telling and chilling analyses of those who participate in atrocities that often include torturing and mutilating civilians as well as enemy soldiers. Another corpus of American historiography, that which discusses the American treatment of the Indians, helps make sense of this dark ground—that treatment being one portion of the far broader picture of European treatment of aboriginal peoples whenever and wherever they expanded.[14]

Annihilating the very face and body of the enemy was in part rage and in part mutual release, through which an inner circle of warriors sought to tighten their knot of brotherhood. Totally crazy in a peaceful world, such behavior made perverse emotional sense in the counterculture of guerrilla war—this was a reaching toward the dystopia of nihilism, where the essence of life was to be purely destroyed.

And yet even men falling into the nihilist nightmare, I would argue, needed at some level to believe that they were doing what they were doing not out of pure malevolence but for some twisted version of general cultural good. Therefore, they always argued that they were preserving the true people when taking vengeance against inhuman destroyers, that they were defending by any means necessary those higher values which defined their culture. This set of values included the home, women, their own manliness—the sum of which, they believed, was honor, maintained within the wider context of a belief in Christian purification and in the

identification of the honor of the good people with service of God's true
servants. Bertram Wyatt-Brown has given us a lively and greatly sugges-
tive, if sometimes wild, analysis of some aspects of honor, aspects which
he argues, unnecessarily, were especially true of the American South.[15] To
my knowledge, no one has analyzed in depth the subject of the Christian
God of war in nineteenth-century American history; and I know little
about the Inquisition, the Crusades, or later so-called wars of religion, or
for that matter the Puritans, though knowledge of these doubtless would
be of great help methodologically.

This general sensibility of multiple capacities, and these mid-range
theoretical tools, enabled me to some extent to work through the dread-
ful data which had nearly overwhelmed me. The guerrillas who held Mary
Hall while they slaughtered her son did not rape her niece or her, which
they easily could have done, nor did the Union militiamen who invaded
and vandalized Mrs. Singleton's bedchamber rape her or her nieces.
Mayhem, slaughter of other men, near rape and symbolic rape, but why
not rape? Of course men on each side feared that turnabout would mean
that their women kin might be raped later on. But more profoundly this
omission of rape was one key piece of evidence that, to a limited degree
at least, the guerrillas meant what they said when they proclaimed that
they were fighting alien invaders in defense of the South, at the center
of which was family, home, and, on the pedestal in the center, women.
Killing and mutilating enemy men was done in service to a warrior version of these higher embodiments of male honor.

Women shared these basic values, which they knew offered them a
certain general protection from men and which men did not accord one
another. To give one of the many such stories I have found, Private Hiram
Crandall from Iowa noted in his diary, while his regiment was waiting for
a ferry across a Missouri river, "[A] number of the boys amused themselves
by talking to a number of secessionist ladies. One of these *ladies* was very
bloodthirsty and said she hoped we would all get killed, for which expression of good will I thanked her as kindly as I knew how and politely as I
could."[16] Even though this was in his opinion no real lady, Crandall,
through playfulness and irony, reigned in his anger and responded as befit
a gentleman serving the code of honor. His assailant knew the code as
well, and the latitude it accorded her.

The strikingly blase reporting of local events that I mentioned earlier, that only the odd person had been killed lately and so things were tolerable calm, was a clear example of psychic numbing. Another example of this cold tone evincing numbness came from just over the Kansas border in 1863, where Samuel Ayres wrote a friend, "The most we have to complain of is the operations of bushwhackers . . . they pay us a visit occasionally and levy a tax to the amount of one or more horses—sometimes plunder houses—run off cattle—kill a few men and burn some houses."[17] The coldness is in the words "kill a few men"—meaning, in part, not me or my kin—and in the notion of this activity as a species of taxation, a vexatious but normally irritating price for living. Ayres was a rather nice man, actually, but he could not afford to feel too much.

"Doubling" helps explain Sardius Smith's attack of conscience and self-awareness when he realized, gun in hand, how he was hardening into a soldier who could smile and politely ask a lady whose home he was invading the whereabouts of her husband so he could blast him away. Many other fighters shocked themselves with the tough soldier they found growing inside them. Charles Falker, a former store clerk in a small town in Wisconsin, wrote his wife about the Union toughs in his camp, which was far away from any enemy. They were, in his opinion, "little better than bushwhackers." All went around armed and "every few days somebody gets shot. . . . It seems a little odd at first to wear a sword and revolvers but I soon got used to it," he wrote. Immersed in this environment, Iowa private Henry Dysart held a kind of internal dialogue in his diary between the threatened, nice, home boy Henry and the emerging soldier Henry: "'Isn't that wrong?' 'Not for a soldier.' 'Are you breaking the sabbath?' 'There is no sabbath in the army, were I at home I would not do it.' The result of this instability is that we become so accustomed to a looseness of character our consciences become so seised, that we do daily what we would be ashamed of at home."[18]

As well as being markers of revenge, acts of mutilation and exaltation over disfigured corpses served as a means of binding together those still living within the brotherhood of fighters. This was, I believe, the psychological import of Brigadier General Clinton B. Fisk's order that after a drumhead court-martial the captured bushwhacker was to be shot "by every soldier" in the regiment when he was found guilty, "as he doubtless [was]"; and the import of a Kansas cavalry sergeant's casual notation that the previous morning they had captured "a few Rebs . . . who [they] hung or shot both at the same time."[19] Hanging *or* shooting would have been sufficient; a firing squad rather then the whole regiment would have sufficed. These formulations suggest that vengeance was to go beyond mere killing into a realm where solidarity in blood would be diffused and shared by all the soldiers. This was human sacrifice, sanctification through blood, a kind of instinctive religious ceremony for an ancient and buried but still accessible faith.

Although Sherman Bodwell, a Christian warrior, was far more systematic in his theology than most of the fellow soldiers with whom he shared the range of experiences and feelings I have been describing, he was rendered, if anything, even more determined and efficient by his more fully developed set of beliefs. He hunted, coldly shot and debased the enemy, and rejoiced in his actions; he could without ambivalence separate the children of God from the children of the devil; he could quite comfortably create a doubled soldier persona, the better to reinforce the code of honor and of God. For me, Bodwell is the intellectual as warrior, one who was in fact rather like one of *us* professors. We may have been lucky enough to avoid the terrain, but we are not off the hook.

Crossing this blood-red ground has been an intense subjective experience for me, as it proves to be, I hope, for my readers as well, though it was a far more intense subjective experience for those involved. This subject called up, amplified, and directed a wide range of not only my feelings about anger, but also my own angry feelings. Anger over Vietnam, the bitterest personal and cultural event of my young manhood, the background of the Holocaust (and I am a Jew born in America in 1943), and, not easily admissible to an ostensibly nice Jewish boy, a more immediate anger growing from a mutually hostile divorce which occurred at the end of a long and painful marriage and during the gestation and writing of the book—all these were personal sources which without doubt deepened the angry subjectivism of this topic for me. I would be the last to reduce history writing to autobiography or therapy, but I would not deny that it is also those things. I believe that every book that is alive must be animated in part by the subjective passions of the author-in-protest. Methodologically, this admission breaks the unstated historian's code of pretended objectivity; but I think it important that we follow the lead of anthropologists on this issue and

move beyond naive objectivism to a fuller realization of the intensely subjective nature of our authorship, a quality which enriches our work and
which does not deny for a moment the reality of the suffering of others,
nor reduce history to endlessly optional and therefore amoral postmod-
ern story construction.

As I have already noted, my subjective experience was also about the
intense subjective experience of my subjects. Especially during times of
crisis, the normal persona slips, as it is no longer as fully explanatory or
functional; and then one not only doubles in character, but also glimpses
further into a range of alternative images of self that lie beneath one's
more polite constructs. I do not believe in original sin, however; and I do
not believe that most Missourians simply capitulated to some newborn
(or reborn) monster beneath. Rather I believe that I observed them desperately mediating alternative selves with older ones in a manner which
would reach some sort of equilibrium between the needs for survival in a
harsh place and continuing maintenance of values acceptable to the older
self and, if possible, to other people. I am not a cynic who believes that
personality is like an onion with no center, nor do I believe that many of
my subjects were cynics, though that would have been a relatively comfortable mentality under the circumstances. I believe that I observed an
enormous need to somehow maintain a self which had moral continuity
and integrity—even as the means to attempt to achieve this maintenance
were often its effective opposite. Destruction could not service construction but could only lead to intensifying cycles of destruction, which
pushed peace back beyond the horizon of attainment.

During living nightmares such as guerrilla war, personalities in such
crisis parallel a culture in crisis. That is an understatement. As personalities take shape within a culture, and absorb and reflect its values in belief
and in action, in a very real sense, these personal crises *are* a cultural crisis. War is the objective correlative of these subjective crises. Looked at
as a collective experience, war was not an aberration for these Missourians,
but an unavoidable cultural crisis which caused the subjective crises from
which I drew my primary evidence. Whatever caused the war is a separate
question. Whatever disasters might have befallen my subjects or been
made by them in peacetime is moot. Extreme wartime experience reveals
much about personality and cultural values which remain muted during
more "normal" times.

Wartime experience is akin to madness, and sometimes leads to madness; but individual madness is not the source of the experience: human (not inhuman), social (not anti- or ante-social), collective destructive activity is the source, as Joseph Conrad knew. Our problem, therefore, is not just the problem of Iago, or even Hitler, but one for everybody, for us. Hannah Arendt reduced this form of every person's war when she analyzed Adolph Eichmann.[20] The problem is not just bureaucratic and banal. Under certain not so extraordinary circumstances, the problem is a fully human creation, our *fleur de mal*.

# Notes

## Introduction: The Desperate Side of War

The author wishes to thank John C. Inscoe for his helpful comments on an earlier version of this introduction.

1. Albert Burton Moore, *Conscription and Conflict in the Confederacy* (New York: Macmillan, 1924); Ella Lonn, *Desertion during the Civil War* (New York: Century, 1928); Georgia Lee Tatum, *Disloyalty in the Confederacy* (Chapel Hill: University of North Carolina Press, 1934); Richard Beringer, Herman Hattaway, Archer Jones, and William Still, eds., *Why the South Lost the Civil War* (Athens: University of Georgia Press, 1984); E. Merton Coulter, *The Confederate States of America, 1861–1865* (Baton Rouge: Louisiana State University Press, 1950). So forceful were the arguments of Beringer et al. that military historians have responded by reminding us not to lose track of the military side of the war. Gary W. Gallagher, *The Confederate War* (Cambridge, Mass.: Harvard University Press, 1997).

2. Frank W. Klingberg, *The Southern Claims Commission* (Berkeley: University of California Press, 1955), 1–19, treated the general subject only briefly in his examination of the Southern Claims Commission. Carl Degler, *The Other South: Southern Dissenters in the Nineteenth Century* (New York: Harper and Row, 1974); Steven E. Woodworth, ed., *The American Civil War: A Handbook of Literature and Research* (Westport, Conn.: Greenwood, 1996), 494–504, 530–43, reviews the scope, quality, and significance of the recent work on Southern Unionism.

3. Daniel W. Crofts, *Reluctant Confederates: Upper South Unionists in the Secession Crisis* (Chapel Hill: University of North Carolina Press, 1989), 359.

4. Richard L. Toutman, *The Heavens Are Weeping: The Diaries of George Richard Browder, 1852–1886* (Grand Rapids, Mich.: Zondervan Publishing, 1987), 114.

5. Stephen V. Ash, *When the Yankees Came: Conflict and Chaos in the Occupied South, 1861–1865* (Chapel Hill: University of North Carolina Press, 1995), 109–10.

6. W. Todd Groce, "The Social Origins of East Tennessee's Confederate Leadership," and Martin Crawford, "The Dynamics of Mountain Unionism: Federal Volunteers of Ashe County, North Carolina," both in *The Civil War in Appalachia: Collected Essays*, ed. Kenneth W. Noe and Shannon H. Wilson (Knoxville: University of Tennesse Press, 1997), 48, 62–64, 68; Richard N. Current, *Lincoln's Loyalists: Union Soldiers from the Confederacy* (Boston: Northeastern University Press, 1992), 133, 138.

7. Daniel E. Sutherland, "Getting the 'Real War' into the Books," *Virginia Magazine of History and Biography* 98 (April 1990): 193–220.

8. Current, *Lincoln's Loyalists*, 133.

9. Richard S. Brownlee, *Gray Ghosts of the Confederacy: Warfare in the West, 1861–1865* (Baton Rouge: Louisiana State University Press, 1958); Virgil C. Jones, *Gray Ghosts and Rebel Raiders* (New York: Holt, 1956); Albert Castel, "The Guerrilla War, 1861–1865," *Civil War Times Illustrated*, Special Issue (October 1974). For a pair of early reflective pieces on the guerrilla war see Virgil C. Jones, "The Problem of Writing about Guerrillas," *Military Affairs* 21 (summer 1958): 21–25; and Carl E. Grant, "Partisan Warfare, Model 1861–65," *Military Review* 8 (November 1958): 42–56. For the new historiographical trends, see John Keegan, *The Face of Battle: A Study of Agincourt, Waterloo, and the Soome* (New York: Viking Press, 1976); Maris A. Vinovskis, "Have Social Historians Lost the Civil War? Some Preliminary Demographic Speculations," *Journal of American History* 76 (June 1989): 34–58. Vinovskis followed his original article with a book of edited essays, *Toward a Social History of the American Civil War: Exploratory Essays* (Cambridge: Cambridge University Press, 1990). For an early attempt to combine both the "new" military history and the new "social" focus on the war with the advantages offered by a community study see Daniel E. Sutherland, *Seasons of War: The Ordeal of Confederate Community, 1861–1865* (New York: Free Press, 1995).

10. Phillip Shaw Paludan, *Victims: A True Story of the Civil War* (Knoxville: University of Tennessee Press, 1981); Michael Fellman, *Inside War: The Guerrilla Conflict in Missouri during the American Civil War* (New York: Oxford University Press, 1989); Benjamin Franklin Cooling, *Fort Donelson's Legacy: War and Society in Kentucky and Tennessee, 1862–63* (Knoxville: University of Tennessee Press, 1997); Noel C. Fisher, *War at Every Door: Partisan Politics and Guerrilla Violence in East Tennessee, 1860–1869* (Chapel Hill: University of North Carolina Press, 1997).

11. For instance, see David Paul Smith, *Frontier Defense in the Civil War: Texas' Rangers and Rebels* (College Station: Texas A&M University Press, 1992); David B. McCaslin, *Tainted Breeze: The Great Hanging at Gainesville, Texas, 1862* (Baton Rouge: Louisiana State University Press, 1994); William C. Davis, "A Different Kind of War: Fighting in the West," in *The Cause Lost: Myths and Realties of the Confederacy* (Lawrence: University Press of Kansas, 1996), 53–70. Altina L. Waller, "Feuding in Appalachia: Evolution of a Cultural Stereotype," in *Appalachia in the Making: The Mountain South in the Nineteenth Century*, ed. Mary Beth Pudup et al. (Chapel Hill: University of North Carolina Press, 1995), 347–76, while focusing on the postwar period, portrays the violence of the eastern mountains in softer tones.

12. James M. McPherson, *Battle Cry of Freedom: The Civil War Era* (New York: Oxford University Press, 1988), 284–97; Richard A. Martin, "Defeat in Victory: Yankee Experience in Early Civil War Jacksonville," *Florida Historical Quarterly* 53 (July 1974): 1–32; Kenneth C. Barnes, "The Williams Clan: Mountain Farmers and Union Fighters in North Central Arkansas," *Arkansas Historical Quarterly* 52 (autumn 1993): 286–317; Robert S. Davis Jr., "Forgotten Union Guerrilla Fighters

from the North Georgia Mountains," *North Georgia Journal* 5 (summer 1988): 30–40; Ralph Mann, "Ezekiel Counts's Sand Lick Company: Civil War and Localism in the Mountain South," and Jonathan D. Sarris, "An Execution in Lumpkin County: Localized Loyalties in North Georgia's Civil War," both in *Civil War in Appalachia*, ed. Noe and Wilson, 78–103, 131–57; Vernon H. Crow, *Storm in the Mountains: Thomas' Confederate Legion of Cherokee Indians and Mountaineers* (Cherokee, N.C.: Museum of the Cherokee Indian, 1982).

13. Kenneth W. Noe, "Exterminating Savages: The Union Army and Mountain Guerrillas in Southern West Virginia, 1861–62," in *Civil War in Appalachia*, ed. Noe and Wilson, 105–6; Noel G. Harrison, "Atop and Anvil: The Civilians' War in Fairfax and Alexandria Counties, April 1861–April 1862," *Virginia Magazine of History and Biography* 106 (spring 1998): 133–64.

14. Daniel E. Sutherland, "Guerrillas: The Real War in Arkansas," *Arkansas Historical Quarterly* 52 (fall 1993): 257–85, and "Without Pity, and Without the Blessing of God," *North & South* 1 (September 1998): 12–21.

# Telling and Retelling the Legend of the "Free State of Jones"

Several residents of Jones and Covington County deserve special thanks for helping me to better understand the Free State of Jones: Earle Knight shared memories, family stories, and research materials; Carliona Forsyth extended great hospitality and kindly arranged interviews for me with Knight descendants; Ethel Knight, DeBoyd Knight, and Julius Huff shared their opinions and insights with me. Gregg Andrews assisted me in conducting interviews and visits and provided ongoing editorial suggestions. An earlier version of this article was presented at the 1997 OAH Convention in San Francisco, where Daniel Sutherland and Philip Paludan offered helpful critiques. Participants in Rice University's Houston Area Southern Historians seminar of January 1998, especially Jane Dailey, Evelyn Thomas Nolen, John Boles, and Elizabeth H. Turner, offered encouragement and advice that further improved this article.

1. Jackson *Daily News*, August 1, 1974; B. D. Graves, Hebron Community Meeting, June 17, 1926, Special Collections, Lauren Rogers Museum of Art, Laurel, Mississippi, 6, 7.

2. Graves, Hebron Community Meeting, 6, 7. Benjamin Knight, Newton Knight, and Sil Coleman were related through their ties to John "Jackie" Knight, who in 1860 owned twenty-two slaves and 700 acres in Covington County. Benjamin Knight was Jackie's grandson through William H. Knight of Jones County; William in 1860 claimed real estate valued at $1,500 and personal property valued at $2,730. He owned two slaves. In 1860, Ben Knight lived in Jones County, owned 310 acres valued at $600, personal property valued at $295, and no slaves. Living with him were sixteen-year-old Louisa, presumably his wife, and two-year-old Sarah, presumably the couple's daughter. Newton Knight owned no slaves,

was the son of Albert Knight, and the grandson of Jackie Knight. He was twenty-three in 1860, married, the father of one son, and lived on the Jasper County side of Leaf River. Sil Coleman was a cousin-in-law to Ben and Newton Knight. His aunt, Elizabeth Coleman, married Daniel Knight, a son of Jackie Knight. In 1860, Daniel owned ten slaves, seven of which he appeared to gain through his marriage to Elizabeth Coleman. Bureau of the Census, *Federal Manuscript Censuses, Population, Agricultural and Manufacturing, and Slave Schedules, 1860, Covington, Jasper, and Jones Counties, Mississippi*, M653, MF4721, National Archives and Records Service (hereafter cited as NA); Winnie Knight Thomas et al, *The Family of John "Jackie" Knight and Keziah Davis Knight, 1773–1985* (Magee, MS: Robert and DeLores Knight Vinson, 1985), 335–40; Jan Sumrall and Kenneth Welch, *The Knights and Related Families* (Denham Springs, La.: privately published by authors, 1985), 151.

3. Graves, Hebron Community Meeting, 7. As Leah Townsend noted in her history of South Carolina Baptists, baptism symbolizes "an actual burial in a watery grave from which the regenerate subject arises a conscious member of Christ." *South Carolina Baptists, 1670–1805* (Baltimore: Genealogical Publishing Company, 1974), 291.

4. The most recent studies of the Civil War's effect on the home front and vice versa include Kenneth W. Noe and Shannon H. Wilson, eds., *The Civil War in Appalachia: Collected Essays* (Knoxville: University of Tennessee Press, 1997); Drew Gilpin Faust, *Mothers of Invention: Women of the Slaveholding South in the American Civil War* (Chapel Hill: University of North Carolina Press, 1996); Daniel E. Sutherland, *Seasons of War: The Ordeal of a Confederate Community, 1861–1865* (New York: Free Press, 1995); LeeAnn Whites, *The Civil War as a Crisis in Gender: Augusta, Georgia, 1860–1890* (Athens: University of Georgia Press, 1995); Catherine Clinton and Nina Silber, *Divided Houses: Gender and the Civil War* (New York: Oxford University Press, 1992); and George C. Rable, *Civil Wars: Women and the Crisis of Southern Nationalism* (Urbana: University of Illinois Press, 1989). Those that specifically study Unionism and desertion within the Confederate South include Wayne K. Durrill, *War of Another Kind: A Southern Community in the Great Rebellion* (New York: Oxford University Press, 1990); James Marten, *Texas Divided: Loyalty and Dissent in the Lone Star State, 1856–1874* (Lexington: University Press of Kentucky, 1990); William T. Auman, "Neighbor against Neighbor: The Inner Civil War in the Randolph County Area of Confederate North Carolina," *North Carolina Historical Review* 61 (January 1984): 60–90; and Phillip S. Paludan, *Victims: A True Story of the Civil War* (Knoxville: University of Tennessee Press, 1981).

5. Ethel Knight, *The Echo of the Black Horn* (privately published by author, 1951), 135–36.

6. Knight, *Echo of the Black Horn*, especially 82–85, 90–95, 126, 142, 168; C. Vann Woodward, *Origins of the New South, 1877–1913* (Baton Rouge: Louisiana State University Press, 1951).

7. Records of Benjamin F. Knight, Company B, Seventh Battalion Infantry, from "Compiled Service Records of Confederate Soldiers Who Served in

Organizations From the State of Mississippi," M269, roll 166, NA. An original
copy of Newton Knight's muster list is contained in the Newton Knight Folder,
H.R. 1814, RG 233, House of Representatives, Accompanying Papers Files, 42nd
Cong., box 15, NA. Clipping of letter from unidentified person, Mobile *Evening
News*, May 3, 1864, contained in James L. Power Scrapbook, Mississippi
Department of Archives and History (hereafter cited as MDAH), Jackson,
Mississippi.

　　8. Mobile *Evening News*, May 3, 1864; Power Scrapbook, MDAH.

　　9. Natchez *Courier*, July 12, 1864.

　　10. G. Norton Galloway, "A Confederacy Within a Confederacy," *Magazine of
American History* (October 1886): 387–90.

　　11. General Dabney Herndon Maury, *Recollections of a Virginian in the Mexican,
Indian, and Civil Wars* (New York: Charles Scribner's Sons, 1894), 200–203, quoted
passage, 246–47.

　　12. For arguments against Jones County's secession from the Confederacy, see
Alexander L. Bondurant, "Did Jones County Secede?" *Publications of the Mississippi
Historical Society* 1 (1898): 103–6; and Goode Montgomery, "Alleged Secession of
Jones County," *Publications of the Mississippi Historical Society* 8 (1904): 13–22. The
myth of secession was perpetuated by Mary Looram, "A Little-Known Republic,"
*The Outlook*, March 17, 1920; James Street, *Look Away! A Dixie Notebook* (New
York: Sun Dial Press, 1936); and Craddock Goins, "The Secession of Jones
County," *American Mercury*, January 1941. Jones's secession was denied by L. R.
Collins, youngest son of Jasper Collins, in a letter to the Mobile *Daily Herald* dated
May 19, 1914 (typed copy of letter in unpublished files of the Works Progress
Administration [WPA], RG 60, v. 316, MDAH). Newton Knight denied it in 1921
(*New Orleans Item*, March 20, 1921).

　　13. Quoted passages from Galloway, "Confederacy Within a Confederacy," 390;
Maury, *Recollections of a Virginian*, 247. On the economic structure of antebellum
Jones County, see Bradley G. Bond, "Herders, Farmers, and Markets on the Inner
Frontier: The Mississippi Piney Woods, 1850–1860," in *Plain Folk of the South
Revisited*, ed. Samuel C. Hyde Jr. (Baton Rouge: Louisiana State University Press,
1997), 73–99. On the connections between republican ideals of independence and
Southern yeomen's "selective" participation in markets, see Joyce Chaplin, *An
Anxious Pursuit: Agricultural Innovation and Modernity in the Lower South,
1730–1815* (Chapel Hill: University of North Carolina Press, 1993), 281, 330–55.

　　14. Earle Knight, descendant of William Martin Knight, a member of the
Knight Company, recalled hearing that the siege of Vicksburg precipitated the
desertions of many Jones County soldiers from the Confederate army (author's conversation with Earle Knight, June 30, 1994, Laurel, Miss., transcript deposited at
the University of Southern Mississippi, Hattiesburg, Miss.). The records of soldiers
who served in Company B, Seventh Battalion Infantry, confirm his assertion.
("Compiled Service Records of Confederate Soldiers Who Served in Organizations
From the State of Mississippi," M269, rolls 165–67, NA). For contemporary reports
on the siege of Vicksburg, see U.S. War Department, *War of the Rebellion: A*

*Compilation of the Official Records of the Union and Confederate Armies,* (Washington, D.C.: GPO, 1891), ser. 1, 24, pt. 2, 146–23, passim (hereafter cited as *Official Records*).

15. Statistics on Mississippi slaveholding are from the Inter-University Consortium for Political and Social Research, "Study 00003: Historical Demographic, Economic, and Social Data: U.S., 1790–1970." Anne Arbor, ICPSR. Local statistics are from the Bureau of the Census, *Federal Manuscript Slave Schedules, 1860, Covington, Jasper, and Jones Counties;* and *Agricultural and Manufacturing Census Records, 1860, Jones, Covington, and Jasper Counties,* M653, MF 4721, NA.

16. Knight, *Echo of the Black Horn,* 82, 115–16. Works that portray Newton Knight and his followers as principled Unionists include Thomas J. Knight (Newton's son), *The Life and Activities of Captain Newton Knight and His Company and the Free State of Jones County* (privately published by author, [1934], 1946); and Jack D. L. Holmes, "The Mississippi County That 'Seceded' from the Confederate States of America," *Civil War Times Illustrated* 3, no. 10 (February 1965). Meigs Frost described Newt as a Unionist but also as the embodiment of "primeval simplicity" in the *New Orleans Item,* March 20, 1921. Likewise, John K. Bettersworth, in his *Confederate Mississippi: The People and Policies of a Cotton State in Wartime* (Baton Rouge: Louisiana State University Press, 1963), 524–25, acknowledged Piney Woods Unionism but characterized its inhabitants as "primitive" poor whites who lacked a political ideology. Though they disagree on numerous facts, both Ethel Knight and Rudy Leverett (*Legend of the Free State of Jones* [Jackson: University Press of Mississippi, 1984]) present Newton Knight and his men as thieves and murderers.

17. L[eonidas] Polk, Lieutenant General, to President [Jefferson] Davis, March 21, 1864; and W. Wirt Thomson, Captain, to Secretary of War James Seddon, March 29, 1864, both in *Official Records,* ser. 1, 32, pt. 3, 662–63, 711–12. A. H. Polk, First Lieutenant and Acting Assistant Inspector General, referred to Jones County deserters as "Tories" to Lieutenant Colonel T. F. Sevier, Assistant Inspector General, March 3, 1864 (*Official Records,* ser. 1, 32. pt. 3, 579).

18. Colonel Brown to Governor Clark, May 5, 1864, Governors' Papers, RG 27, v. 57, MDAH.

19. Lieutenant General L[eonidas] Polk to General [Dabney] Maury, February 7, 1864, *Official Records,* ser. 1, 32, pt. 2, 688–89; Dabney H. Maury, Major-General, Commanding, to Hon. James A. Seddon, Secretary of War, March 3, 1864, *Official Records,* ser. 1, 32, pt. 2, 688–89; L. Polk, Lieutenant General and Adjutant Inspector General, to General S[amuel] Cooper, March 3, 1864, *Official Records,* ser. 1, 32, pt. 3, 580.

20. T. M. Jack, Assistant Adjutant General, by Command of Lieutenant General Polk, Special Orders No. 80, March 20, 1864, *Official Records,* ser. 1, 32, pt. 3, 662–63.

21. Colonel [William N.] Brown to Governor Clark, May 5, 1864, Governors' Papers, RG 27, v. 56, MDAH; Adjutant-General Colonel Robert Lowry to

Lieutenant Colonel T. M. Jack, Assistant General, April 13, 1864, *Official Records*, ser. 1, 52; pt. 2, 657.

22. *New Orleans Item*, March 20, 1921. Newton Knight's roster listed the following men as executed by Colonel Lowry's Cavalry: Tapley Bynum, S. C. Coleman, Tucker Gregg, B. F. Knight, Daniel Redock (Reddock), N. V. Whitehead, T. J. Whitehead, W. W. Whitehead, James Yates (Ates), and Thomas Yates (Ates) (Newton Knight Folder, H.R. 1814, RG 233, box 15, NA). Knight's bill was read before the House of Representatives three times between 1871 and 1873; each time it was referred to a committee where it died. Congress never compensated the men of Knight's Company. See H.R. 41A–B1, H.R. 2775, 41st Cong., 3rd sess., January 16, 1871 (referred to Judiciary Committee); H.R. 42A–B1, H.R. 1814, 42nd Cong., 2nd sess., March 4, 1872 (referred to Military Affairs Committee); and H.R. 43A–B1, H.R. 822, 43rd Cong., 1st sess., December 18, 1873 (referred to Claims Committee), in RG 233, NA.

23. Richard Simmons to Honorable G. C. McKee, December 6, 1870; and B. A. Mathews, Ex-Probate Judge of Jones County, Mississippi, to Honorable L. W. Perce and G. C. Mckee, December 8, 1870, both in Newton Knight Folder, H.R. 1814, RG 233, box 15, NA. In regard to the men that Newton Knight included in his bill, Judge Mathews explained that Knight excluded former members who "did not hold out faithful" to the band.

24. *New Orleans Item*, March 20, 1921.

25. Newton Knight twice enrolled in Confederate army units. From Jasper County, on August 17, 1861, he enrolled as a private in Company K, Eighth Regiment, Mississippi Volunteers (later, Company E, Eighth Mississippi Infantry). On May 12, 1862, he enlisted in Company F, Seventh Battalion Mississippi Infantry, along with many of his neighbors and kin shortly after the first Confederate Conscription Act was passed. Neither of his unit records mentions his having entered as a hospital orderly; in fact, he was detailed as provost guard between September and October 1862. He was first reported AWOL between November and December 1862, which fits his story of having deserted after the Confederacy passed the Twenty Negro Law on October 11, 1862. Jasper Collins enrolled in Company F, Seventh Battalion, in May 1862. He was reported missing from his command on October 13, 1862, two days after passage of the Twenty Negro Law. (This law, it should be noted, discriminated against virtually all Jones County slaveholders as well as nonslaveholders.) All records from "Compiled Service Records of Confederate Soldiers Who Served in Organizations From the State of Mississippi," M269, rolls 165, 166, and 170, NA.

26. *New Orleans Item*, March 20, 1921.

27. *New Orleans Item*, March 20, 1921. Rudy Leverett cited Lieutenant Wilson's use of civilian forces to defeat Federal raiders at the battle of Rocky Creek as additional evidence of Jones's Confederate sympathies (*Legend of the Free State of Jones*, 61). Wilson, however, identified the civilians who *fought* on his side as being primarily from Brookhaven, eighty-six miles away (*Official Records*, ser. 1, 24, pt. 2, 514–15).

28. H. Maury, Colonel, to General [Dabney H. Maury], March 12, 1864, enclosed in letter from Dabney H. Maury, Major General, to Colonel T. M. Jack, Assistant Adjutant General, March 15, 1864, *Official Records*, ser. 1, 32, pt. 3, 632–33; Danl. P. Logan to Major J. C. Denis, Provost Marshall General, April 7, 1864, *Official Records*, ser. 1, 32, pt. 3, 755; W. L. Brandon, Brigadier General, Commanding, to Maj. General D. H. Maury, August 14, 1864, *Official Records*, ser. 1, 39, pt. 3, 777.

29. Address of Mr. M. P. Bush before the meeting of the D.A.R., February 12, 1912, Special Collections, Lauren Rogers Museum, Laurel, Miss. Madison P. Bush served in Company B, Seventh Battalion, alongside many future members of the Knight Company. He served at Vicksburg and was reported AWOL in January 1864 ("Compiled Service Records of Confederate Soldiers Who Served in Organizations From the State of Mississippi," M269, roll 165, NA).

30. Ruby Huff, "A Skirmish—Cavalry Versus Deserters—Wherein Newt Knight's Men Raid Lowrey's Raiders," unpublished WPA files, RG 60, v. 272, MDAH. In 1860, Thomas J. Huff owned one slave. At war's end, he was appointed Jones County sheriff by Governor Sharkey on the advice of Newton Knight and sixty-three petitioners who protested that "rebel cavalry" had prevented them from casting their ballots in the 1864 election of county officers. Forty-one pro-Confederate men signed a counterpetition that branded Huff a deserter. Petitions of July 15, 1865, and July 29, 1865, from Jones County to Governor Sharkey, Governors' Papers, RG 27, v. 61B, MDAH.

31. Interview with B. R. Sumrall, August 31, 1936, unpublished WPA files, RG 60, v. 316, MDAH.

32. Graves, Hebron Community Meeting, 5, 8. Ben Graves's father, Robert Graves Jr., was reported as owning ten slaves in the Bureau of the Census, *Federal Manuscript Census, Slave Schedule, 1860, Jones County, Mississippi*, M653, MF4 721, NA.

33. Knight, *Echo of the Black Horn*, 82, 115; Pension and military records verify that Riley James Collins was a private in Company E, First Regiment of the New Orleans Volunteers (Jean Strickland and Patricia N. Edwards, comps., *Miscellaneous Records of Jones County, MS: Marks and Brands; Final Records of the Chancery Court; Union Army Pension Records, 1843–1890*, [Moss Point, Miss.: n.p., 1992], 148–49). B. R. Sumrall identified the speechmaker as "J. R. Collins." I am inferring that this was Riley James, with the initials inverted, because Sumrall also mentioned that "J. R." died in New Orleans after joining the Union army. (WPA records, RG 60, vol. 316, 11–12, MDAH).

34. Ages of men were calculated from the Bureau of the Census, *Federal Manuscript Censuses, 1850, 1860, Jones County, Mississippi*, M653, MF4721, NA. In his bill to Congress for compensation for services rendered to the United States government, Newton Knight reported that R. J. Collins enlisted on April 30, 1864, in Captain Wolfe's Company, Tisdel's regiment, at New Orleans. (Newton Knight Folder, H.R. 1814, RG 233, box 15, NA). Vinson A. Collins's participation as a delegate at the 1868 convention is reported in the *Journal of the Proceedings in the*

*Constitutional Convention of the State of Mississippi, 1868* (Jackson: E. Stafford, Printer, 1871), 14. On the Unionist views of the Collinses of Hardin County, Texas, see Campbell Loughmiller and Lynn Loughmiller, comps. and eds., *Big Thicket Legacy* (Austin: University of Texas Press, 1977).

35. Unpublished WPA files, RG 60, v. 315, MDAH. Addie West's interview of Martha Wheeler may also be found in George P. Rawick, ed., *The American Slave: A Composite Autobiography*, supplement, series 1, vol. 10, *Mississippi Narratives* (Westport, Conn.: Greenwood, 1972), 5:2262–71. That version, however, does not contain the story of Ben Knight's murder. Quoted remarks of Ben Graves from Graves, Hebron Community Meeting, June 17, 1926.

36. Knight, *Echo of the Black Horn*, 135–36.

37. Ibid., 136–37.

38. Ibid., 138.

39. On the history of Newton and Rachel Knight's relationship, see Victoria Bynum, "Misshapen Identity: Memory, Folklore, and the Legend of Rachel Knight," in *Discovering the Women in Slavery: Emancipating Perspectives on the American Past,* ed. Patricia Morton (Athens: University of Georgia Press, 1996), 29–46; and Victoria Bynum, "'White Negroes' in Segregated Mississippi: Miscegenation, Racial Identity, and the Law," *Journal of Southern History* 64, no. 2 (May 1998): 247–76.

40. Author's conversation with Earle Knight, June 30, 1994.

## "Shot for Being Bushwhackers": Guerrilla War and Extralegal Violence in a North Georgia Community, 1862–1865

1. Emily Hughes Fannie Boyd, July 17, 1861, Madeline Anthony Collection, Lumpkin County Public Library, Dahlonega, Ga.; Depositions of Mary Stansbury, Margaret Stuart, William R. Crisson, Thomas N. Wilson, William A. Twiggs, Francis Williams, and S. B. Boyd, located in U.S. Pension Bureau files of Solomon Stansbury and Iley Stuart, National Archives; Robert S. Davis Jr., "Forgotten Union Guerrilla Fighters from the North Georgia Mountains," *North Georgia Journal* 5 (summer 1988): 30; William S. Kinsland, "The Graves on Bearden's Bridge Hill," in *A North Georgia Journal of History* (Woodstock, Ga.: Legacy Communications, 1989), 304–13; Ethelene Dyer Jones, *Facets of Fannin: A History of Fannin County, Georgia* (Dallas, Tex.: Curtis Media Corp., 1989), 533. Other analyses of Civil War atrocities, analyses which have greatly informed this paper, are Phillip Paludan's *Victims: A True Story of the Civil War* (Knoxville: University of Tennessee Press, 1981) and Michael Fellman's *Inside War: Guerrilla Conflict in Missouri during the American Civil War* (New York: Oxford University Press, 1989).

2. Michael P. Johnson, "A New Look at the Popular Vote for Delegates to the Georgia Secession Convention," *Georgia Historical Quarterly* 56 (summer 1972): 259–76. See also Michael P. Johnson, *Toward a Patriarchal Republic: The Secession of*

*Georgia* (Baton Rouge: Louisiana State University Press, 1977); Roy R. Doyton and Thomas W. Hodler, "Secessionist Sentiment and Slavery: A Geographic Analysis," *Georgia Historical Quarterly* 73 (summer 1989): 323–48.

3. William Martin to Governor Brown, April 12, 1861, Governor's Correspondence, Georgia Department of Archives and History, Atlanta, Ga. (hereafter cited as GDAH); Luke Tate, *History of Pickens County* (Atlanta: Walter Brown Publishing, 1978), 205.

4. James W. Miller to Governor Joseph E. Brown, February 15, 1861, Telamon Cuyler Collection, Hargrett Library, University of Georgia, Athens.

5. Andrew Young to Governor Brown, December 5, 1861, Telamon Cuyler Collection; James Dobson to Governor Brown, September 19, 1861, ibid.; *Athens Southern Watchman*, May 8, 1861; William A. Campbell to Governor Brown, February 23, 1861, Governor's Correspondence, GDAH.

6. George W. Lee to Governor Brown, January 27, 1863, Governor's Correspondence, GDAH; Kinsland, "The Civil War Comes to Lumpkin County," in *A North Georgia Journal of History*, 181–82.

7. T. Conn Bryan, *Confederate Georgia* (Athens: University of Georgia Press, 1953), 90–93; Peter Wallenstein, *From Slave South to New South: Public Policy in Nineteenth-Century Georgia* (Chapel Hill: University of North Carolina Press, 1987), 118–20.

8. U.S. Commissioner of Claims, *Case File of Rickles Stanley, Fannin County, Georgia; Southern Claims Commission Approved Claims*, National Archives microfilm, 1990; Jonathan D. Sarris, "Anatomy of an Atrocity: The Madden Branch Massacre and Guerrilla Warfare in North Georgia, 1861–1865," *Georgia Historical Quarterly* 78 (winter 1993): 694–95. For similar instances of Appalachian women being drawn into mountain warfare, see Ralph Mann, "Guerrilla Warfare and Gender Roles: Sandy Basin, Virginia, as a Test Case," in *Journal of the Appalachian Studies Association*, 5, *Diversity on Appalachia, Images and Realities* (1993): 59–66.

9. Mills Lane, *Times That Prove Men's Principles: Civil War in Georgia, A Documentary History* (Savannah: Beehive Press, 1993), 133.

10. Robert S. Davis Jr, "Memoirs of a Partisan War: Sion Darnell Remembers North Georgia, 1861–1865," *Georgia Historical Quarterly* 80 (spring 1996): 93–116.

11. Report of Special Agent John Wager, March 9, 1877, U.S. Pension Bureau file of Solomon Stansbury, National Archives.

12. James Jefferson Findley to Governor Brown, December 23, 1863, Telamon Cuyler Collection; Huldah Fain to M. C. Briant, April 14, 1863, Huldah Fain Papers, Southern Historical Collection, University of North Carolina, Chapel Hill.

13. Undated petition of Floyd County Citizens to General Braxton Bragg, Simpson Fouche Papers, Southern Historical Collection.

14. Josiah Woody to Joseph Brown, September 6, 1862, Governor's Correspondence, GDAH.

15. George W. Lee to Governor Brown, January 27, 1863, Brown Correspondence, GDAH; February 3, 1863, ibid.; William Harris Bragg, *Joe Brown's Army: The Georgia State Line, 1862–1865* (Macon: Mercer University Press, 1987), 18–21.

16. Lumpkin County Superior Court Minutes, December 1863, May 1864; *State of Georgia v. James Payne and John Woody*, box 38, "Old Court Records," Lumpkin County Courthouse, Dahlonega, Ga.; Weir Boyd to Governor Brown, December 19, 1864, Governor's Correspondence, GDAH.

17. Bertram Wyatt-Brown, *Southern Honor: Ethics and Behavior in the Old South* (Oxford: Oxford University Press, 1982), 435–93; Altina Waller, *Feud: Hatfields, McCoys, and Social Change in Appalachia, 1860–1900* (Chapel Hill: University of North Carolina Press, 1988), 85–93; Richard Maxwell Brown, *Strain of Violence: Historical Studies of American Violence and Vigilantism* (New York: Oxford University Press, 1975), 91–133. The intersection of vigilantism and wartime fears of disloyalty is illustrated in Richard McCaslin's outstanding case of Cooke County, Texas, *Tainted Breeze: The Great Hanging at Gainesville, Texas, 1862* (Baton Rouge: Louisiana State University Press, 1994).

18. Nancy Wimpy to Andrew Reese, August 27, 1863, Madeline Anthony Collection. For a further exploration of civilian commitment to harsh war measures, see Charles Royster, *The Destructive War: William Tecumseh Sherman, Stonewall Jackson, and the Americans* (New York: Alfred A. Knopf, 1991), 232–95.

19. Deposition of Francis Marion Williams, February 28, 1877, U.S. Pension Bureau file of Solomon Stansbury, National Archives; McCaslin, *Tainted Breeze*.

20. Deposition of William Crisson, February 28, 1877, U.S. Pension Bureau file of Solomon Stansbury, National Archives. Richard McCaslin has outlined a very similar incident of Civil War vigilantism; see his *Tainted Breeze*.

21. Deposition of Francis Marion Williams of Lumpkin County, March 8, 1877, U.S. Pension Bureau file of Solomon Stansbury, National Archives; Joel Williamson, *The Crucible of Race: Black-White Relations in the American South since Reconstruction* (New York: Oxford University Press, 1984), 180–220.

22. Lumpkin County Grand Jury Presentments, February and August 1866, Lumpkin County Courthouse, Dahlonega, Ga.

23. James M. McPherson, *What They Fought For, 1861–1865* (Baton Rouge:Louisiana State University Press, 1994); Phillip Paludan, "The American Civil War Considered as a Crisis in Law and Order," *American Historical Review* 77, (October 1972): 1013–34. See also Paludan's *A People's Contest: The Union and the Civil War, 1861–1865* (New York: Harper and Row, 1988), 3–31.

# "In Time of War": Unionists Hanged in Kinston, North Carolina, February 1864

1. U.S. War Department, *War of the Rebellion: A Compilation of the Official Records of the Union and Confederate Armies*, (Washington, D.C.: GPO, 1880–1901) ser. 1, vol. 33, 62–67, 69 (hereafter cited as *Official Records*, all references to series 1); "Narrative of James Mitchell, Co. I, 99th N. Y. S. Vols." in *History of the Naval Brigade: 99th New York Volunteers, Union Coast Guard*, by Philip Corell (New York: published under the auspices of the regimental veteran association, 1905), 17–18;

John G. Smith, "Recollections of Capt. John G. Smith, Co. C, 8th Ga. Cavalry, as to a Trip as a Spy in Newbern, N.C., February 1864," *Carolina and the Southern Cross* 2, no. 1 (April 1914): 3. The total number of men at Beech Grove included fifty-seven men from Company F, 2nd (Union) North Carolina Volunteers; fourteen members of the 132nd New York; and a small detachment from the 99th New York, perhaps sixty men and three officers, who arrived as reinforcements. Some Union soldiers successfully escaped, including John Buck, who served in Company F, 2nd North Carolina (Union) Volunteers and later testified on behalf of Andrew Britton's widow. See Andrew J. Britton, Pension Records, Application 227182; Certificate 179682, RG 15, National Archives (hereafter as NA).

2. Clifford Tyndall, "Lenoir County during the Civil War" (M.A. thesis, East Carolina University, 1981), 75 n. 15; *Raleigh Daily Progress*, February 11, 1864; Corell, *History of the Naval Brigade*, 18; *Raleigh Daily State Journal*, January 16, 1864; Smith, "Recollections," 2; *Executive Document No. 98*, House of Representatives, 39th Cong., 1st sess., 80–81 (hereafter cited as *House Executive Doc. No. 98*).

3. Ulysses S. Grant to Andrew Johnson, March 16, 1866, in *The Papers of Ulysses S. Grant*, ed. John Simon (Carbondale: Southern Illinois University Press, 1988), 16: 120–22. The exact dates of the hangings are unclear; pension records and newspaper accounts differ. Chaplain John Paris recorded hangings on February 5, 12, and 15, in John Paris Diary, Southern Historical Collection, University of North Carolina, Chapel Hill (hereafter cited as SHC). The two sets of brothers were John and Joseph Brock and John and Lewis Freeman. Hodijah Meade alleged that thirteen "were strung up at once." John Paris wrote, "The thirteen were all hanged on one scaffold." See Hodijah Lincoln Meade to Richard Hardaway Meade, February 21, 1864, Meade Family Papers, Virginia Historical Society, Richmond, Va.; Paris Diary, February 15, 1864, SHC.

4. George Rable, *The Confederate Republic: A Revolution against Politics* (Chapel Hill: University of North Carolina Press, 1994), 200–205; William C. Harris, *William Woods Holden: Firebrand of North Carolina Politics* (Baton Rouge: Louisiana State University, 1987), 127–55; William Thomas Auman, "Neighbor against Neighbor: The Inner Civil War in the Randolph County Area of Confederate North Carolina," *North Carolina Historical Review* 61 (January 1984): 68; Michael K. Honey, "The War within the Confederacy: White Unionists of North Carolina," *Prologue: Journal of the National Archives* 18 (summer 1986): 79. For example, on January 19, 1864, the *Raleigh Daily State Journal* condemned Holden and his followers for corrupting "public sentiment through the powerful agency of the press" and instigating treason.

5. Georgia Lee Tatum, *Disloyalty in the Confederacy* (Chapel Hill: University of North Carolina Press, 1934), viii; Frank W. Klingberg, *The Southern Claims Commission* (1955; reprint, New York: Octagon Books, 1978), 2–4, quote from 4; Philip Shaw Paludan, *Victims: A True Story of the Civil War* (Knoxville: University of Tennessee Press, 1981), 59–62; Auman, "Neighbor against Neighbor," 70 n. 43; Richard Nelson Current, *Lincoln's Loyalists: Union Soldiers from the Confederacy* (New York: Oxford University Press, 1992), 64, 144–46, quote from 146; Stephen V. Ash,

*When the Yankees Came: Conflict and Chaos in the Occupied South, 1861–1865* (Chapel Hill: University of North Carolina Press, 1995), 11. Michael Fellman, Richard McCaslin, and Noel Fisher have found examples of anti-Union violence in Missouri, Texas, and Tennessee. See Michael Fellman, *Inside War: The Guerrilla Conflict in Missouri during the American Civil War* (New York: Oxford University Press, 1989); Richard McCaslin, *Tainted Breeze: The Great Hanging at Gainesville, Texas, 1862* (Baton Rouge: Louisiana State University Press, 1994); Noel Fisher, *War at Every Door: Partisan Politics and Guerilla Violence in East Tennessee* (Chapel Hill: University of North Carolina, 1997).

6. Studies that highlight North Carolina's class tensions, disaffection, desertion, Unionism, and violent inner Civil War include Paul Escott, *Many Excellent People: Power and Privilege in North Carolina, 1850–1900* (Chapel Hill: University of North Carolina Press, 1985); John G. Barrett and W. Buck Yearns, eds., *North Carolina Civil War Documentary* (Chapel Hill: University of North Carolina Press, 1980); Ella Lonn, *Desertion during the Civil War* (Gloucester, Mass.: Peter Smith, 1966); Albert Burton Moore, *Conscription and Conflict in the Confederacy* (New York: Hilary House Publishers, 1963), 279–96; Current, *Lincoln's Loyalists*, 61–73; Wayne Durrill, *War of Another Kind: A Southern Community in the Great Rebellion* (New York: Oxford University Press, 1990); Paludan, *Victims;* Richard Bardolph, "Confederate Dilemma: North Carolina Troops and the Deserter Problem," pts. 1–2, *North Carolina Historical Review* 66 (January/April 1989): 61–86, 179–210; Honey, "The War within the Confederacy," 75–93; Auman, "Neighbor against Neighbor," 59–92; Robin E. Baker, "Class Conflict and Political Upheaval: The Transformation of North Carolina Politics during the Civil War," *North Carolina Historical Review* 69 (April 1992): 148–78; Norman C. Delaney, "Charles Henry Foster and the Unionists of Eastern North Carolina," *North Carolina Historical Review* 37 (July 1960): 348–66; Richard Reid, "A Test Case of the 'Crying Evil': Desertion among North Carolina Troops during the Civil War," *North Carolina Historical Review* 58 (July 1981): 234–55; Tatum, *Disloyalty in the Confederacy,* 107–35; Jeffrey J. Crow, "Thomas Settle Jr., Reconstruction, and the Memory of the Civil War," *Journal of Southern History* 62 (November 1996): 689–726.

7. Lenoir County's prime importance to the Confederacy was the railroad that ran through Kinston. Wartime manufacturing included a shoe factory and grist mills. Quote from William H. Cocke Diary, October 21, 1863, Cocke Family Papers, Virginia Historical Society, Richmond, Va. For more on wartime Kinston and Lenoir County see David Jackson Logan to *Enquirer*, December 1, 1862, David Jackson Logan Letters, Heritage Place Lenoir Community College, Kinston, N.C.; William S. Powell, *Annals of Progress: The Story of Lenoir County and Kinston, North Carolina* (Raleigh: State Department of Archives and History, 1963), 5, 7, 36, 41, 45–47; also Edward Jervey, ed., *Prison Life among the Rebels: Recollections of a Union Chaplain* (Kent, Ohio: Kent State University Press, 1990), 23; *Official Records,* 33:1068; Daniel Crofts, *Reluctant Confederates: Upper South Unionists in the Secession Crisis* (Chapel Hill: University of North Carolina Press), 41, 150.

8. U.S. Bureau of the Census, *Eighth Census of the United States, 1860,*

Schedule 1 (Population), Lenoir and Jones County, North Carolina, NA. I found about ten of the victims in the census, including Jesse Summerlin, John Stanly, Stephen Jones, William Haddock, Amos Armyett, William Irving, John Freeman, Lewis Freeman, Lewis Taylor, John Brock.

9. *House Executive Doc. No. 98*, 38–39, 56, quotes from 38–39. A. J. Lofton, a member of the same home guard unit, stated that he joined the battalion "soon after the fall of New Bern" in early 1862. See Lewis Freeman, Pension Record, Application 132278, Certificate 187672, RG 15, NA; and Louis H. Manarin, *A Guide to Military Organizations and Installations in North Carolina, 1861–1865* (Raleigh: North Carolina Confederate Centennial Commission, 1961), 16.

10. George M. Rose, "Sixty-Sixth Regiment," in *Histories of the Several Regiments and Battalions from North Carolina in the Great War, 1861–65*, ed. Walter Clark (Goldsboro, N.C.: Nash Brothers, Book and Job Printers, 1901), 4: 685.

11. Ibid., 685–87; also W. H. C. Whiting to Zebulan Vance, October 24, 1863, Zebulon Vance Papers, North Carolina Division of Archives and History, Raleigh, N.C.

12. For a discussion of self-interest as a determinant of loyalty see David Potter, *The South and the Sectional Conflict* (Baton Rouge: Louisiana State University Press, 1968), 36–83; also Rable, *Confederate Republic*, 7. The *Raleigh Daily State Journal* reported on January 16, 1864: "One small regiment of infantry numbering about 500 men known by the Yankees as the 2d North Carolina Troops made up of deserters chiefly from Nethercutt's battalion does most hazardous picketing and scouting duty along our lines, being as they are, thoroughly acquainted with the people and every nook and corner of the county lying between New Bern and this place." See *Official Records*, 29, pt. 1, 979–81, 989, for evidence of the Federal army seeking to protect and even rescue families of the Second North Carolina from Confederate attack; also *Official Records*, 33:484, for positioning of unit in defense of New Bern. The Union newspaper *North Carolina Times* advertised a $302 bounty to join the Second Regiment North Carolina Union Volunteers on January 23, 1864. For more on the Second North Carolina and a discussion of these men's military status, see *North Carolina Times*, January 9 and 23,1864; *House Executive Doc. No. 98*, 38–39, 56–58; Tyndall, "Lenoir County," 74; Current, *Lincoln's Loyalists*, 67–69, 135; Delaney, "Charles Henry Foster," 362–64; Francis MacDonnell, "The Price of Loyalty: Unionist Families in Eastern North Carolina," unpublished paper in possession of author. George Pickett asked Governor Vance about Lincoln offering amnesty to Confederate deserters in August of 1863. See George E. Pickett to Zebulan Vance, November 17, 1863, Zebulon Vance Papers, North Carolina Division of Archives and History, Raleigh, N.C. Lincoln's Amnesty Proclamation was dated December 8, 1863, and quickly began appearing regularly in the pro-Union New Bern newspaper, *North Carolina Times*. Pension and census records indicate that some of these men joined the Second North Carolina as early as November 24 and as late as December 22, 1863. See Andrew J. Britton Pension Records, Application 227182, Certificate 179682, RG 15, NA; U.S. Bureau of the Census, *Eleventh Census of the United States, 1890*, Schedules Enumerating Union Veterans and Widows of Union Veterans of Civil War, Jones County, N.C., NA.

13. Jervey, *Prison Life among the Rebels*, 22; *House Executive Doc. No. 98*, 28–32.

14. Harrison also insisted that the condemned were not conscripts but willing volunteers in the Confederate army. See Walter Harrison to Andrew Johnston, June 15, 1865, Pickett Family Typescript Notebook, Virginia Historical Society, Richmond. Lee A. Wallace Jr. in his *Seventeenth Virginia Infantry*. (Lynchburg, Va.: H. E. Howard, 1990), 58, cites Brigadier General and Virginian Montgomery Corse as "president" of the court-martial, along with seven other unnamed Virginia officers.

15. Richard Bardolph argues that the court-martials' denial of clemency, haste, and the sheer number of men executed at Kinston made this episode "uncommon." Despite "Leiber's Code," which sanctioned the execution of deserters captured in the enemy's ranks, the size, spectacle, and polarized public reaction to these deaths make this an unusual episode. See Bardolph, "Confederate Dilemma," pt. 2, 205, 207; also *House Executive Doc. No. 98*, 30; Tyndall, "Lenoir County," 76; *House Executive Doc. No. 98*, 45; Current, *Lincoln's Loyalists*, 118.

16. *Official Records*, 33:867–68.

17. John Paris, "Note" to *A Sermon: Preached Before Brig.-Gen. Hoke's Brigade, at Kinston, N.C. on the 28th Day of February, 1864* (Greensboro, N.C.: A. W. Ingold & Co., 1864); John Paris Diary, February 11, 14, and 15, 1864, SHC; *Fayetteville North Carolina Presbyterian*, April 13,1864; James O. Hall, "Atonement," *Civil War Times Illustrated* 29 (August 1980): 20; Paris, *A Sermon*, 5–7. Hoke's North Carolina brigade had only recently returned from rounding up deserters and draft evaders in the North Carolina piedmont, where they encountered strong anti-Confederate feeling. See Auman, "Neighbor against Neighbor," 77. For evidence of Baptist ministers besides the Methodist Chaplain Paris visiting men, see *House Executive Doc. No. 98*, 34–35; and *Fayetteville North Carolina Presbyterian*, April 13,1864.

18. *House Executive Doc. No. 98*, 16.

19. Jervey, *Prison Life among the Rebels*, 27.

20. *Raleigh Daily Confederate*, February 8, 10, 11, 16, and 20, 1864; *Fayetteville Observer*, February 8, 1864. Some papers simply reprinted portions of Paris's sermon, silently giving approval to his views. See *Fayetteville North Carolina Presbyterian*, April 14,1864; and *Americus (Georgia) Sumter Republican*, May 13, 1864. Holden denied any wrong doing in his *Weekly Standard*, February 24, 1864. For an example of his paper's support of executions see *Raleigh Daily Standard*, February 15, 1864.

21. The melodramatic novel appeared in segments in the *Raleigh Mercury* in June 1864 and later sold five thousand copies as a separate book. Ironically, Herrington himself deserted to the Union in February 1865 and disappeared. See William D. Herrington, *The Captains Bride, A Tale of the War, and The Deserter's Daughter*, facsimile edition edited by W. Keats Sparrow (Raleigh: Division of Archives and History, North Carolina Department of Cultural Resources, 1990), quotes from 17, 23.

22. *Official Records*,33:865.

23. *Official Records*,33:869. See also *Official Records*, 33:867–70; Current, *Lincoln's Loyalists*, 121. Union officials' immediate and postwar responses to the hangings are compiled in *House Executive Doc. No. 98*, and *Executive Document No.*

11, House of Representatives, 39th Cong., 2d sess. W. P. Derby, a former Federal officer from the Department of North Carolina, remembered "the fear felt for New Berne at the time of that attack and also the horror with which a short time after we learned of the execution of the brave Union men of the 2d N.C." In W. P. Derby to Mary Freeman Kendall, November 15, 1886, John Freeman Pension Records, Application 322383, Certificate 271892, RG 15, NA. When the Confederacy retook Plymouth later that spring, demoralization again swept the ranks of the North Carolinian Unionists. See *Official Records,* 33:299, 948–49,959–60; *Official Records,* 51, pt. 1, 1289; Current, *Lincoln's Loyalists,* 166–67; Delaney, "Charles Henry Foster," 364–65.

24. *New Bern North Carolina Times,* March 9,1864. The paper's headline was "Cold Blooded Murder of Twenty-Three Patriotic Men." Mark Grimsley notes, "Both sides asserted repeatedly that they were conducting the struggle according to the established laws and usages of war (usually in the course of accusing the other side of violating these same norms)." He adds that the controversial question of the Confederacy's legal status was "never entirely settled." See Mark Grimsley, *The Hard Hand of War: Union Military Policy toward Southern Civilians, 1861–1865* (Cambridge: Cambridge University Press, 1995), 12–13.

25. In the latter story the drummer boy's name was Joey Neal, an orphan who was fourteen rather than fifteen, with a fair complexion and blue eyes. See *New York Times,* March 11 and 18, 1864. Another Northern paper claimed that the event started a riot among Union prisoners in Goldsboro and Confederate troops had to quiet the disturbance. See *Washington Star News,* March 11, 1864.

26. Investigation and proceedings of both boards found in *House Executive Doc. No. 98.* See also Current, *Lincoln's Loyalists,* 121–22. I was unable to find any newspaper coverage of the proceedings in Raleigh or New Bern newspapers from October 1865 to March 1866.

27. Eighteen of the twenty-two men killed had wives, mothers, or children who filed for pensions. By 1883 seven of these family members continued to collect small pension ranging from four to eight dollars per month. See *List of Pensioners on the Roll, January 1, 1883; Giving the Name of Each Pensioner, the Post Office Address, The Rate of Pension Per Month, and the Date of Original Allowance, As Called by Senate Resolution of December 8, 1862,* 5 vols. (Baltimore: Genealogical Publishing Company, 1970), 5:166, 170.

28. For examples of victims' Unionism and accounts of their being forced into the Confederate army, see Charles Cuthrell, Pension Record, Application 151963, Certificate 155267, RG 15, NA; William Irvin Hill, Pension Record, Lewis Freeman Pension Record, Application 132278, Certificate 187672, RG 15, NA; *House Executive Doc. No. 98,* 28. Wayne Durrill discusses Confederates illegally and forcefully "recruiting" North Carolinians into the army in early 1864, in *War of Another Kind,* 186–87. John H. Haddock, the father of William Haddock, successfully sought restitution from the Southern Claims Commission for the loss of property. In his claims file he attested to his family's Unionism and recounted the hanging of his son at Kinston. About the same time as his son's capture and death, Confederates

arrested and imprisoned Haddock for his Union sentiments. He resided about eight miles from Kinston. See John H. Haddock Southern Claims Commission File, Application 15076, RG 217, NA. Klingberg describes difficulties claimants faced in seeking restitution from Southern Claims Commission in *The Southern Claims Commission*, 17–18, 84, 89, 209. It seems likely that widows of Southern Unionists would face similar obstacles.

29.  David Jones, Pension Record, Application 180796, Certificate 179439, RG 15, NA. Paris commented that Jones "though quite a young man" never "shed a tear." See *Fayetteville North Carolinian Presbyterian*, 13 April 1864; Joseph L. Haskett, Pension Record, Application 168014, Certificate 129629, RG 15, NA; Gil Hill notes from Lewis Bryan, Pension Record, RG 15, NA, in possession of author; *House Executive Doc. No. 98*, 31; John J. Brock, Pension Record, Application 130492 and 215776, Certificate 144731 and 194242, RG 15, NA; Charles Cuthrell, Pension Record, Application 151963, Certificate 155267, RG 15, NA; John Freeman, Pension Record, Application 322383, Certificate 271892, RG 15, NA; Andrew Britton, Pension Records, Application 227182, Certificate 179682, RG 15, NA; *House Executive Doc. No. 98*, 28, 30–31.

30.  Talmage C. Johnson and Charles R. Holloman, *The Story of Kinston and Lenoir County* (Raleigh: Edwards & Broughton Company, 1954), 97–112, quote from 102; and Powell, *The Annals of Progress*, 42–51; Tyndall, "Lenoir County," 81; Crow, "Thomas Settle Jr.," 600, 726. For more on longevity of the myth of the "solid South" and forgotten Southern Unionists see Honey, "The War within the Confederacy," 76; Klingberg, *The Southern Claims Commission*, 194; Current, *Lincoln's Loyalists*, 199–203; Charles Royster, *The Destructive War: William Tecumseh Sherman, Stonewall Jackson, and the Americans* (New York: Alfred A. Knopf, 1991), 172. As this article was going to press Kinston suddenly became very topical. Three forthcoming studies on Kinston include Gerald Patterson, *Justice or Atrocity: General George E. Pickett and the Kinston, N.C., Hangings* (Gettysburg, Penn.: Thomas Publications, 1998); and Donald Collins, "War Crime or Justice? General George Pickett and the Mass Execution of Deserters in Civil War Kinston, North Carolina," in *The Art of Command in the Civil War*, ed. Steven E. Woodworth (Lincoln: University of Nebraska Press, 1998). Francis MacDonnell is also at work on the subject. For my own view of George Pickett's role in the Kinston hangings, see *General George E. Pickett in Life and Legend* (Chapel Hill: University of North Carolina Press, 1998).

31.  I visited Kinston in July 1996 and October 1996 and spoke to Everett C. Wilkie Jr., Head Librarian and Crofut Curator of Rare Books and Manuscripts, Connecticut Historical Society, and W. Keats Sparrow, Dean, College of Arts and Science, East Carolina University, both former residents of Lenoir County. Officials at the CSS Neuse State Historic Site in Kinston told me in October 1996 that the museum wanted to incorporate the full story of the Kinston hanging into an exhibit, but up to that time, it had not.

32.  *New York Times*, March 11, 1864.

33.  Paludan, *Victims*, 115–16.

## The Politics of Violence: Unionist Pamphleteers in Virginia's Inner Civil War

1.  Cecil D. Eby Jr., ed., *A Virginia Yankee in the Civil War: The Diaries of David Hunter Strother* (Chapel Hill:University of North Carolina Press, 1961), 198, 199, 201, 207, 213–14. Also see *Calendar of the Arthur Ingram Boreman Letters in the State Department of Archives and History* (Charleston, W.Va.: Historical Records Survey, 1939).

2.  Anna Pierpont Sivitar, *Recollections of War and Peace, 1861–1868* (New York: G. P. Putnam's Sons, 1938), 69, 94, 107, 376. Also see Francis H. Pierpont, *Letter . . . to His Excellency the President and the Honorable Congress of the United States on the Subject of Abuse of Military Power in the Command of General Benjamin Butler in Virginia and North Carolina* (Washington, D.C.: McGill and Witherow, Printers and Stereotypers, 1864); Governor Pierpont's Scrapbook is in the West Virginia University Library, Morgantown. For other eyewitnesses to Virginia's border inner civil war see John Minor Botts, *The Great Rebellion* (New York: Harper and Bros., Publishers, 1866). Botts used martial language throughout to describe the events in his part of Virginia. Also see Rebecca Harding Davis, *Margaret Howth: A Story of Today* (Boston: Ticknor and Fields, 1862); James W. Hunnicut, *The Conspiracy Unveiled: The South Sacrificed; or, the Horrors of Secession* (Philadelphia: J. B. Lippincott, 1863).

3.  Edward Conrad Smith, *The Borderland in the Civil War* (New York: Macmillan Co., 1927), 186, 188, 199. Although Smith did not use the leaders' pamphlets, he acknowledges their importance. He points out that "a pamphlet prepared by Carlile was distributed all over western Virginia," 199. The best discussion to follow up Smith's suggestion of a leadership vacuum in local government is in *When the Yankees Came: Conflict and Chaos in the Occupied South, 1861–1865*, by Stephen V. Ash (Chapel Hill: University of North Carolina Press, 1995). Alas, Ash leaves out any discussion in his fine book of events in western Virginia.

4.  Richard Orr Curry, *A House Divided: A Study of Statehood Politics and the Copperhead Movement in West Virginia* (Pittsburg: University of Pittsburg Press, 1964), 68. Also see Charles Henry Ambler, *Waitman Thomas Willey: Orator, Churchman, Humanitarian* (Huntington, W.Va.: Standard Printing and Publishing, 1954); and Charles H. Ambler and Festus P. Summers, *West Virginia, The Mountaineer State* (Englewood Cliffs, N.J.: Prentice Hall, 1958), 207, 223.

5.  For local studies that suggest the uses of pamphlets and a politics of violence see George Selden Wallace, *Cabell County Annals and Families* (Richmond: Garrett and Massie, 1935),41, 77, 86; William Grifee Brown, *History of Nicholas County, West Virginia* (Richmond: Dietz Press, 1954), 113, 121, 154. Brown points out that "during the time of more than four years, there were no public officials to control crime, enforce legal rights, or keep records," 119. See also Hila Appleton Richardson, "Raleigh County, West Virginia, in the Civil War," *West Virginia History* 10 (April 1949): 213–98; and John D. Shaffer, "Loyalties in Conflict: Union and Confederate Sentiment in Barbour County," *West Virginia History* 50 (1991): 109–28.

6. See Bernard Bailyn, ed., *Pamphlets of the American Revolution* (Cambridge: Harvard University Press, 1965); Frank Freidel, ed., *Union Pamphlets of the Civil War*, 2 vols. (Cambridge: Harvard University Press, 1967); Jon L. Wakelyn, ed., *Southern Pamphlets on Secession, November 1860–April 1861* (Chapel Hill; University of North Carolina Press, 1996).

7. Ambler, *Willey*, 39. See also the excellent comments on the relationship between pamphlets and the newspaper press in *Politics and the People: A Study in English Political Culture, c. 1815–1867*, by James Vernon (Cambridge: Cambridge University Press, 1993).

8. All of those who study the lives of the people at war owe a large debt to recent quality writings on the subject. For the border of Virginia, see Gary W. Gallagher, "Homefront and Battlefield: Some Recent Literature Relating to Virginia and the Confederacy," 135–68; Stephen V. Ash, "White Virginians under Federal Occupation, 1861–1865," 169–192; Daniel E. Sutherland, "Getting the 'Real War' into Books," 193–220; all in *Virginia Magazine of History and Biography* 98 (April 1990). Some of this work has begun to appear in book form. See Daniel W. Crofts, *Old Southampton: Politics and Society in a Virginia County, 1834–1869* (Charlottesville: University Press of Virginia, 1992); and Daniel E. Sutherland, *Seasons of War: The Ordeal of a Confederate Community, 1861–1865* (New York: Free Press, 1995).

9. George W. Thompson, *Secession Is Revolution: The Dangers of the South; the Barrier States . . .* (Wheeling, Va.: n.p., 1861), 23, 24, delivered December 1, 1860. See also "Judge Thompson's Proclamation," in *The Political History of the United States during the Great Rebellion*, by Edward McPherson (1865; reprint, New York: DaCapo Press, 1971), 293–96. For excellent commentary on the Virginia secession convention see Daniel W. Crofts, *Reluctant Confederates: Upper South Unionists in the Secession Crisis* (Chapel Hill: University of North Carolina Press, 1989). Also see Wakelyn, *Southern Pamphlets on Secession*, xii–xxix.

10. Samuel McD. Moore, *Substance of a Speech . . . in the Convention of Virginia . . . on Federal Relations* (Richmond: Whig Book and Job Office, 1861), 14, 15.

11. Sherrard Clemens, *State of the Union* (Washington, D.C.: Office of the Congressional Globe, 1861). See also John P. Kennedy, "An Appeal to Maryland," in *Political History of the Rebellion*, by McPherson, 368–74.

12. Biographical information on these and other leaders mentioned in this study may be found in *The Biographical Guide to the Congress of the United States*, new ed. (Washington, D.C.: GPO, 1994). Most helpful in evaluating the rhetoric in these pamphlets is Andrew W. Robertson, *The Language of Democracy: Political Rhetoric in the United States and Britain, 1790–1900* (Ithaca: Cornell University Press, 1995).

13. John S. Carlile, *Speech in the Virginia State Convention* (Richmond: Whig Book and Job Office, 1861). For comment on Carlile's and other Virginia pre-secession pamphlets see Wakelyn, *Southern Pamphlets on Secession*, 399–400.

14. Joseph Eggleston Segar, *Speech Delivered in the House of Delegates of Virginia, March 30th, 1861* ((Richmond: State Printers, 1861), 6, 17, 19, 22.

15.  "Speech of John S. Carlile in the Wheeling Convention, June 14, 1861," in *Political History of the Rebellion*, by McPherson, 374, 375.

16.  Joseph Segar, *Letter to a Friend in Virginia, in Vindication of His Course in Declining to Follow His State into Secession* (Washington, D.C.: William H. Moore, Printer, 1862), 3.

17.  John H. Carlile, *Speech on the Bill to Confiscate the Property and Free the Slaves of Rebels* (Washington, D.C.:Office of the *Congressional Globe*, 1862), 13. The pamphlet versions of these wartime addresses given in Congress for the most part were reprinted from the official version in the *Congressional Globe*.

18.  Ambler, *Willey*, 44–45.

19.  "Western Virginia on the Seizure of Sherrard Clemens," in *Political History of the Rebellion*, by McPherson, 52.

20.  Carlile, *Speech on the Bill to Confiscate Property*, 10.

21.  Carlile, *Speech on the Bill to Confiscate Property*, 13. In melodramatic language Carlile wailed that "assassins sought [his] life" and on April 13, 1861, "one hundred men came to hang [him]."

22.  Carlile, *Speech on the Bill to Confiscate Property*, 7.

23.  Waitman T. Willey, *Speech on the Abolition of Slavery in the District of Columbia* (Washington, D.C.: Lemuel Towers, Printer, 1862). Also see Waitman T. Willey, *Speech on the Object of the War* (Washington, D.C.: Office of the *Congressional Globe*, 1862); Ambler, *Willey*, 39, 63. Unfortunately, Ambler did not analyze Willey's important pamphlets, so he missed the subtlety in relating abolition to the protection of western Virginia.

24.  Carlile, *Speech on the Bill to Confiscate Property*, 9, but see also 8 and 10.

25.  Kevin K. V. Whaley, *Speech Delivered in the House of Representatives, July 11, 1862, on a Bill to Provide for the Admission of West Virginia into the Union as a State* (Washington, D.C.: Gammell and Co., Printers, 1862), 4.

26.  Joseph E. Segar, *To the Voters of Accomac and Northampton* (n.p., 1863), 2,3.

27.  John S. Carlile, *Repeal of the Fugitive Slave Acts, March 1, 1864* (Washington, D.C.: Office of the *Congressional Globe*, 1864), 33, 34.

28.  Carlile, *Speech on the Bill to Confiscate the Property*, 8.

29.  Pierpont, *Letter to His Excellency the President*, 8. Also see Charles H. Ambler, *Francis H. Pierpont, Union War Governor of Virginia* (Chapel Hill: University of North Carolina Press, 1937).

30.  Joseph E. Segar, *Speech on Ship Canals* (Washington, D.C.: Office of the *Congressional Globe*, 1863), 2,7. Almost nothing has been written on this remarkable speech. Yet, Segar sent copies of it all over the Norfolk region. One should look at how he used the rhetorical device of question and answer to make his point.

31.  Joseph E. Segar, *Report to the Committee on Elections* (Washington, D.C.: Office of the *Congressional Globe*, 1863), 5–8. This speech was delivered in November 1861 and mailed in January. Also bound with the pamphlet were comments of Governor Francis Pierpont of October 12, 1861, requesting that Segar be seated.

32.  Joseph E. Segar, *Speech in the House of Representatives of the United States, May 17, 1864, in Defense of His Claim to a Seat in that Body* (Baltimore: John

Murphy and Co., 1864), 24. Segar used that particular refrain to invoke sympathy
from his friends and to identify with the folks back home. See also p. 21 of the
pamphlet in which he talked about what it meant to stay in the Union. "In the
name of the Union," he said, " do not ignore our young and maybe feeble government, by denying us representation in this body."

33. Pierpont, *Letter to His Excellency the President,* esp. 4.

34. Pierpont, *Letter to His Excellency the President,* 8, 38, 50, 55.

35. Ambler, *Willey,* 52, 87, 108–9. For Willey's use of the newspaper press to
work for statehood from Washington see John Lewis Kiplinger, "The Press in the
Making of West Virginia," *West Virginia History* 6 (January 1945): 127–76. It
should be mentioned that William O. Curry's fine study of state making does not
analyze the pamphlet arguments of the leaders from Washington, and thus over-
looks how other Virginia border politicians had a stake in the division of Virginia.

36. Whaley, *Speech Delivered in the House of Representatives, July 11, 1862,* 6, 7.

37. Curry, *A House Divided,* 139.

38. Segar, *Letter to a Friend in Virginia,* 1, 5.

39. Peter G. Van Winkle, *Speech on the Reorganization of Viirginia, and the
Admission of West Virginia* (Washington, D.C.: Gibson Brothers, Printers, 1864), 4,
11, 12, 17. Van Winkle remained true to his constituents even after the war. See
Thomas W. Howard, "Peter G. Van Winkle's Vote on the Impeachment of
President Andrew Johnson," *West Virginia History* 35 (July 1974): 290–95.

40. Van Winkle, *Speech,* 29.

41. Segar, *Speech in Defense of His Claims,* 18.

42. Joseph E. Segar, *Address on the War, the Union, and the Restoration of the
Union* (Richmond: Richmond Republic, 1865), 1. In the speech Segar relived the
personal violence, the sacrifices, and all the other themes which linked him with
his followers. Also see Francis H. Pierpont, *Address to the People of Virginia*
(Washington, D.C.: McGill and Witherow, 1865), 1, where he said, "Our state has
been made the seat of domestic violence."

43. Willey, *Speech on the Object of the War,* 4, also see 12.

44. Segar, *Letter to a Friend in Virginia,* 55.

45. Whaley, *Speech on the Bill to Provide,* 7.

# The Absence of Violence: Confederates and Unionists in Culpeper County, Virginia

1. For reviews of the literature see the essays by Bradley G. Bond and Bill
Cecil-Fronsman in *The American Civil War: A Handbook of Literature and Research,*
ed. Steven E. Woodworth (Westport, Conn.: Greenwood Press, 1996). Michael W.
Fitzgerald provides a succinct statement of the issues in "Class Conflicts," in
*Encyclopdia of the Confederacy,* ed. Richard N. Current (New York: Simon &
Schuster, 1993), 1:344–47. Historians who tend to stress the role of class conflict
include Fred A. Bailey, Robin E. Baker, Bill Cecil-Fronsman, Daniel W. Crofts,
Wayne K. Durrill, Paul D. Escott, Eric Foner, Steven Hahn, Michael K. Honey,

Randall C. Jimerson, Michael J. Johnson, Carl H. Moneyhon, Phillip S. Paludan, George C. Rable, Richard Reid, James L. Roark, and David Williams. Those who place limits on its application include Stephen E. Ambrose, Stephen V. Ash, William T. Auman, Richard Bardolph, William L. Barney, William Blair, Richard N. Current, William C. Harris, James Penn, Emory M. Thomas, Peter Wallenstein, and Bell I. Wiley. Even Durrill, who generally sympathizes with the class interpretation, cautions against interpreting community divisions along rigid class lines in *War of Another Kind: A Southern Community in the Great Rebellion* (New York: Oxford University Press, 1990), 230.

   2.  U.S. Bureau of the Census, *Population Schedule of the 8th Census of the United States, 1860, Culpeper County, Virginia*, National Archives microfilm publication, microcopy no. 653, roll 1341, 500–501, 504–5, 510–11; U.S. Bureau of the Census, *Productions of Agriculture of the 8th Census of the United States, 1860, Schedule 4, Culpeper County, Virginia*, roll 234, 109–10; and U.S. Bureau of the Census, *Agriculture of the United States in 1860; Compiled from the Original Returns of the Eighth Census* (Washington, D.C., 1864), 155–62. For Culpeper's wartime experience see Daniel E. Sutherland, *Seasons of War: The Ordeal of a Confederate Community, 1861–1865* (New York: Free Press, 1995).

   3.  Edward Elly (no. 15,468), James B. Kirk (no. 636), Archibald Shaw (no. 14,135), Southern Claims Commission Case Files, 1877–83, Records of Government Accounting Office, Records of Third Auditor's Office, RG 217, NA (hereafter cited as Southern Claims). The records of the Southern Claims Commission must be used with care when reconstructing the wartime opinions of people, but scholars who have studied or used the claims affidavits have found them to be reliable sources of evidence when used in conjunction with other sources. See Frank W. Klingberg, *The Southern Claims Commission* (Berkeley: University of California Press, 1955); Gary B. Mills, *Southern Loyalists in the Civil War: The Southern Claims Commission* (Baltimore: Genealogical Publishing, 1994), vii–xiii; Steven Hahn, *The Roots of Southern Populism: Yeoman Farmers and the Transformation of the Georgia Upcountry, 1850–1890* (New York: Oxford University Press, 1983), 129–30; Carl Degler, *The Other South: Southern Dissenters in the Nineteenth Century* (New York: Harper and Row, 1974), 179–84; Sarah Larson, "Records of the Southern Claims Commission," *Prologue* 12 (winter 1980): 207–18; Michael K. Honey, "The War within the Confederacy: White Unionists in North Carolina," *Prologue* 18 (summer 1986): 76–77; James Penn, "Geographical Variation of Unionism in Louisiana: A Study of the Southern Claims Data," *Louisiana History* 30 (fall 1989): 402–3.

   4.  William A. Soutter (no. 17,756) and Archibald Shaw (no. 14,135), Southern Claims; Matilda G. Hudson (no. 15,194), Claims Disallowed by Commissioners of Claims (Southern Claims Commission), Records of the U.S. House of Representatives, 1867?–1889, RG 233, National Archives (hereafter cited as Southern Claims Disallowed).

   5.  Simeon B. Shaw (no. 14,136), Southern Claims; Delila Day (no. 2858), Southern Claims Disallowed.

   6.  These statistics were compiled from the Southern Claims Commission

records (see note 3 above) and the 1860 population, agricultural, and slave censuses for Culpeper County (see note 2 above).

7. The survey of Culpeper soldiers is based on the rosters of the Seventh, Eleventh, and Thirteenth Virginia Infantry Regiments and the Fourth Virginia Cavalry Regiment provided in *7th Virginia Infantry*, 2nd ed., by David F. Riggs (Lynchburg: H. E. Howard, 1982); *13th Virginia Infantry*, by David F. Riggs (Lynchburg: H. E. Howard, 1988); *11th Virginia Infantry*, by Robert T. Ball (Lynchburg: H. E. Howard, 1985); and *4th Virginia Cavalry*, 2nd ed., by Kenneth L. Stiles, (Lynchburg: H. E. Howard, 1985).

8. Paul D. Escott, *After Secession: Jefferson Davis and the Failure of Confederate Nationalism* (Baton Rouge: Louisiana State University Press, 1978), 127–28; William Blair, *Virginia's Private War: Feeding Body and Soul in the Confederacy, 1861–1865* (New York: Oxford University Press, 1998), 60–68, 88–91; Bill Cecil-Fronsman, *Common Whites: Class and Culture in Antebellum North Carolina* (Lexington: University Press of Kentucky, 1992), 215–16; Kevin Conley Ruffner, "Civil War Desertion from a Black Belt Regiment: An Examination of the 44th Virginia Infantry," in *The Edge of the South: Life in Nineteenth-Century Virginia* , ed. Edward L. Ayers and John C. Willis (Charlottesville: University Press of Virginia, 1991), 100.

9. Kenneth Radley, *Rebel Watchdog: The Confederate States Army Provost Guard* (Baton Rouge: Louisiana State University Press, 1989), 147–52; John W. Stevens, *Reminiscences of the Civil War: A Soldier in Hood's Texas Brigade, Army of Northern Virginia* (Hillsboro, Tex.: Hillsboro Mirror, 1902), 492–93. It is interesting to compare three studies of desertion by North Carolina troops, both for the variety of influences at work and for the differences in interpretation: See William T. Auman, "Neighbor against Neighbor: The Inner Civil War in the Randolph County Area of Confederate North Carolina," *North Carolina Historical Review* 61 (January 1984): 59–92; Richard Bardolph, "Confederate Dilemma: North Carolina Troops and the Deserter Problem," *North Carolina Historical Review* 66 (January 1989): 61–86, and (April 1989): 179–210; and Richard Reid, "A Test Case of the 'Crying Evil': Desertion among North Carolina Troops during the Civil War," *North Carolina Historical Review* 58 (July 1981): 234–62.

10. Bardolph, "Confederate Dilemma," 78–80, 86; Fanny Brown to Margaret W. Barnes, January 19, 1864, Barnes Family Papers, College of William and Mary, Williamsburg, Va.

11. Richard Wallach (no. 10,182), Southern Claims; [William D. Wallach] to Henry W. Halleck, August 14, 1862, Consolidated Correspondence File, box 222, RG 92, National Archives. Carl H. Moneyhon, in "Disloyalty and Class Consciousness in Southwestern Arkansas, 1862–1865," *Arkansas Historical Quarterly* 52 (autumn 1993): 231 n.17, in a rare slip, misses the significance of his own terms and data when he identifies the same group of Unionists—all of whom owned respectable amounts of both real and personal property—as "poor men" in one paragraph and as members of the "yeoman class" in the next.

12. W. Todd Groce, "The Social Origins of East Tennessee's Confederate Leadership," in *The Civil War in Appalachia: Collected Essays*, ed. Kenneth W. Noe

and Shannon H. Wilson (Knoxville: University of Tennessee Press, 1997), 40–41, 48; Charles L. Wagandt, ed., "The Civil War Journal of Dr. Samuel A. Harrison," *Civil War History* 13 (June 1967): 133. The Arkansans mentioned in the preceding note averaged about forty years of age, also.

13. Martha Bailey (no. 18,467), John Brown (no. 15,556), Lucy M. Colvin (no. 21,015), and Sarah E. Thomas (no. 13,821), Southern Claims.

14. Statement by Hiram L. Amiss in William Heflin (no. 20,597), Southern Claims.

15. Soutter, Southern Claims; Isham B. Chewning (no. 10,507) and Hudson, Southern Claims Disallowed.

16. Stephen V. Ash, "White Virginians under Federal Occupation, 1861–1865," *Virginia Magazine of History and Biography* 98 (1990): 183–84; Henry R. Pyne, *Ride to War: History of the First New Jersey Cavalry* (1871; reprint, New Brunswick, N.J.: n.p., 1961), 42–46; Susan P. W. Hall (no. 15,192), Southern Claims.

17. Ash, *When the Yankees Came,* 171–76. Ash in "Poor Whites in the Occupied South," 40–41, 47–48, acknowledges this Northern bias but occasionally accepts such judgments. Grady McWhiney in *Cracker Culture: Celtic Ways in the Old South* (Tuscaloosa: University of Alabama Press, 1988), 23–35, 156–57, 235–40, 264–69, demonstrates some of the problems of accepting Northern interpretations of Southern society and culture.

18. U.S. War Department, *War of the Rebellion: A Compilation of the Official Records of the Union and Confederate Armies,* (Washington, D.C.: GPO, 1888–1901), ser. 1, vol. 12, pt. 1, 453–54; Daniel A. Grimsley, *Battles in Culpeper County, Virginia, 1861–1865* (Culpeper: Exponent Printing Office, 1900), 4–5.

19. Mary L. Payne (no. 22,128), Southern Claims.

20. Thomas R. Rixey (no. 20,612), Southern Claims Disallowed; Margaret Jeffries, "Redwood," in Works Progress Administration of Virginia, Historical Inventory for Culpeper County (typescript), Clerk's Office, Culpeper County Circuit Court; Cecil D. Eby Jr., ed., *A Virginia Yankee in the Civil War: The Diaries of David Hunter Strother* (Chapel Hill: University of North Carolina Press, 1961), 81; Mrs. Berkeley G. Calfee, *Confederate History of Culpeper County in the War between the States* (Culpeper: n.p., 1948), 5–6; J. W. Hewitt to Nathaniel P. Banks, August 13, 1862, Nathaniel Prentice Banks Papers, Library of Congress.

21. Rixey, Southern Claims Disallowed; William Heflin (no. 20,597), Southern Claims.

22. [William D. Wallach] to Henry W. Halleck, August 14, 1862, Consolidated Correspondence File, box 222, RG 92, National Archives; John C. Green (no. 20,613), Southern Claims.

23. Calfee, *Confederate History of Culpeper,* 7–8; George M. Neese, *Three Years in the Confederate Horse Artillery* (New York: Neale Publishing, 1911), 210–11; George R. Agassiz, ed., *Meade's Headquarters 1863–1865: Letters of Colonel Theodore Lyman from the Wilderness to Appomattox* (Boston: Atlantic Monthly, 1922), 48.

24. Riggs, *13th Virginia Infantry,* 101, 133; William Y. Mordecai to Mother, October 20, 1863, William Young Mordecai Papers, Virginia Historical Society, Richmond.

25. Spencer G. Welch, *A Confederate Surgeon's Letters to His Wife* (New York: Neale Publishing, 1911), 82–83; James I. Robertson, ed., *The Civil War Letters of General Robert McAllister* (New Brunswick, N.J.: Rutgers University Press, 1965), 357.

26. William F. Zornow, "Aid for the Indigent Families of Soldiers in Virginia, 1861–1865," *Virginia Magazine of History and Biography* 66 (October 1958): 454–58; Culpeper County Circuit Court Minute Books, book no. 24 (1858–64), 343–46, 426, book no. 25 (1864–69), 1, 5–6, Clerk's Office, Culpeper County Circuit Court, Va.; Calfee, *Confederate History of Culpeper*, 11–12.

27. Culpeper County Circuit Court Minute Books, book no. 25, 9, 11–12, 18.

28. Heflin, Kirk, and Richard Wallach, Southern Claims.

# Definitions of Victory: East Tennessee Unionists in the Civil War and Reconstruction

1. David Madden, "Unionist Resistance to Confederate Occupation: The Bridge Burners of East Tennessee," *East Tennessee Historical Society Publications* 52 (1980): 42–53, and 53 (1981): 22–39; Jesse C. Burt Jr., "East Tennessee, Lincoln, and Sherman," *East Tennessee Historical Society Publications* 34 (1962): 3–25, and 35 (1963): 54–75; "President Lincoln's Plan of Campaign—1861—undated," U.S. War Department, *War of the Rebellion: A Compilation of the Official Records of the Union and Confederate Armies*, (Washington, D.C.: GPO, 1880–1900), ser. 1 vol. 52, pt. 1, 191–92 (hereafter cited as *Official Records*).

2. Charles F. Bryan, "The Civil War in East Tennessee: A Social, Political, and Economic Study" (Ph.D. diss., University of Tennessee, 1978); Eric R. Lacy, *Vanquished Volunteers: East Tennessee Sectionalism from Statehood to Secession* (Johnson City: East Tennessee State University Press, 1965); Stanley J. Folmsbee, Robert E. Corlew, and Enoch L. Mitchell, *History of Tennessee* (New York: Lewis Historical Publishing Company, 1960), 3:56–78; Oliver P. Temple, *East Tennessee and the Civil War* (Cincinnati: Robert Clarks Company, 1899), 4–38.

3. David C. Hsiung, *Two Worlds in the Tennessee Mountains: Exploring the Origins of Appalachian Stereotypes* (Lexington: University Press of Kentucky, 1997); Mary Beth Pudup, Dwight B. Billings, and Altina L. Waller, eds., *Appalachia in the Making: The Mountain South in the Nineteenth Century* (Chapel Hill: University of North Carolina Press, 1995); Robert Tracy McKenzie, *One South or Many: Plantation Belt and Upcountry in Civil War–Era Tennessee* (New York: Cambridge University Press, 1994); Blanch Henry Clark, *The Tennessee Yeomen, 1840–1860* (Nashville: University of Vanderbilt Press, 1942); Frank L. Owsley and Harriet C. Owsley, "The Economic Structure of Rural Tennessee, 1850–1860," *Journal of Southern History* 8 (May 1942): 161–82.

4. Durwood Dunn, *An Abolitionist in the Appalachian South: Ezekiel Birdseye on Slavery, Capitalism, and Separate Statehood in East Tennessee. 1841–1846* (Knoxville: University of Tennessee Press, 1997); Kenneth W. Noe, *Southwest Virginia's Railroad: Modernization and the Sectional Crisis* (Champaign: University of Illinois

Press, 1994); W. Todd Groce, "Mountain Rebels: East Tennessee Confederates and the Civil War, 1860–1870" (Ph.D. diss., University of Tennessee, 1993); John C. Inscoe, *Mountain Masters: Slavery and the Sectional Crisis in Western North Carolina* (Knoxville: University of Tennessee Press, 1989); U.S. Census Bureau, *Statistics of the United States in 1860, Compiled from the Original Returns of the Eighth Census* (Washington, D.C.: GPO, 1866).

5. Daniel Crofts, *Reluctant Confederates: Upper South Unionists in the Secession Crisis* (Chapel Hill: University of North Carolina Press, 1989), 144–53; Mary Emily Robertson Campbell, *The Attitude of Tennesseans toward the Union, 1847–1861* (New York: Vantage Press, 1961), 158–79; Temple, *East Tennessee,* 147–49.

6. Campbell, *Attitude,* 194–99; Thomas B. Alexander, *Thomas A. R. Nelson of East Tennessee* (Nashville: Tennessee Historical Commission, 1956), 76–83; Temple, *East Tennessee,* 179–204.

7. *Knoxville Whig,* January 12, 1861; D. Young to Governor William B. Campbell, June 3, 1861, Campbell Family Papers, William R. Perkins Library, Manuscript Department, Duke University, Durham, N.C..

8. *Knoxville Whig,* January 26, 1861; A. W. Howe to T. A. R. Nelson, April 14, 1861, T. A. R. Nelson Papers, McClung Collection, Lawson McGhee Library, Knoxville, Tenn.

9. William Randolph Carter, *History of the First Regiment of Tennessee Volunteer Cavalry in the Great War of the Rebellion* (Knoxville, Gant-Ogden, 1902), 14–19; Temple, *East Tennessee,* 179–204.

10. Charles F. Bryan, "A Gathering of Tories: The East Tennessee Convention of 1861," *Tennessee Historical Quarterly* 39 (spring 1980): 27–48; Temple, *East Tennessee,* 340–65; Thomas William Humes, *The Loyal Mountaineers of Tennessee* (Knoxville: Ogden Brothers, 1888), 103–19.

11. John C. Inscoe, "'Moving through Deserter Country': Fugitive Accounts of the Inner Civil War in Southern Appalachia," in *The Civil War in Appalachia,* ed. Kenneth W. Noe and Shannon H. Wilson,(Knoxville: University of Tennessee Press, 1997); Robert A. Ragan, *Escape from East Tennessee to the Federal Lines* (Washington, D.C.: J. H. Doney, 1910); Humes, *Loyal Mountaineers,* 184–85, 364–66; Daniel Ellis, *Thrilling Adventures of Daniel Ellis* (New York: Harper, 1867); Thomas Doak Edington Diary, March 2–7, 1862, University of Tennessee Library, Special Collections, Knoxville.

12. Richard Nelson Current, *Lincoln's Loyalists: Union Soldiers from the Confederacy* (Boston: Northeastern University Press, 1992), 29–60, 213–15; Major General Edmund Kirby Smith to Major T. A. Washington, April 26, 1862, *Official Records,* 10, pt. 2, 23, 453–54.

13. G. M. Hall to Callie Stakely, March 23, 1862, Hall-Stakely Family Papers, McClung Collection, Lawson McGhee Library, Knoxville, Tenn.; Kirby Smith to Brigadier General Danville Leadbetter, March 27, 1862, and Kirby Smith to Adjutant and Inspector General Samuel Cooper, April 19, 1862, RG 109, National Archives (hereafter cited as NA).

14. Brigadier General Felix K. Zollicoffer, General Orders 5–15, August 29– September 15, 1861, RG 109, NA; Elvie Eagleton Skipper and Ruth Gove, eds.,

"'Stray Thoughts': The Civil War Diary of Ethie M. Fonte Eagleton," *East Tennessee Historical Society Publications* 41 (1969): 119–26; J. S. Hurlbut, *History of the Rebellion in Bradley County, East Tennessee* (Indianapolis: Downey and Brouse, 1866), 130–33 and appendix, 6–13; Peter Smith to William B. Reynolds, December 8, 1864, and January 17, 1865, William B. Reynolds Papers, William R. Perkins Library, Manuscript Department, Duke University, Durham, N.C. For similar conflicts in other parts of the South, see Kenneth W. Noe, "Exterminating Savages: The Union Army and Mountain Guerrillas in Southern West Virginia, 1861–1862," and Jonathan D. Sarris, "An Execution in Lumpkin County: Localized Loyalties in North Georgia's Civil War," in *Civil War in Appalachia*, ed. Noe and Wilson; Stephen V. Ash, *When the Yankees Came: Conflict and Chaos in the Occupied South, 1861–1865* (Chapel Hill: University of North Carolina Press, 1996); Michael Fellman, *Inside War: The Guerrilla Conflict in Missouri during the American Civil War* (New York: Oxford University Press, 1989); Stephen V. Ash, *Middle Tennessee Society Transformed, 1860–1870: War and Peace in the Upper South* (Baton Rouge: Louisiana State University Press, 1988); William T. Auman, "Neighbor against Neighbor: The Inner Civil War in the Randolph County Area of Confederate North Carolina," *North Carolina Historical Review* 61 (January 1984): 59–92; Phillip Shaw Paludan, *Victims: A True Story of the Civil War* (Knoxville: University of Tennessee Press, 1981).

15. Kirby Smith to Washington, April 3, 1862, RG 109, NA; Major General Sam Jones to Secretary of War George W. Randolph, September 23 and 24, October 4, 14, 17, and 18, 1862, RG 109, NA; Major General John. P. McCown to Randolph, September 3, 1862, RG 109, NA; Major General Daniel S. Donelson to Colonel Ewell, February 10, 1863, *Official Records*, 23, pt. 2, 631.

16. Thomas B. Hall to his father, August 18, 1862, Hall Family Papers, Tennessee State Library and Archives, Nashville; Stephen F. Whitaker to his father, August 2, 1863, Stephen F. Whitaker Papers, North Carolina State Archives, Raleigh; William Williams Stringfield, "History of the Sixty-Ninth North Carolina," William Williams Stringfield Papers, North Carolina State Archives, Raleigh; Campbell Wallace and John R. Braemen to President Jefferson Davis, July 17, 1863, Jefferson Davis Papers, William R. Perkins Library, Manuscript Department, Duke University, Durham, N.C.

17. Kirby Smith to Colonel William Mackell, March 14, 1862, RG 109, NA; Major General Ambrose Burnside to Colonel Foster, September 4, 1863, RG 393, NA; Temple, *East Tennessee*, 498–510; Samuel P. Carter Memoirs, University of Tennessee Library, Special Collections, Knoxville.

18. Madden, "Unionist Resistance;" Burt, "East Tennessee;" Temple, *East Tennessee*, 370–401; Secretary of War Judah P. Benjamin to Colonel W. B. Wood, Colonel Danville Leadbetter, and Brigadier General William Carroll, November 25, 1861, RG 109, NA; William G. Brownlow, *Sketches of the Rise, Progress, and Decline of Secession* (Philadelphia: J. B. Lippincott, 1862), 280–381.

19. Brigadier General George W. Morgan to Secretary of War Edwin M. Stanton, May 24, 1862, *Official Records*, 10, pt. 2, 213; Colonel William Clift to Adjutant General United States Army, October 28, 1862, *Official Records*, 16, pt.

1, 858–59; Major General John M. Schofield to Major George W. Kirk, February 13, June 12, July 24, 1864, RG 393, NA; L. Cowles to Mary, July 24, 1864, Calvin J. Cowles Papers, North Carolina State Archives, Raleigh.

20. Alexander, *Nelson*, 87–93; Oliver P. Temple, *Notable Men of Tennessee from 1833–1875* (New York: Cosmopolitan Press, 1912), 123–27; Temple, *East Tennessee*, 367–69.

21. Bryan, "Tories;" Temple, *East Tennessee*, 343–65; Humes, *Loyal Mountaineers*, 115–19.

22. James Welch Patton, *Unionism and Reconstruction in Tennessee, 1860–1869* (Chapel Hill: University of North Carolina Press, 1934), 44–45; Temple, *East Tennessee*, 44–47; Mary Jane Reynolds to S. B. Reynolds, April 17, May 1, 1864, Mary Jane Reynolds Letters, University of Tennessee Library, Special Collections, Knoxville.

23. Thomas B. Alexander, *Political Reconstruction in Tennessee* (Nashville: Vanderbilt University Press, 1950), 18–32; Patton, *Unionism*, 48–50.

24. Alexander, *Reconstruction*, 73–77; Patton, *Unionism*, 70–102; U.S. District Court, Eastern District, Knoxville, Tennessee, Minute Book A, 1864–65, Minute Book B, 1865–70, NA, Southeast Region, Atlanta, Ga.

25. Alexander, *Reconstruction*, 99–140; Patton, *Unionism*, 114–95.

26. David W. Bowen, *Andrew Johnson and the Negro* (Knoxville: University of Tennessee Press, 1989); Eric L. McKitrick, *Andrew Johnson and Reconstruction* (Chicago: University of Chicago Press, 1960); D. C. Trewitt to L. C. Houk, May 23, 1866, and Nat B. Owens to Houk, September 22, 1866, Leonidas Campbell and John C. Houk Papers, McClung Collection, Lawson McGhee Library, Knoxville, Tenn.

27. Alexander, *Reconstruction*, 198–225; Patton, *Unionism*, 226–34; Barbour Lewis to John Eaton, December 20, 1868, John Eaton Papers, University of Tennessee Library, Special Collections, Knoxville; Lieutenant A. A. Carter to William B. Stokes, August 11, 1869, William B. Stokes Correspondence, Tennessee State Library and Archives, Nashville.

28. Gordon B. McKinney, *Southern Mountain Republicans, 1865–1900: Politics and the Appalachian Community* (Chapel Hill: University of North Carolina Press, 1978), 33–41, 77–86.

29. E. Merton Coulter, *William G. Brownlow: Fighting Parson of the Highlands* (Chapel Hill: University of North Carolina Press, 1934), 205–42; Brownlow, *Secession*, 337–444; Humes, *Loyal Mountaineers*, 301–33.

# A People's War: Partisan Conflict in Tennessee and Kentucky

1. Stig Forster and Jorg Nagler, eds., *The Road to Total War: The American Civil War and the German Wars of Unification, 1861–1871* (Washington: German Historical Institute and Cambridge University Press, 1997), introduction.

2. Jill K. Garrett, "Guerrillas and Bushwhackers in Middle Tennessee during the Civil War," 1–11, unpublished manuscript in Jill K. Garrett collection, miscellaneous collections, Union and Confederate Accounts, box 11, Tennessee State Library and Archives, Nashville (hereafter cited as TSLA); Richard Stone, *A Brittle Sword: The Kentucky Militia, 1776–1912* (Lexington: University Press of Kentucky, 1977), chap. 7, esp. 68–69.

3. Noel C. Fisher, *War at Every Door: Partisan Politics and Guerrilla Violence in East Tennessee, 1860–1869* (Chapel Hill: University of North Carolina Press, 1997), chap. 2–5 esp.

4. Ulysses S. Grant, *Personal Memoirs* (New York: Charles Webster and Company, 1885), 1:368–69; telegrams, U. S. Grant to Henry Halleck, Halleck to Grant, both March 11, 1862, entries 2602; telegrams received, November 1861–March 1862 and entry 2587; telegrams sent, November 1861–March 1862; telegrams from RG 393, U.S. Army Continental Commands, Department of the Missouri, National Archives and Records Service; U.S. War Department, *War of the Rebellion: A Compilation of the Official Records of the Union and Confederate Armies,* (Washington, D.C.: GPO, 1880–1901), ser.1 vol. 10, pt.2, 30 (hereafter cited as *Official Records*).

5. Benjamin Franklin Cooling, *Fort Donelson's Legacy: War and Society in Kentucky and Tennessee, 1861–1863* (Knoxville: University of Tennessee Press, 1997), chap. 2.

6. James M.McPherson, *Drawn with the Sword: Reflections on the American Civil War* (New York: Oxford University Press, 1996), esp. 76–86; Noel Fisher, "'Prepare Them for My Coming': General William T. Sherman, Total War, and Pacification in West Tennessee," *Tennessee Historical Quarterly* 51 (summer 1992): 75–86; John Keegan, "Rules of Engagement," *Economist* (October 23, 1993): 8; Mark Grimsley, *The Hard Hand of War: Union Military Policy toward Southern Civilians, 1861–1865* (Cambridge: Cambridge University Press, 1995), 98–101, 114–18.

7. Hunter B. Whitesell's series of articles in volume 63 of the *Kentucky Historical Society Register* underscore these conclusions: see "Military Operations in the Jackson Purchase Area of Kentucky, 1862–1865," (April 1965): 141–67; (July 1965): 240–67; and (October 1965): 323–45.

8. David Hubbard, February 25, 1861; Theodore Harris, June 12, 1861; A. O. W. Lattern, June 14, 1861; S. J. Rudd, June 15, 1861; B. B. Seat, June 17, 1861; J. W. McHenry, August 4, 1861; all to Isham G. Harris, Harris papers, TSLA; John S. Daniel Jr., "Special Warfare in Middle Tennessee and Surrounding Areas, 1861–1862" (master's thesis, University of Tennessee, 1971), 35–38.

9. L. C. Porter diary, 103–8, Filson Club, Louisville, Ky.

10. *Official Records*, ser. 1, 7:4–6 and 52:229; Brian Steel Wills, *A Battle from the Start: The Life of Nathan Bedford Forrest* (New York: Harper Collins, 1992), 52–53.

11. Diary of Robert S. Montgomery cited in Charles R. Gunter Jr., "History of the Civil War in Bedford County" (master's thesis, University of Tennessee, 1965), 48.

12. Cooling, *Fort Donelson's Legacy,* 50-53, 60–64.

13. Ibid., 64–78.

14. *Official Records*, ser. 4, 1:1094–99; James A. Ramage, *Rebel Raider: The Life of General John Hunt Morgan* (Lexington: University Press of Kentucky, 1986), 67–70; Emory M. Thomas, *The Confederate Nation* (New York: Harper and Row, 1979), chap. 7, and *The Confederacy as a Revolutionary Experience* (Englewood Cliffs, N.J.: Prentice-Hall, 1977), 51–57, 61–62, 67–68; Paul D. Escott, *After Secession; Jefferson Davis and the Failure of Confederate Nationalism* (Baton Rouge: Louisiana State University Press, 1978), 63–64.

15. Comparison between Morgan and Forrest as representatives of the people can be made through recent biographies, including Ramage, *Rebel Raider;* Wills, *Battle from the Start;* Lonnie E. Maness, *An Untutored Genius: The Military Career of General Nathan Bedford Forrest* (Oxford, Miss.: Guild Bindery Press, 1990); and Jack Hurst, *Nathan Bedford Forrest: A Biography* (New York: Alfred A. Knopf, 1993).

16. Richard P. Gildrie, "Guerrilla Warfare in the Lower Cumberland River Valley, 1862–1865," *Tennessee Historical Quarterly* 49 (fall 1990): 161–76; Stephen V. Ash, *When the Yankees Came: Conflict and Chaos in the Occupied South, 1861–1865* (Chapel Hill: University of North Carolina Press, 1995), and *Middle Tennessee Society Transformed, 1860–1870* (Baton Rouge: Louisiana State University Press, 1988), chap. 5–7.

17. Lewis Collins and Richard H. Collins, *History of Kentucky* (Covington, Ky.: Collins and Company, 1882), 1:102.

18. *Memphis Appeal*, June 19, 1862.

19. *Official Records*, ser. 4, 2:1003; Michael Fellman, "At the Nihilist Edge: Reflections on Guerrilla Warfare during the American Civil War" in *Road to Total War*, ed. Forster and Nagler, 519–40.

20. For a comparison of guerrilla warfare in the countryside with civil resistance in the cities, see Ash, *Middle Tennessee Society Transformed;* and Walter T. Durham, *Nashville, the Occupied City: The First Seventeen Months, February 16, 1862, to June 1863* (Nashville: Tennessee Historical Society, 1985), *Rebellion Revisited: A History of Sumner County, Tennessee, from 1861 to 1870* (Nashville: Sumner County Museum Association, 1982), and *Reluctant Partners: Nashville and the Union, July 1, 1863, to June 30, 1865* (Nashville: Tennessee Historical Society, 1987).

21. James T. Siburt, "Colonel John M. Hughs: Brigade Commander and Confederate Guerrilla," *Tennessee Historical Quarterly* 51 (summer 1992): 87–95.

22. *Official Records*, ser. 1, 37, pt. 1, 55–57.

23. See Fellman, "At the Nihilist Edge"; as well as McPherson, *Drawn with the Sword*, esp. chap. 6.

24. Stephen V. Ash, "Sharks in an Angry Sea: Civilian Resistance and Guerrilla Warfare in Occupied Middle Tennessee, 1862–1865," 45 *Tennessee Historical Quarterly* (fall 1986): 217–29.

25. See Gildrie, "Guerrilla Warfare," for a locally focused discussion of the matrix; while Ash provides an intriguing if incomplete schematic representation of the occupied South, illustrating this result in *When the Yankees Came*, 78.

26. Cooling, *Fort Donelson's Legacy*, 190–91, 195, 226–27, 251.

27. Francis Lieber, "Guerrilla Parties Considered with Reference to the Laws and Usages of War," in *Official Records*, ser. 3, 2:301–9, and 3:148–64 for General Order

Number 100; Frank Freidel, "General Orders 100 and Military Government," *Mississippi Valley Historical Review* 32 (March 1946): esp. 541–46; Richard S, Hartigan, *Lieber's Code* (South Holland, Ill.: Precedent Publishing, 1983), 1–26; Grimsley, *Hard Hand of War*, 145, 148–51.

28. *Official Records*, ser. I, 49, pt. 2, 1124–26; Whitesell, "Military Operations," (October 1965): 342–43.

29. Whitesell, "Military Operations," (October 1965): 345–48.

30. Edward E. Leslie, *The Devil Knows How to Ride: The True Story of William Clarke Quantrill and His Confederate Raiders* (New York: Random House, 1996), chap. 14; O. S. Barton, *Three Years with Quantrill; A True Story Told by His Scout John McCorkle* (Norman: University of Oklahoma Press, 1992), chap. 13.

31. Worthington Davis, *Camp-fire Chats of the Civil War* (Hartford, Conn.: Park Publishing Company, 1887), 157–59.

32. Reid Mitchell captures this tone in *Civil War Soldiers: Their Expectations and Their Experience* (New York: Viking, 1988), 132–45.

33. Richard L. Troutman, ed., *The Heavens Are Weeping: The Diaries of George Richard Browder* (Grand Rapids, Mich.: Zondervan Publishing House, 1987) 172, 183–84, 197–98.

34. U.S. Navy Department, *Official Records of the Union and Confederate Navies in the War of the Rebellion*, (Washington, D.C.: GPO, 1894–1927), ser. 1 vol. 25, 540–41, 469.

35. For a recent view concerning Americans and the extremities of violence, see Russell F. Weigley, "The Necessity of Force: The Civil War, World War II, and the American View of War," in *War Comes Again; Comparative Vistas on the Civil War and World War II*, ed. Gabor Boritt (New York: Oxford University Press, 1995), esp. 232–34.

# The Limits of Dissent and Loyalty in Texas

1. McCulloch to S. B. Davis, March 3, 1862, in *War of the Rebellion: A Compilation of the Official Records of the Union and Confederate Armies*, ed. Robert N. Scott et al. (Washington, D.C.: GPO, 1880–1901; reprint, Harrisburg, Pa.: , 1971), ser. 1 vol. 9, 701 (hereafter cited as *Official Records*).

2. Claude Elliott, "Union Sentiment in Texas, 1861–1865," *Southwestern Historical Quarterly* 50 (April 1947): 458.

3. McCulloch to Bourland, October 29, 1863, Bourland Papers, Manuscripts Division, Library of Congress.

4. Stephen D. Yancey to McCulloch, November 6, 1863, *Official Records*, ser. 1, 26, pt. 2, 394.

5. Richard B. McCaslin, *Tainted Breeze: The Great Hanging at Gainesville, Texas, 1862* (Baton Rouge: Louisiana State University Press, 1994), 1–6; James Alan Marten, "Drawing the Line: Dissent and Disloyalty in Texas, 1856 to 1874" (Ph.D. diss., University of Texas, Austin, 1986), 142–43.

6. Robert L. Kerby, *Kirby Smith's Confederacy: The Trans-Mississippi South, 1863–1865* (New York: Columbia University Press, 1972), 92; McCulloch to S. B. Davis, March 25, 1862, and McCulloch to S. B. Davis, March 31, 1862, *Official Records*, ser. 1, 9:704–5.

7. Excellent general accounts of German opposition to the war are found in *The History of the German Settlements in Texas*, by Rudolph L. Biesele (Austin: Von Boeckmann-Jones, 1930); *Foreigners in the Confederacy*, by Ella Lonn (Chapel Hill: University of North Carolina Press, 1940); and "German Unionism in Texas during the Civil War and Reconstruction," by Robert W. Shook (master's thesis, University of North Texas, 1957). The best treatment of the killing on the Nueces River is Robert W. Shook's "The Battle of the Nueces, August 10, 1862," *Southwestern Historical Quarterly* 66 (July 1962): 31–42.

8. For a more detailed treatment of the activities of the Texas Mounted Rifles, see David P. Smith, *Frontier Defense in the Civil War: Texas' Rangers and Rebels* (College Station: Texas A&M University Press, 1992), 21–40.

9. James M. Day, ed., *House Journal of the Ninth Legislature, Regular Session, November 4, 1861–January 14, 1862* (Austin: Texas State Library, 1964), 49–50; C. W. Raines, ed., *Six Decades in Texas: The Memoirs of Francis R. Lubbock, Confederate Governor of Texas* (1900; reprint, Austin: Pemberton Press, 1968), 337–38, 357.

10. The best source, by far, of the great hanging at Gainesville is McCaslin, *Tainted Breeze*. Any study of dissent and disaffection in north Texas should begin with this work.

11. Claude Elliot, "Union Sentiment in Texas, 1861–1865," *Southwestern Historical Quarterly* 50 (April 1947): 453; Ella Lonn, *Desertion during the Civil War* (1911; reprint, Gloucester, Mass.: Peter Smith, 1966), 4–7, 14–16.

12. McCaslin, *Tainted Breeze*, 14–19, 58–59; Marten, "Drawing the Line," 230–31. See also James M. McPherson, *Battle Cry of Freedom: The Civil War Era* (New York: Oxford University Press, 1988), 611–17; and James Oakes, *Slavery and Freedom: An Interpretation of the Old South* (New York: Alfred K. Knopf, 1990), 128–36.

13. Thomas Barrett, "The Great Hanging at Gainesville," typescript, Barker Texas History Center, University of Texas, Austin, 4–5; Sam Acheson and Julie Ann Hudson O'Connell, eds., *George Washington Diamond's Account of the Great Hanging at Gainesville* (Austin: Texas State Historical Association, 1963), 6–7; L. D. Clark, ed., *Recollections of James Lemuel Clark* (College Station: Texas A & M Univeristy Press, 1984), 96.

14. McCaslin, *Tainted Breeze*, 66.

15. "Hangman" quotation found in *Encyclopedia of the New West*, ed. William S. Speer and John Henry Brown (Marshall, Tex.: United States Biographical Publishing Co., 1881), 573; "good hater" quotation found in "Notes on the Great Hanging in Cooke Co., Texas, October, 1862," typescript, 298, Lillian Gunter Papers, Morton Museum, Gainesville, Tex.

16. Bourland to William Quayle, July 19, 1864, William Quayle Papers, Rare Book Room, University of Alabama, Tuscaloosa (hereafter cited as Quayle Papers).

17. Acheson and O'Connell, *Diamond's Account*, 36–40, 44–53; Barrett, "The Great Hanging at Gainesville," 9–12, 19–22; Clark, *Recollections of James Lemuel Clark*, 97–99; McCaslin, *Tainted Breeze*, 81–83.

18. Acheson and O'Connell, *Diamond's Account*, 99; James Smallwood, "Disaffection in Confederate Texas: The Great Hanging at Gainesville," *Civil War History* 22 (December 1976): 357–58; Michael Collins, *Cooke County, Texas: Where the South and the West Meet* (Gainesville, Tex.: Cooke County Heritage Society, 1981), 14–15; McCaslin, *Tainted Breeze*, 84–89.

19. General Orders Number 76, May 30, 1863, *Official Records*, ser. 1, 26, pt. 2, 25; General Orders Number 82, June 5, 1863, ibid., ser. 1, 26, pt. 2, 38; quotation found in Raines, *Six Decades in Texas*, 503.

20. O. M. Roberts, *Texas*, vol. 11, *Confederate Military History*, ed. Clement Evans (1899; reprint, New York: Thomas Yoseloff, 1962), 105.

21. They were often called "brush men" or "bush men" by contemporaries. This author leans with the majority and will use "brush."

22. General Orders Number 38, August 26, 1863, *General Orders of the Trans-Mississippi Department* (Houston: E. H. Cushing, 1865), 23.

23. McCulloch to Magruder, September 18, 1863, *Official Records*, ser. 1, 26, pt. 2, 236.

24. Benjamin H. Epperson and James W. Throckmorton were the influential former Unionists who heeded McCulloch's request to help with the situation. E. S. C. Robertson to Mary Robertson, October 11, 1863, Sutherland Collection, Department of Special Collections, University of Texas at Arlington Library; Samuel Roberts to B. H. Epperson, October 7, 1863, Epperson Papers, Barker Texas History Center, Austin, Tex.; John H. Brown to Wife, September 14, 1863, John H. Brown Papers, Barker Texas History Center, Austin. Quotation found in *Clarksville Standard*, October 10, 1863.

25. McCulloch to Epperson, September 29, 1863, Epperson Papers, Barker Texas History Center, Austin.

26. Kirby Smith to McCulloch, October 2, 1863, *Official Records*, ser. 1, 26, pt. 2, 285.

27. McCulloch to Magruder, October 11, 1863, *Official Records*, ser. 1, 26, pt. 2, 303; McCulloch to Magruder, October 21, 1863, ibid., ser. 1, 26, pt. 2, 344–45.

28. E. S. C. Robertson to Mary Robertson, October 13, 1863, Sutherland Collection, Department of Special Collections, University of Texas at Arlington Library; Thomas Lanagin to McCulloch, November 28, 1863, James G. Bourland Papers, Manuscripts Division, Library of Congress.

29. William Elsey Connelley, *Quantrill and the Border Wars* (1910; reprint, New York: Pageant Book Co., 1956), 436; Lary C. Rampp, "Incident at Baxter Springs on October 6, 1863," *Kansas Historical Quarterly* 36 (summer 1970): 183–97.

30. E. S. C. Robertson to Mary Robertson, October 24, 1863, Sutherland Collection, Department of Special Collections, University of Texas at Arlington Library.

31. McCulloch to E. P. Turner, October 22, 1863, *Official Records*, ser. 1, 26, pt. 2, 348.

32. Smith to McCulloch, November 1, 1863, *Official Records*, ser. 1, 26, pt. 2, 383.

33. Connelley, *Quantrill and the Border Wars*, 439; Roberts, *Texas*, 105; quotation found in E. Cunningham to McCulloch, November 19, 1863, *Official Records*, ser. 1, 22, pt. 2, 1073.

34. McCulloch to Magruder, February, 3, 1864, *Official Records*, ser. 1, 34, pt. 2, 942.

35. Throckmorton to Murrah, March 28, 1864, Governor Pendleton Murrah Records, Archives, Texas State Library, Austin (hereafter cited as TSL); A. Cameron Petree to Ellen Galbraith, March 30, 1864, Galbraith Family Papers, in possession of Charles Eversole Jr., Grapevine, Tex. Quotation found in McCulloch to E. P. Turner, April 6, 1864, *Official Records*, ser. 1, 34, pt. 3, 742.

36. McCulloch to E. P. Turner, January 6, 1864, *Official Records*, ser. 1, 53, 923–25; McCulloch to Magruder, January 23, 1864, ibid., ser. 1, 34, pt. 2, 909.

37. John W. Hale to James Bourland, *Official Records*, ser. 1, 34, pt. 2, 911. "Jayhawkers" was a common term used to describe any Unionist or abolitionist who made war on Southern sympathizers. Its Southern counterpart was "bushwhacker."

38. H. P. N. Gammel, ed., *Laws of Texas, 1822–1897* (Austin: Gammel Book Co., 1898), 5:677–78, 688–89.

39. Erath to Culberson, April 28, 1864, Adjutant General's Records, TSL; Erath to Burney, May 6, 1864, Quayle Papers.

40. Erath to Culberson, April 28, 1864, and Erath to Culberson, June 30, 1864, Adjutant General's Records, TSL; Erath to George Burney, May 6, 1864, and Erath to Burney, May 7, 1864, Quayle Papers.

41. Hunter to Murrah, May 1, 1864, Dorman Winfrey and James Day, eds., *The Indian Papers of Texas and the Southwest, 1825–1916* (Austin: Pemberton Press, 1961), 4:83–84; Hunter to Culberson, May 13, 1864, and Hunter to Culberson, May 25, 1864, Adjutant General's Records, TSL; William Banta and J. W. Caldwell Jr., *Twenty-Seven Years on the Texas Frontier* (1893; reprint, Council Hill, Okla.: L. G. Park, n.d.), 189–94.

42. S. B. Gray to Murrah, May 28, 1864, Governor Pendleton Murrah Records, TSL.

43. McAdoo to Culberson, September 15, 1864, Adjutant General's Records, TSL.

44. W. A. Pitts to E. S. C. Robertson, January 8, 1864, Sutherland Collection, Department of Special Collections, University of Texas at Arlington Library.

45. McCulloch to Murrah, March 20, 1864, Governor Pendleton Murrah Records, TSL.

46. Quayle passed this information along to James Bourland, whose border regiment operated within the state's First Frontier District. Bourland passed the information up the Confederate chain of command, in Bourland to McCulloch, April 13, 1864, Quayle Papers. Only two secondary accounts of the Frontier Conspiracy have been published; see McCaslin, *Tainted Breeze*, 139–43; and Smith, *Frontier Defense in the Civil War*, 112–15.

47. McCulloch to Bourland, April 14, 1864, Bourland Papers, Manuscripts Division, Library of Congress.

48. McCulloch to Quayle, April 14, 1864, Quayle Papers.

49. Special Orders Number 19, April 15, 1864; McCulloch to Bourland, April 15, 1864; and McCulloch to Quayle, April 15, 1864; all found in Quayle Papers. Quotation found in Bourland to Quayle, April 16, 1864, ibid.

50. Statements of J. Charles Adair and T. L. Stanfield to D. Howell, Chief Justice of Wise County, December 19, 1864, Governor Pendleton Murrah Records, TSL.

51. Muster Roll of Lt. Thomas Smith's Company, First Frontier District, February 1–June 1, 1864, Adjutant General's Records, TSL.

52. McCulloch to Bourland, July 14, 1864, Quayle Papers.

53. Eight pages of the "Charges and Specifications prepared against James Bourland, Col. Comdg. Border Reg." are located in the Quayle Papers.

54. McCaslin, *Tainted Breeze*, 150.

55. Speer and Brown, *Encyclopedia of the New West*, 281–82, 343; McCaslin, *Tainted Breeze*, 150.

56. C. l. Sonnichsen, *Ten Texas Feuds* (Albuquerque: University of New Mexico Press, 1957), 3–5; Donald C. Brown, "The Great Gun-Toting Controversy, 1865–1910: The Old West Gun Culture and Public Shootings" (Ph.D. diss., Tulane University, 1983), 29; Walter P. Webb, *The Texas Rangers: A Century of Frontier Defense* (1935; reprint, Austin: University of Texas Press, 1965), 220–21, 226.

57. McCaslin, *Tainted Breeze*, 170, 175–76.


# "Out of Stinking Distance": The Guerrilla War in Louisiana

1. An excellent recent treatment of the entire history of Louisiana is *Louisiana: A History*, ed. Bennett H. Wall (Arlington Heights, Ill.: Forum Press, 1990).

2. In Stephen Michot's "War Is Still Raging in This Part of the Country: Oath Taking, Conscription, and Guerilla War in Louisiana's Lafourche Region," *Louisiana History* 38 (September 1997): 157–84, the author does a thorough job of explaining the dilemma facing most blacks in Civil War Louisiana as they faced conscription into U.S. armies on one side and starvation on the other.

3. The best single book on Louisiana in the Civil War is *The Civil War in Louisiana*, by John D. Winters (Baton Rouge: Louisiana State University Press, 1987); other books to consider, although older in terms of research and publication, would include *Louisiana in the Confederacy*, by Jefferson Davis Bragg (Baton Rouge: Louisiana State University Press, 1941), *Secession and Restoration of Louisiana*, by Willie M. Caskey (Baton Rouge: Louisiana State University Press, 1938), and *The Mississippi Valley in the Civil War*, by John Fiske (Boston: Houghton Mifflin Company, 1900).

4. Winters, *The Civil War in Louisiana*, 104–5.

5. As quoted in "The Lafourche District in 1861–1862: A Problem in Local Defense,"by Barnes Lathrop, *Louisiana History* 1 (spring 1960): 119. Stephen Michot's "Society at War: Sectionalism, Secession, and Civil War in Louisiana's Lafourche Region" (Ph.D. diss., Mississippi State University, 1994) is an in depth look at this region as it suffered through the war.

6. See Lathrop, "The Lafourche District in 1861–1862," 99–129, where the author describes the disarray present among Confederate war planners after the surprise occupation of the Lafourche country by Federal troops.

7. Winters, *The Civil War in Louisiana*, 125–48; see also the various biographies of Benjamin Butler, including Chester G. Hearn's *When the Devil Came Down to Dixie: Benjamin Butler in New Orleans* (Baton Rouge: Louisiana State University Press, 1997); and Robert S. Holzman's *Stormy Ben Butler* (New York: Octagon Books, 1978). Butler's autobiography is entitled *Autobiography and Personal Reminiscences of Major General Benjamin F. Butler* (Boston: A. M. Thayer and Co., 1892).

8. Charles P. Roland, *Louisiana Sugar Plantations during the Civil War* (Baton Rouge: Louisiana State University Press, 1997), 72–73; Winters, *The Civil War in Louisiana*, 125–48.

9. Lathrop, "The Lafourche District in 1861–1862," 119; Winters, *The Civil War in Louisiana*, 125–48.

10. The work of Barnes Lathrop, including his "The Lafourche District in 1862: Militia and Partisan Rangers," *Louisiana History* 1 (summer 1960): 300–319, sets out the changing Confederate strategy in southern Louisiana in reaction to the Union invasion. See also Winters, *The Civil War in Louisiana*, 150–51.

11. William B. Ratliff to R. C. Martin, June 26, 1862, Martin-Hugh Papers, box 3, no. 262, Special Collections, Hill Memorial Library, Louisiana State University, Baton Rouge (hereafter cited as HML).

12. J. K. Gaudet to R. C. Martin, June 28, 1862, Martin-Pugh Papers, box 3, no. 265, HML.

13. W. W. Pugh to R. C. Martin, July 8, 1862, Martin-Pugh Papers, box 3, no. 268, HML; see also Lathrop, "The Lafourche District in 1862: Militia and Partisan Rangers," 310–12.

14. Lathrop, "The Lafourche District in 1862: Militia and Partisan Rangers," 312.

15. D. G. Farragut "To the People of Donaldsonville," *War of the Rebellion: A Compilation of the Official Records of the Union and Confederate Armies*, (Washington, D.C.: GPO; reprint, Gettysburg: National Historical Society, 1972), ser. 1, vol. 15, 796 (hereafter cited as *Official Records*, with all references to series 1).

16. Winters, *The Civil War in Louisiana*, 123; Benjamin F. Butler to Secretary of War, May 8, 1862, *Official Records*, 6:506.

17. For more information on Governor Thomas O. Moore as he struggled to resist the Federal invasion of Louisiana, see Edwin Adams Davis, *Heroic Years: Louisiana in the War for Southern Independence*, WBRZ-TV 1964 Lectures in Louisiana History (Baton Rouge: Bureau of Educational Materials and Research, Louisiana State University College of Education, 1964); and Van D. Odom, "The Political Career of Thomas Overton Moore, Secession Governor of Louisiana,"

*Louisiana Historical Quarterly* 26 (October 1943): 975–1054. See also *Official Records*, 15:795–96.

18. For a compelling argument regarding the importance of the loss of New Orleans to the Confederacy's hopes for independence, see Charles L. Dufour's *The Night the War Was Lost* (Lincoln: University of Nebraska Press, 1994); and, more recently, Chester G. Hearn's *The Capture of New Orleans, 1862* (Baton Rouge: Louisiana State University Press, 1995).

19. G. T. Beauregard, Bladen, Alabama, to Ed Gotheil, Richmond, Virginia, August 15, 1862, *Official Records*, 15:799.

20. The only biography on Taylor is T. Michael Parrish's *Richard Taylor: Soldier Prince of Dixie* (Chapel Hill: University of North Carolina Press, 1992); see also Richard Taylor, *Destruction and Reconstruction: Personal Experiences of the Late War* (New York: D. Appleton and Company, 1879).

21. Barnes Lathrop, "The Lafourche District, 1862: Confederate Revival," *Louisiana History* 1 (fall 1960): 300–319.

22. Barnes Lathrop, "The Lafourche District in 1862: Invasion," *Louisiana History* 2 (spring 1961): 175–202.

23. Several books stand out as being excellent sources for a preliminary exploration of the transformation of the Africa-American population in Louisiana. These include C. Peter Ripley's *Slaves and Freedmen in Civil War Louisiana* (Baton Rouge: Louisiana State University Press, 1976); see also Joe Gray Taylor, *Negro Slavery in Louisiana* (Baton Rouge: Louisiana Historical Association, 1963).

24. Roland, *Louisiana Sugar Plantations*, 72–73, 101–14.

25. Donald S. Frazier, "Texans on the Teche: The Texas Brigade at the Battles of Bisland and Irish Bend, April 12–14, 1863," *Louisiana History* 32 (fall, 1991): 417–35.

26. William Randolph Howell, Camp Stonewall Jackson near Washington, Louisiana, to Editor, August 17, 1863, *Houston Tri-Weekly Telegraph*, August 31, 1863, 2.

27. Ibid.; J. W. Watkins, Washington, Louisiana, to Irene Watkins, Marlin, Texas, August 18, 1863, Watkins Letters, Harold B. Simpson Confederate Research Center, Hillsboro, Tex. (hereafter cited as Watkins Letters).

28. William Randolph Howell, Camp Stonewall Jackson near Washington, Louisiana, to Editor, August 17, 1863, *Houston Tri-Weekly Telegraph*, August 31, 1863, 2, J. W. Watkins, Washington, Louisiana, to Irene Watkins, Marlin, Texas, August 18, 1863, Watkins Letters.

29. William Randolph Howell, Camp Stonewall Jackson near Washington, Louisiana, to Editor, August 17, 1863, *Houston Tri-Weekly Telegraph*, August 31, 1863, 2; J. W. Watkins, Washington, Louisiana, to Irene Watkins, Marlin, Texas, August 18, 1863, Watkins Letters.

30. William Randolph Howell, Camp Stonewall Jackson near Washington, Louisiana, to Editor, August 17, 1863, *Houston Tri-Weekly Telegraph*, August 31, 1863, 2.

31. For a short account of this campaign, with a valuable annotated bibliography,

see Richard Lowe, *The Texas Overland Expedition of 1863* (Abilene, Tex.: McWhiney Foundation Press, 1997).

32. W. L. Robards, Washington, Louisiana, to Editor, July 27, 1863, *Houston Tri-Weekly Telegraph*, August 10, 1863, 2.

33. Michot, "War Is Still Raging in This Part of the Country," 166–68.

34. Captain H. U. M. C. Brown had served in the Seventeenth Arkansas Cavalry against Union troops in the Port Hudson Campaign and had been captured. Upon his parole, he renewed his efforts, this time west of the river; see Michot, "War Is Still Raging in This Part of the Country," 157. A sizable number of the troops in the Seventh Louisiana Cavalry were pardoned deserters from Valsin Fouret's Tenth Louisiana (Yellow Jacket) Battalion; see Arthur W. Bergeron Jr., *Guide to Louisiana Confederate Military Units, 1861–1865* (Louisiana State University Press, 1989), 48–52.

35. Roland, *Louisiana Sugar Plantations*, 71–72; *New Orleans Daily True Delta*, March 26, 1864; Michot, "War Is Still Raging in This Part of the Country," 169–70.

36. A number of reports relating the fights against guerillas can be found in *Official Records*, 48, pt.1, 77–82.

37. Michot, "War Is Still Raging in This Part of the Country," 179–82.

# Bushwhackers, Provosts, and Tories: The Guerrilla War in Arkansas

1. William L. Shea, "1862: A Continual Thunder," in *Rugged and Sublime: The Civil War in Arkansas*, ed. Mark E. Christ (Fayetteville: University of Arkansas Press, 1995), 37–38. See also Michael Dougan, *Confederate Arkansas: The People and Politics of a Frontier State in Wartime* (Port Washington, N.Y.: Kennikat Press, 1976), 90, on the confusion surrounding Hindman's appointment.

2. U.S. War Department, *War of the Rebellion: A Compilation of the Official Records of the Union and Confederate Armies*, (Washington, D.C.: GPO, 1880–1901), ser. 1, vol. 13, 835 (hereafter cited as *Official Records*, with all references to series 1). The best summaries of the guerrilla war in Arkansas are Leo E. Huff, "Guerrillas, Jayhawkers, and Bushwhackers in Northern Arkansas during the Civil War," *Arkansas Historical Quarterly* 24 (spring 1965): 127–48; and Daniel E. Sutherland, "Guerrillas: The Real War in Arkansas," *Arkansas Historical Quarterly* 52 (autumn 1993): 257–85.

3. *Official Records*, 22, pt. 2, 197–98.

4. The lack of proper mounts became an issue of contention between the War Department and Major General Frederick Steele, Union commander in Arkansas in 1864. Apparently Steele liked to race the best horses in his command for the entertainment of himself and his officers. U.S. Senate, "Administration of the Department of Arkansas," 38th Cong., 2nd sess., 1864, serial 1214, S. Rept. 142, 78.

5. James A. Campbell Diaries, January 1, March 28, 1864, Civil War Collection, item H-16, box 1, file 4, Archives and Special Collections, University of Arkansas at Little Rock (hereafter cited as UALR-SC).

6. Record of Event cards, Company A, First Arkansas Cavalry, April 12, 1863, Company E, First Arkansas Cavalry, January–February 1864, microfilm M594, roll 1, Records of the Adjutant General's Office, War Department, RG 94, National Archives (hereafter cited as RG 94, NA); Report of Company M, Third Arkansas Cavalry, January–February 1864, Civil War Collection, item A5, series 1, box 1, file 6, UALR-SC.

7. *Official Records*, 22, pt. 2, 197–98; 34, pt. 2, 51–52; 48, pt. 1, 1008.

8. Michael Fellman, *Inside War: The Guerrilla Conflict in Missouri during the Civil War* (New York: Oxford University Press, 1989), 33–34, 78, 93–94.

9. 17. Orders and Accounts, April 26, 1864, Provost Marshal General of Arkansas, Headquarters Department of Arkansas, vol. 111, General Order No. 6, January 14, 1865, Department of Arkansas General Orders, vol. 20 (1865–1867), RG 393, NA, emphasis added; James William Demby, *The War in Arkansas, or A Treatise on the Great Rebellion of 1861* (Little Rock: Egis Printing Co., 1864), 12.

10. U.S. Senate, "Administration of the Department of Arkansas," S. Rept. 142, 78, 81–82, 85.

11. Lieutenant Colonel John L. Chandler to Major General Frederick Steele, October 1, 1863, Department of Arkansas, vol. 108, pt. 1, Letters of the Provost Marshal General, RG 393, NA; *Official Records*, 41, pt. 1, 898–99.

12. Barry Popchock, ed., *Soldier Boy: The Civil War Letters of Charles O. Musser, Twenty-Ninth Iowa* (Iowa City: University of Iowa Press, 1995), 53.

13. *Official Records*, 22, pt. 2, 238; Case 91 and Case 93, Office of the Judge Advocate General, Department of Arkansas and Seventh Army Corps and Fourth Military District, 1862–1870, RG 153, NA.

14. Popchock, *Soldier Boy*, 85; "Classification of Prisoners," Orders and Accounts, Provost Marshal General of Arkansas, Department of Arkansas and Seventh Army Corps and Fourth Military District, 1862–1870, vol. 111, RG 393, NA; General Register of Prisoners, New Orleans, 1863–65, Records of the Provost Marshal General, RG 109, NA.

15. David D. Porter, *The Naval History of the Civil War* (New York: Sherman Publishing Company, 1886), 333; Anne J. Bailey, "The Mississippi Marine Brigade: Fighting Guerrillas on Western Waters," *Military History of the Southwest* 22 (spring 1992): 34.

16. Bailey, "Mississippi Marine Brigade," 34–6.

17. Jesse L. Chapman, "The Ellet Family and Riverine Warfare in the West, 1861–1865" (M.A. thesis, Old Dominion University, 1985), 61, 63–64.

18. "Mississippi Marine Brigade, General and Staff Muster Roll, May & June 1863," Records of the Record and Pension Office of the War Department, 1784–1919, General Records, Service Histories of the Volunteer Force of the United States Army, 1861–1865, Mississippi Marine Brigade, microfilm M594, RG 94, NA; "Report of Brigadier General Ellet, commanding Marine Brigade," June 5, 1863, U.S. Navy Department, *Official Records of the Union and Confederate Navies in the War of the Rebellion* (Washington, D.C.: GPO, 1884–1922), ser. 1, vol. 25, 128–29 (cited hereafter as ORN); *Official Records*, 22, pt. 1, 232.

19. William W. Heartsill, *Fourteen Hundred and 91 Days in the Confederate Army: A Journal Kept by W. W. Heartsill of the W. P. Lane Rangers*, Bell I. Wiley, ed., (1876; reprint, Jackson, Tenn.: McCowat-Mercer Press, 1954), 101; Mark Grimsley, *The Hard Hand of War: Union Military Policy toward Southern Civilians, 1861–1865* (New York: Cambridge University Press, 1995), 113–19.

20. *ORN*, 25:175; Porter to Welles, April 2, 1863, Letters Received by the Secretary of the Navy from Squadron Commanders, Mississippi Squadron, 1861–1865, Civil War Military Collection, Arkansas Historical Commission, Little Rock, Ark.

21. *Official Records*, 34, pt. 2, 768; *ORN*, 25:524, 697–98; Bailey, "Mississippi Marine Brigade," 39–41.

22. Richard N. Current, *Lincoln's Loyalists: Union Soldiers from the Confederacy* (Boston: Northeastern University Press, 1992), 73–79, 167–69, 216.

23. Popchock, *Soldier Boy*, 85; Wiley Britton, *The Civil War on the Border* (New York: G. P. Putnam and Sons, 1904), 2:521; *Official Records*, 34, pt. 1, 876, 1053.

24. *Official Records*, 34, pt. 1, 658.

25. Daniel E. Sutherland, "1864: A Strange, Wild Time," and Carl H. Moneyhon, "1865: A State of Perfect Anarchy," in *Rugged and Sublime*, ed. Christ, 12–23, 146–49; *Official Records*, 34, pt. 3, 109, 548, 562–63.

26. *Official Records*, 41, pt. 1, 266–70; Michael A. Hughes, "Wartime Gristmill Destruction in Northwest Arkansas and Military Farm Colonies," *Arkansas Historical Quarterly* 46 (summer 1987): 175–76.

27. U.S. Senate, "Report of the Adjutant General of Arkansas for the Period of the Late Rebellion, and to November 1, 1866," 39th Cong., 2nd sess., 1867, S. Doc. 53, 267; Hughes, "Wartime Gristmill Destruction," 184–86.

28. *Official Records*, 48, pt. 1, 1177–79, 1293–94.

29. Hans Mattson, *Early Days of Reconstruction in Northeast Arkansas; An Address Delivered by Colonel Hans Mattson before the Loyal Legion at St. Paul, Minnesota, March 6, 1889* (St. Paul, Minn.: Pioneer Press Co., 1889), 7; Diane Neal and Thomas W. Kremm, "An Experiment in Collective Security: The Union Army's Use of Armed Colonies in Arkansas," *Military History of the Southwest* 20 (fall 1990): 173, 175–76; *Official Records*, 48, pt. 1, 1185, 1193–94, 1221–22.

30. 34. Wendy Richter, "The Impact of the Civil War on Hot Springs, Arkansas," *Arkansas Historical Quarterly* 43 (summer 1984): 134–35.

# Inside Wars: The Cultural Crisis of Warfare and the Values of Ordinary People

This chapter is a revised version of an essay with the same title, which appeared in the *Australasian Journal of American Studies* 10 (December 1991): 1–9, and was delivered in July 1991 at the Centenary Conference: Setting Historical Agendas, Department of History, University of Sydney, Australia. The opening epigraph is from Joseph Conrad's *Heart of Darkness* (1902; reprint, London: Penguin Books, 1995), 61–63.

1. Notable among the books which have begun to open up the cultural meanings of war are John Keegan, *The Face of Battle* (New York: Viking, 1976); Gerald F. Linderman, *Embattled Courage: The Experience of Combat in the American Civil War* (New York: Free Press, 1987); Reid Mitchell, *Civil War Soldiers: Their Expectations and Experiences* (New York: Viking, 1989); and Joseph T, Glatthaar, *The March to the Sea: Sherman's Troops in the Savannah and Carolina Campaigns* (New York: New York University Press, 1985). My contribution, upon which this essay reflects, is *Inside War: The Guerrilla Conflict in Missouri during the American Civil War* (New York: Oxford University Press, 1989).

2. Deposition of Mrs. Mary Hall, Franklin County, Letters Received File 2593, Records of U.S. Army Continental Commands, 1821–1920, Department of the Missouri, RG 393, National Archives. Hall made her report three days after the event.

3. M. G. Singleton to Col. James S. Rollins, February 9, 1863, James S. Rollins Papers, Joint Collection, University of Missouri, Western Historical Manuscript Collection, State Historical Society of Missouri Manuscripts, Columbia (hereafter cited as JC).

4. John to Dr. J. F. Snyder, Boliver, June 16, 1864, John F. Snyder Papers, Illinois State Historical Library, Springfield; J. W. Woods to Aunt Zelia, Newton County, June 2, 1864, Woods-Holman Family Papers, JC.

5. Entry for May 28, 1862, Sardius Smith Dairy, Illinois State Historical Library, Springfield.

6. Entry for July 30, 1863, Civil War Diary of Francis Springer, Illinois State Historical Library, Springfield.

7. Major Emory S. Foster to Lieutenant D. A. Thatcher, Warrensburg, June 18, 1862, in *War of the Rebellion: A Compilation of the Official Records of the Union and the Confederate Army*, by the U.S. War Department (Washington, D.C.: GPO, 1880–1902), ser. 1, vol. 13, 125 (hereafter cited as *Official Records*).

8. Entry for February 2, 1863, Forseyth, Diary of Timothy Phillips, Wisconsin State Historical Society, Madison.

9. Entries for October 1 and 24, 1863, and September 20, 1865, Diary of Sherman Bodwell, Kansas State Historical Society, Topeka.

10. J. Glenn Gray, *The Warriors: Reflections on Men in Battle* (New York: Harcourt, Brace, 1959).

11. Richard Slotkin, *Regeneration through Violence: The Mythology of the American Frontier, 1600–1860* (Middletown, Conn.: Wesleyan University Press, 1973); James Axtell, *The European and the Indian: Essays in the Ethnohistory of North America* (New York: Oxford University Press, 1981); Nicholas P. Canny, "The Ideology of English Colonization: From Ireland to America," *William and Mary Quarterly*, 3rd ser., 30 (October 1973): 575–98.

12. Robert Jay Lifton, *The Nazi Doctors: Medical Killing and the Psychology of Genocide* (New York: Basic Books, 1986).

13. Robert Jay Lifton, *Death in Life: Survivors of Hiroshima*, 2nd ed. (New York: Basic Books, 1982). Other books by Lifton which are of great help to cultural historians include *Thought Reform and the Psychology of Totalism: A Study of Brainwashing*

*in China*, 2nd ed. (Chapel Hill: University of North Carolina Press, 1989); *Explorations in Psychohistory: The Wellfleet Papers* (New York: Simon and Shuster, 1974); and *The Broken Connection: On Death and the Continuity of Life* (New York: Simon and Shuster, 1979). On the whole Lifton is tougher-minded than the earlier generation of ego-psychologists, including his great teacher, Erik Erikson. He also has a better feel for historical and cultural contexts. Lifton is an antiwar activist, which I honor, but which sometimes leads to a certain tendency, in his case a subtle one, of loading the cultural dice to point to preferred outcomes. He is, on the other hand, quite realistic about actual behavior.

14. William Barry Gault, "Some Remarks on Slaughter," *American Journal of Psychiatry* (October 1971): 450–54; William Goldsmith and Constantine Cretekos, "Unhappy Odysseys: Psychiatric Hospitalizations among Vietnam Returnees," *Archives of General Psychiatry* 30 (January 1969): 78–83; Sarah A. Haley, "When the Patient Reports Atrocities: Specific Considerations of the Vietnam Veteran," *Archives of General Psychiatry* (February 1974): 191–96; Joel Yager, "Personal Violence in Infantry Combat," *Archives of General Psychiatry* (February 1975): 257–61. On the slaughter and mutilation of American Indians by Union cavalrymen in Colorado in 1864, see John M. Carroll, ed., *The Sand Creek Massacre: A Documentary History* (New York: Sol Lewis, 1973); Stan Hoig, *The Sand Creek Massacre* (Norman: University of Oklahoma Press, 1961); and, more generally, Slotkin, Axtell, and Canney, cited in note 11. A note on all such European treatments of "the other," including their own lower orders, would include about 25 percent of contemporary historical literature.

15. Bertram Wyatt-Brown, *Southern Honor: Ethics and Behavior in the Old South* (New York: Oxford University Press, 1982).

16. Entry for December 8, 1862, Hiram C. Crandall Diary, Illinois State Historical Library, Springfield. A good analysis of the development of the American Victorian notion of women's domestically based claims for moral superiority is Mary P. Ryan, *The Empire of the Mother: American Writing about Domesticity, 1830–1860* (New York: Haworth Press, 1982).

17. Samuel Ayres to L. Langdon, Koueka, Kansas, June 1, 1863, Kansas State Historical Society, Topeka.

18. Charles W. Falker to his wife, Ft. Scott, Kansas, May 2, 1865, Wisconsin State Historical Society; entry for April 19, 1862, Henry Dysert Diary, Iowa State Historical Society, Iowa City.

19. Brigadier General Clinton B. Fisk to Lieutenant Colonel Daniel M. Draper, Macon, April 18, 1864, *Official Records*, 34, pt. 3, 216; entry for October 20, 1864, Diary of Webster W. Moses, Kansas State Historical Society, Topeka.

20. Hannah Arendt, *Eichmann in Jerusalem: A Report on the Banality of Evil* (New York: Viking Press, 1963).

# Index

146–47, 165; violence by, 23, 142–43,
147–48
desertion: causes of, 11, 21, 22–23, 24,
25–26, 35, 49, 54–55, 78–79, 103, 205
Doggett, Delila, 77
Donaldsville, La., 158, 169
draft dodgers, 35, 136, 138, 139–40, 163,
164, 215
Duff, James, 135
Duval, Alexander, 125
Dysart, Henry, 196

East Tennessee, 13, 89; unionism in, 4–5,
6, 90–92, 93–95
economic markets, 21, 90
Ellet, Alfred W., 178, 180
Elly, Edward, 76
Emancipation Proclamation, 106
Erath, George B., 143

Fain, Huldah, 38
Falker, Charles, 196
farm colonies, 14, 183–84
Farragut, David Glasgow, 152, 155, 158
Fayetteville, Ark., 173, 182, 183
Fellman, Michael, 9, 15, 124
Ferguson, Champ, 125
Fisher, Noel C., 9, 13, 115, 116
Fisk, Clinton B., 196
Fitch, Leroy, 128
Fleming, Andrew, 103
Forrest, Nathan Bedford, 115, 117,
119–20, 122, 124, 129
Forster, Stig, 113
Foster, Charles, 53
Foster, Emory S., 191
Fouche, Simpson, 38
Fournet, Valsin A., 157
Frazier, Donald S., 14
Fredericksburg, Tex., 144
Freeman, John, 56, 212
Freeman, Lewis, 212
Freeman, Mary, 56
Freeman, Mary B., 56
Free State of Jones, 11–12, 18–19, 20, 29.
See also Jones County, Miss.
Frontier Conspiracy (Tex.), 145–46

Frontier Organization (Tex.), 143–44
Frost, Meigs, 23, 24, 25
Fry, David, 95

Gainesville, Tex., 137; hanging at, 10,
136–38, 145
Galloway, G. Norton, 20, 21
Garrett, Jill K., 114–15
geography: and guerrilla warfare, 152–54;
factor in unionism, 9–10, 14
Georgia: protest in, 33–38; unionism in,
4, 12, 33–34. See also place names
Georgia troops: militia, 31, 32, 36, 38,
41–42
Germans: in Louisiana, 151; in Texas, 5,
133, 134–35
Gildrie, Richard, 122
Gordon, Lesley J., 12
Grant, Ulysses S., 46, 54, 116, 120, 179
Graves, Benjamin D., 17–18, 26–27, 29
Gray, J. Glenn, 193
Green, Tom, 165–66
Greene County, Tenn., 95, 99
Gregg, Tucker, 19, 207
gristmills, 182
Groce, W. Todd, 6
guerrillas: blacks as, 116, 118, 163; roles
of, 8–9, 97, 98–99, 167–68
guerrillas, Confederate, 8, 10–11, 13,
14, 66, 67, 68, 71–72, 115–17,
158, 162–63, 166–67, 172, 178–79,
181–82, 188–89, 191; effectiveness of,
124, 128–26, 128–29, 167–68, 172,
182–83, 184–85; treatment of, 60,
176–77, 196–97
guerrillas, Unionist, 8, 10, 11–12, 13, 18,
39, 41, 66, 67, 97, 98–101, 102–3,
119, 125–26, 163–64; effectiveness of,
99–103; execution of, 165
guerrilla warfare, 10–11, 32, 118; character of, 113–15, 122, 123, 126, 130–31,
163, 188–89, 189–92, 195–97,
198–99

Haddock, John H., 216–17
Haddock, William, 216–17
Hall, Mary, 188, 195